CHRISTIAN SACRAMENTS
IN A
POSTMODERN WORLD

A Theology for the Third Millennium

KENAN B. OSBORNE, O.F.M.

PAULIST PRESS
New York / Mahwah, N.J.

Cover design by Bruce Crilly

Library of Congress Cataloging-in-Publication Data

Osborne, Kenan B.
    Christian sacraments in a postmodern world / Kenan B. Osborne.
      p. cm.
    Includes bibliographical references and index.
    ISBN 0-8091-3904-9 (alk. paper)
      1. Sacraments—Catholic Church. 2. Postmodernism—Religious aspects—Catholic Church.
3. Catholic Church—Doctrines. I. Title.
BX2200.075 1999
234′.16—dc21   99-44727
                                                        CIP

Published by Paulist Press
997 Macarthur Boulevard
Mahwah, New Jersey 07430

www.paulistpress.com

Printed and bound in the
United States of America

Contents

Preface

There is no doubt that postmodern philosophy has already reshaped the thinking of many people both in the West and, at least indirectly, in other areas of the globe as well. Since postmodern thought will play a major role in the third millennium, I want to pursue the discussion with a focus on sacramental theology. Postmodern thought has already brought new and serious challenges to theology in general and to sacramental theology in particular. These challenges have created a shaking of the foundations, as Paul Tillich once wrote. Postmodern thought does this since postmodern philosophy has shaken the very foundation of the way through which Western people have thought. The epistemology and onto-epistemology of the Western world have been seriously challenged, and the "standard" Western epistemology and onto epistemology are currently being dismantled. If Christian theologians do not advert to this and do not seek a bridge between postmodernity and sacramental theology, the result, in my view, will be profoundly shortsighted.

I present this volume as a possible basis of discussion. Postmodern thought itself is not an "absolute," nor is its presentation in these pages meant to be understood as such. Rather, the focus on postmodern thought simply indicates that this way of approach, both epistemologically and onto-epistemologically, is so widespread at this present time that some sort of *Horizontsverschmelzung* between the theological and the philosophical world must continue to take place. Many contemporary theological writings have been entitled: "Toward a theology of..." and no doubt this present volume should be seen in the same category. That the challenges of postmodern thought clearly

1

make one radically rethink sacramental theology will be seen in the remaining pages, and this radical rethinking in itself might be interpreted negatively as a denial of "true" Christian sacramental theology. My basic hope, however, is to indicate that postmodern ways of thinking and onto-thinking truly have something powerful to say to the ways in which we Christians in the third millennium not only theologize about sacraments but also live sacraments.

Two small issues should be noted. "Postmodern" remains a fairly undefined word. It seems that Federico de Osnis first used it in a Spanish essay around 1934. Arnold Toynbee, in *A Study of History,* expressed the notion that the "modern historical period" ends somewhere between 1850 and 1918, thus indicating that after this period there is a "postmodern" period. In many ways, this dating coincided with Toynbee's cyclical view of history, and this view found some affirmation in the writings of T. S. Eliot, James Joyce, Thomas Mann, and many others, whose writings in the early part of the twentieth century all asked a similar question: Is there a way out, in French an *issue,* from this present ending world? On the other side of the "way out" is something one can call postmodern. The term "postmodern" arose with ambiguity and continues to exude ambiguity. One could look at the entire area of contemporary Western philosophy, beginning with Edmund Husserl down to the present, and although there are many post-Husserlians, post-structuralists, and so forth, there are a few ties of continuity between all of these thinkers. In some postmodern thought it is even a contradiction of terms to "define" postmodern. Thus, I have allowed my use of "postmodern" to cover a certain trend of Western philosophical thought that moves from Husserl to the present.

Second, the era in which many authors who are cited in the following pages lived was not an era of inclusive language. To reconstruct their texts does not honor their work. Consequently, when I have cited such authors I have left the text as it appeared either in its original or in its authorized translation. No effort has been made to edit these texts. In my own text, however, I have tried to be as inclusive as possible.

After the text of this book was being prepared for publication, the encyclical of John Paul II, *Fides et Ratio,* was promulgated. This present volume deals with the same issue which the pope addresses, namely, the interrelationship of revelation and philosophy (no. 4). Although John Paul II is more at home in a philosophy that relies heavily on the insights of Aristotle and Thomas Aquinas (no. 43), he clearly states that "the Church has no philosophy of her own nor does she canonize any one particular philosophy in preference to others" (no. 49). There is an autonomy of philosophy that must be respected, he goes on to say, and this autonomy and respect must also be accorded to what in a general way is called postmodern philosophy. Using the fundamental insights on trinitarian theology of sacraments found in the *Catechism of the Catholic Church* (nos. 1076–1109), I will consider several key issues of postmodern philosophy and also several key issues of medieval Franciscan philosophy and place them in a relationship with the trinitarian theology of sacraments as found in the *Catechism*.

I would like to express my deep appreciation to Fr. Regis Duffy, O.F.M., who has graciously taken his valuable time to read drafts of this manuscript and has offered many insightful suggestions. I am grateful to Jeanette Holmes for all the editing work she carefully provided. I also wish to thank the editors of Paulist Press for their solid assistance on the several drafts of this volume.

The Twentieth-Century Legacy
of Sacramental Revolution

During the last one hundred years the Christian Church in its entirety—the Roman Catholic Church, the several Eastern Churches, the Anglican Church, and the many Protestant churches—has experienced a major revolution and renewal in both its sacramental theology and its sacramental liturgical celebration. A large number of converging factors contributed to this extensive change. In this chapter, we will detail some of the major factors involved. Such an overview helps us understand the reasons why, at the beginning of the third millennium, there will be many differences between sacramental theology in the twenty-first century and the sacramental theology which was in place during the first half of the twentieth century.

1900–1959

From 1900, the turn of the century, down to 1959, the announcement of Vatican II, five issues were of major significance for the sacramental renewal of the twentieth century:

1. The history of the sacraments
2. Jesus as primordial sacrament
3. The liturgical renewal
4. *La nouvelle Théologie*
5. Contemporary philosophies

The History of the Sacraments

Although there had been some study of the history of various Christian doctrines prior to 1900, it was the publication of Henry Charles Lea's three-volume work *A History of Auricular Confession and Indulgences in the Latin Church*[1] that occasioned a sustained study on the history of each of the seven sacraments in the Roman Catholic Church. In 1896 the Roman Catholic Church was ill-prepared to respond to Lea, whose work was heavily anti-Catholic. A French canonist, A. Boudinhon, was the first to reply to Lea in a lengthy article on the history of the sacrament of penance down to the eighth century: "Sur l'histoire de la pénitence: À propos d'un livre récent."[2] More scholarly and more detailed studies were needed, and as a result, F. X. Funk,[3] P. Battifol,[4] E. V. Vacandard[5] and P. A. Kirsch[6] published solid historical works on the subject of the history of the sacrament of penance. In 1906, F. Loofs, a Protestant scholar, also wrote on the subject and aligned himself more with the Catholic authors than with Lea.[7] Nonetheless, all of these authors in many ways tended to agree with Lea on the basic historical interpretation of the sacrament of penance, and thus these replies were, in part, not a refutation but a substantiation of Lea's views.

Some Roman Catholic dogma professors reacted both to Lea and to the Roman Catholic patristic scholars in a highly negative way. Professors, such as J. Gartmeier in Germany,[8] P. Pignataro[9] and A. Di Dario[10] in Italy, wrote monographs in which erroneous historical statements were made in defense of the status quo. The First World War paused scholarship, but after the peace a new group of scholars approached the same subject, the history of the sacrament of penance. This new group included such scholars as P. Galtier,[11] B. Poschmann,[12] A. D'Alès,[13] K. Adam,[14] J. A. Jungmann,[15] and K. Rahner.[16] In the writings of these authors, as well as others, a more balanced and clarified approach to the history of the sacrament of penance was developed.

The historical studies on the sacrament of penance raised issues about the history of baptism. As a result, scholars began to research baptismal history as well.[17] Because baptism is connected to the eucharist, impetus also was given to study the history of the eucharist. Jungmann became a major writer in this field.[18] The historical studies on the eucharist encouraged a historical study of ordained ministry.[19] Because of its relation to baptism, the sacrament of confirmation formed a part of this historical endeavor as well.[20] These five sacraments received the lion's share of research prior to Vatican II, and only in more recent times has the history of the sacraments of marriage[21] and the anointing of the sick[22] received equal study. In the period just after Vatican II many studies on sacraments were produced that integrated the historical dimensions of sacramental life into the theological and pastoral dimensions of sacramental thought and praxis.[23] As a result of this historical research, scholars today have at their fingertips a vision of the history of each sacrament that Thomas Aquinas, Luther, Calvin, and the bishops at the Council of Trent did not have. Because of this, the sacramental theologies of these medieval and reformation figures no longer have the normative weight they once enjoyed. In the twentieth century this far-reaching historical data has truly been an integral part of both the revolution and the renewal of contemporary sacramental theology and liturgy.

Implications

This historical study has major implications. First of all, it is clear that Jesus in his lifetime did not "institute" the seven sacraments. This is particularly clear for confirmation, reconciliation, marriage, ordination, and the anointing of the sick.[24] These five sacramental actions developed gradually over many centuries, and consequently the Tridentine position that Jesus "instituted" the seven sacraments needs rethinking.

Second, history indicates again and again that pastoral need at the local or regional level led to changes and developments. Most often changes and developments in the sacraments did not occur because of a central authority; rather local or regional situations occasioned and developed changes, with papal or conciliar approbation occurring only later. Nor can one say that changes and developments took place because of a well-formulated theological position. The theological academy generally provided a theological base only after the rituals had changed. Scholastic sacramental theology is itself a reflection on an already-in-place liturgical praxis. The scholastic position on sacraments is, then, simply one way of viewing sacramental life. When the praxis in the church changes, as it is doing today, the theological rationale for the new praxis also changes.

Third, the historical material implies that since major aspects of each sacrament have changed in the past, major aspects can be changed in the future. Historical studies relativize many aspects of Roman Catholic, Eastern Catholic, Anglican, and Protestant sacramental theologies and sacramental practice. This relativization must be acknowledged. The brief mention of historical material in the *Catechism of the Catholic Church,* with no subsequent operative role in its theological discussion, is fundamentally inadequate.[25]

Finally, the historical material indicates that in the sequencing of the sacraments there has never been consistency other than the placing of baptism first. In the history and tradition of the Christian-Catholic Church, a variety of sequences can be found. The current sequence in the Roman Catholic Church—baptism, first reconciliation, first eucharist, confirmation—has only a very modern tradition to substantiate it. Other sequences have a much lengthier tradition. There is, moreover, no "golden age" in church history serving as a benchmark or norm for sacramental theology, sacramental ritual, and sacramental sequencing.

The following is a graph of the history of the origins of the seven sacramental rituals. It is based on the first dating when, according to the most reliable contemporary scholars, there is clear extant data on individual sacramental rituals.

A.D. 27	150	200	400	1000	1150
Baptism					
Eucharist					
	Reconcili-ation				
		Orders			
		Anointing			
		of the Sick	[Marriage]		
				Confirma-tion	
					Marriage

The actual dates in this diagram are generalized. The sacraments of baptism and eucharist seem to go back to the time of Jesus, or at least to the time of the apostolic church. It is in the writings of Hermes (140–50) that we have the first clear reference to a rite of reconciliation after baptism.[26] The *Apostolic Tradition* of Hippolytus (c. 215) gives us the first extant indication of ordination and its ritual.[27] In the same work, we have the first clear evidence of a blessing of oil for the sick.[28] We have reliable historical data that church officials began to enter into the marriage celebration around 400.[29] However, only from the time of Peter Lombard (1150) do we have a clear indication that marriage was accepted as a true sacrament in the Western church.[30] In the year 1000 there is clear evidence that confirmation, generally and only in the West, was celebrated as a rite separate from baptism.[31] Prior to 1000 in the West, a separate rite of confirmation can be found, but prior to 800 the separate rite slowly disappears.

Jesus as Primordial Sacrament

It is remarkable how quickly the theological presentation on Jesus as primordial sacrament and the church as a fundamental sacrament became popular in the Roman Catholic Church and, at least as regards the understanding of the church as a fundamental sacrament, a part of the ordinary magisterium of the church itself. In 1953 a Jesuit professor at the Hochschule Sankt Georgen in Frankfurt, Otto Semmelroth, published a work entitled *Die Kirche als Ursakrament (The Church as Original Sacrament).*[32] Shortly before this book appeared, a fellow Jesuit, Karl Rahner, in a manuscript on penance, had spoken of the church as a "radical sacrament." Although Semmelroth refers to this manuscript, he deserves the credit for coining the phrase "church as original sacrament." It was Rahner's subsequent writings, together with Edward Schillebeeckx's works, that brought the idea of Jesus as the primordial sacrament and the church as a basic sacrament into international prominence. In 1961 Rahner published his work *Kirche und Sakrament,*[33] while Schillebeeckx had published *Christus, Sacrament van de Godsontmoeting (Christ the Sacrament of the Encounter with God)* in 1960.[34]

In all of these writings, the idea of the church as a basic sacrament makes no sense unless Jesus, in his humanity, is also seen as a fundamental or primordial sacrament. The two ideas are understandable only in their mutuality. One cannot really call Jesus the primordial sacrament unless one also accepts the church as a basic sacrament, and vice versa, the church as a sacrament presupposes Jesus as the primordial sacrament. In the documents of Vatican II, we find that the bishops accepted the understanding of the church as a basic sacrament. No mention is made directly that Jesus is the primordial sacrament.

In a later section of this volume, we will return in greater detail to the issue of Jesus as primordial sacrament and the church as a basic sacrament. For the moment, it is of importance to note that from 1953, when Semmelroth published his small volume, to 1965, the conclusion of Vatican II, these theological issues shot into prominence and seriously changed the Christian understanding of sacramentality.

Implications

Since the understanding of the church as a basic sacrament is part of the teaching of the ordinary magisterium of the church (the documents of Vatican II), a Roman Catholic cannot speak of the church today without making this sacramentality of the church central. In his explanation of *Lumen gentium,* Gérard Philips, one of the main architects of the document, notes that there is no contradiction between the statement of Trent, which solemnly proclaimed and enumerated seven ritual sacraments, and the idea of the church as a fundamental sacrament. "A valid theology of the seven sacraments," he writes, "always presupposes this openness to the sacramentality of the Church."[35] *The Catechism of the Catholic Church* in its section on "The Sacramental Economy" mentions the church as sacrament only in no. 1118. This lone reference indicates clearly that in the *Catechism* the notion of the church as a basic sacrament does not play a major role for an understanding of the sacramental economy. Moreover, the notion of the church as a basic sacrament plays absolutely no role at all when the *Catechism* goes on to discuss the ritualized sacraments in its most lengthy sacramental section, nos. 1210–1690.[36] When one compares these two different statements of the magisterium of the church—the Vatican II documents on the one hand, and the *Catechism* on the other—one hears perplexing mixed signals. One can only ask, after this comparison of texts, "Is the true magisterium in the text of the council or in the text of the *Catechism?*"

The Liturgical Renewal

In 1903, Pius X issued a *Motu proprio, Tra le sollecitudini,* which has often been cited as the beginning of the modern liturgical movement in the Roman Catholic Church. In 1914, the Benedictine Lambert Beauduin published *La piété de l'église,* which enumerated fundamental principles for the liturgical movement.[37] His monastery of Mont César became a center of liturgical renewal, publishing *Les questions liturgiques* (later called *Les questions liturgiques et paroissiales*) and hosting a series of conferences, *Semaines liturgiques.* When the liturgical leaders at Mont César advocated and used such innovations as vernacular liturgies and an altar facing the people, the monastery became a source of controversy.

At another abbey, Maria Laach in Germany, Ildephonse Herwegen and Odo Casel initiated a number of liturgical renewals. The *Ecclesia orans* series began in 1918 with Romano Guardini's *The Spirit of the Liturgy,*[38] followed by the establishment of an association, *Verein zur Pflege der Liturgiewissenschaft.* Through these media, Casel developed his ideas, which found expression in his major work *Das christliche Kultmysterium.*[39]

Klosterneuburg in Austria, under the direction of Pius Parsch, also became a liturgical center with Parsch's *Das Jahr des Heiles* (1923)[40] and, subsequently, the publication of a journal, *Bibel und Liturgie,* which first appeared in 1926. The Benedictine Abbey of Ampleforth, under the leadership of Bernard McElligott, began the Society of St. Gregory in England and also introduced a journal called *Music and Liturgy.* J. D. Crichton became one of its main editors and writers.[41] In 1926, Virgil Michel at St. John's Abbey in Minnesota began the journal *Orate Fratres,* later renamed *Worship.* He also established the Liturgical Press. From 1940 onward, a series of annual meetings of liturgical scholars began to take place, which developed into the North American Liturgical Conference.[42]

In 1943, French Dominicans established the *Centre de pastorale liturgie* in Paris, and in 1945, began to edit *La Maison-Dieu.* During the Second World War, European Catholics celebrated the eucharistic liturgy in difficult circumstances. Some of these celebrations were in the vernacular or in the form of a dialogue Latin mass. In 1943, Pius XII issued *Mystici corporis,* and, in 1947, *Mediator Dei,* the first encyclical entirely focused on the liturgy. In many ways, this latter encyclical was the papal charter for this century's liturgical movement. Pius XII also established a pontifical commission for general liturgical restoration with such leaders as Ferdinand Antonelli, Joseph Loew, and Annibale Bugnini.

In 1951, the Sacred Congregation of Rites issued its decree *De solemni vigilia paschali instauranda,* calling for a renewal of the paschal vigil and, in 1955, another decree, *Cum nostra hac aetate,* simplified the rubrics for this vigil. The decree, *Maxima redemptionis nostrae,* brought about major liturgical changes for Holy Week. In 1958, an instruction, *De musica sacra,* focused both on music and on lay participation in the liturgy. Add to all of this the highly influential national and international meetings of liturgists, particularly the Assisi-Rome congresses, and it becomes clear that the liturgical movement from the beginning of the century onward was one of intense fermentation. Not only was the need for liturgical reform a product of this intense activity, but in official and unofficial ways, liturgical reforms were already taking place prior to Vatican II. This change in liturgy, with its call for the use of vernacular language, for more participation by the lay person, for a better understanding of the history of liturgical practices and rituals in the Christian-Catholic tradition was a tremendous catalyst for the revolutionary renewal of the church's sacramental life.[43]

Implications

Sacramental theology invariably remains an isolated academic study unless it is intrinsically connected to liturgical praxis. Sacramental and liturgical theology/practice are intrinsically united. Indeed, the only time that one can speak of baptism or eucharist is in an actual baptismal ritual or in an actual eucharistic celebration. These actual, localized, existential events of liturgy are the only moments when baptism, eucharist, confirmation, and so on exist. All books—this present volume is no exception—and all decrees and encyclicals, all canonical laws, and collections of rubrics are simply *about* sacraments. Sacraments only exist in the *doing,* in the *celebrating.* The mere fulfillment of various laws and rubrics *about* sacraments in no way allows Christians to say that a sacramental action truly takes place. One must "unpack" the liturgical experience to understand sacramental life.

Another implication of this liturgical movement in the twentieth century was a desire on the part of some (for example, in the United States, Virgil Michel, Hans A. Reinhold, Reynold Hillenbrand) to include a social dimension to liturgical life.[44] To experience liturgy only within a "Jesus and me" spirituality runs counter to the idea of lay participation, dialogical celebration, and the union of liturgy to daily life. This implication was more fully emphasized in the period after Vatican II, when various forms of liberation theology became highly influential.[45]

La Nouvelle Théologie

During the first half of the twentieth century, one of the most nagging theological issues was the development of doctrine. Answers that were based on the logical deductions made from originally revealed truths began to be developed by such authors as M. Tuyaerts, R. Schulte, and F. Marín-Solá. In their view, newness of insight came from reasoned deduction based on divinely inspired revelation. How could this square with historical research? L. Charlier moved away from the idea that God revealed truths, stating rather that revelation was actually "God, giving himself to us through Christ in the mystery of the incarnation, of which the mystery of the Church is only the extension."[46] That God's revelation was a revelation of God's own self, not a revelation of truths, was further developed by theologians, even though their positions were not acceptable to many Roman Catholic Church leaders. These "new" writers indicated that the concepts in which revealed truths were normally and almost normatively expressed were time-conditioned and often did not express the full meaning of the revelatory message. Henri de Lubac, one of the leaders of *La nouvelle théologie,* noted that the mystery of salvation shatters our human concepts.[47]

The Jesuit professors at Fourvière near Lyon and Dominican professors from Le Saulchoir in Étoilles were key to this movement; they began to use categories from scripture and patristic literature which they found to be closer to Christian experience. Particularly the typological and allegorical interpretations of scripture seemed to convey a richer understanding of the revelation of God's own self. Besides De Lubac, other scholars were J. Daniélou, H. Bouillard, Y. Congar, and M. D. Chenu. The series *Sources chrétiennes* provided critical editions of early patristic writings. *La nouvelle Théologie* was not simply a retreat to the past and to history. Rather, it was an attempt to orient theology, not only along the biblical-patristic tradition, but also toward the horizon of modern thought and the needs of contemporary thinking. In particular, theologians grouped under this label, *La nouvelle théologie,* operated under the following principles:

1. There is an inadequacy in every era to define truth for future eras.
2. The traditional neo-scholastic view of revelation as the transmission of fixed concepts was replaced by a God who encounters the total person and communicates with that person in a historical dialogue.
3. No formula of faith can therefore exhaust the truth; it only can be exchanged for another formula more meaningful to the contemporary mind.
4. Every formulation of a divine mystery is only the beginning, never the end.
5. A theory of the development of dogma was suggested that emphasized the social, historical, and non-conceptual forces impinging in this process (a position close to that of Cardinal Newman).[48]

Although the focus of these theologians was not specifically on the sacraments, this movement had a major influence on Vatican II. Throughout Vatican II and its aftermath, many of the key positions of *La nouvelle théologie* have helped shape the reformulation of sacramental thought and liturgy.

Implications

With the introduction of biblical-patristic modes of thinking, the framework of neo-scholastic sacramental language came into question. Is neo-scholastic conceptual language adequate for sacramental theologizing or for liturgical expression? Most theologians in the Catholic Church today who write on either sacramental theology or sacramental liturgy do not employ the conceptual terms of the neo-scholastic approach.[49]

Nonetheless, the impetus the broad movement called *La nouvelle théologie* brought into theological thought continued to influence sacramental thinking in the latter part of the twentieth century. The emphasis on patristic writings, especially the development of critical editions, has occasioned a rethinking of the entire patristic period, including its sacramental worship, and this has had profound repercussions on the various Eastern churches and their traditional liturgy. These insights also have helped the dialogue between the Roman Church and the various Eastern churches.

New Forms of Philosophical Thinking

With some overlap from the nineteenth century, the Western world in the twentieth century experienced a remarkable philosophical rebirth: existentialism, phenomenology, process thought, Marxism, linguistics, semiotics, and postmodern philosophy. Although the twentieth century has been a century of technological advancement, it has also been one of profound philosophical renewal.[50]

Various theologians have engaged in dialogue with these philosophical currents. R. Bultmann, for instance, clearly incorporated existential thought into his exegetical endeavors. In the Roman Catholic Church, Karl Rahner unabashedly incorporated many of the insights of Heidegger into his theology. Nonetheless, the Christian churches, *precisely as church institutions,* have not faced the challenges of this philosophical endeavor in any major way. Indeed, the churches, *ecclesiastically* or *institutionally,* have been less than open to the implications this renewed philosophical thought has involved.

In these philosophical endeavors, key issues have been reformulated to some degree: the return to the subject; historicity and existentiality of *Dasein;* nothingness; the phenomenon of speech-acts with all its linguistic and hermeneutical ramifications; the challenge to the traditional analytical philosophy of science by a new preoccupation with the problem of the constitution of scientific knowledge and by the effect of the historical and cultural world context in science on the social constitution of scientific knowledge.[51] Whitehead, for example, began to formulate a process philosophy that developed strongly between 1950 and 1970. On the other hand, we are in only a beginning stage toward a process theology, and even this inchoative endeavor has not been overwhelmingly accepted.

Postmodernist philosophers argue that "any 'grand narrative' or foundational theory necessarily tends to homogenize the absolute heterogeneity and specificity of singular events, thereby robbing the event of its full ontological or historical status and, more importantly for a philosopher, denying the very possibility of genuine thinking."[52] But if there is no "grand narrative," for example, what does the Christian Church do with God's "plan of salvation" or with the *economia?*

Implications

In some areas of the Roman Catholic Church, contemporary philosophy as well as modern philosophy have been judged to be counterproductive. Those who take this negative stance generally operate from a standpoint that there is and has been within Roman Catholic circles a *philosophia perennis,* an eternal philosophy.[53]

First of all, the movement from Descartes to Kant to contemporary philosophical studies has emphasized again and again the return to the subject. The so-called objectivity of scholastic theology, at least in its expression from the sixteenth century on, has been seriously challenged. The strength of such an "objective" philosophical position has less and less backing as we move into the new millennium.

Second, the profound philosophical study of time has helped bring about a major acceptance of historicity. Historicity means a relativization of *all* finite elements. In the many forms of contemporary philosophy, relativity is central, in some philosophies more and in others less. For theology, this means a total rethinking of eternal truths, particularly if these involve anything finite. Many of these so-called eternal truths are seen as relative statements, more dependent on the time and place in which they were written than on any unchangeable, ahistorical, or acultural specificity.

Third, epistemological issues have come to the fore, and the possibility of knowing anything beyond a human framework has been questioned. What we know is humanly known, based on a phenomenology of human perception, and what nonhuman elements and realities in themselves might be remains epistemologically far beyond human capabilities. Thus, the human person finds himself or herself within a human, perceptible world.

A sacrament is not theoretical, since sacraments only exist in the actual doing, in the sacramental event itself. But each sacramental event, like all other events in human life, is disparate, not homogenous. Postmodern philosophy would ask: If each sacramental event is a discrete and individualized event, then what is meant by terms such as "baptism" or "eucharist"? Is there not simply a multitude of baptismal events or eucharistic events, similar to some extent, but not mere episodic replications of a predetermined essence? We will explore this later.

1959–1965

Between 1959 and 1965, the Second Vatican Council was a watershed for the renewal of the sacraments.[54] Both in the documents of Vatican II themselves and in their aftermath, certain issues were of major significance. We will consider four of the more important ones that had a profound influence on sacramental theology and liturgy.

1. Official conciliar criteria
2. The church as a basic or universal sacrament
3. The enhanced role of the lay person
4. The endorsement of the ecumenical movement

Official Conciliar Criteria

On the basis of statements made in the documents of Vatican II, the following criteria have served as the guiding principles for the renewal of the sacramental rites. All the pontifical committees that worked on the renewed rituals took these criteria into account, and these remain normative for the liturgical life of the church as we begin the third millennium.

*General Norms (*Sacrosanctum Concilium *[hereafter* SC*], nos. 22–25)*

1. All liturgical formulations are the joint responsibility of the Holy See and the bishops. This has made the oversight of the liturgy a collegial responsibility. No longer is the Holy See the sole authority; conferences of bishops and individual bishops share in this task. "No other person…may add, change or remove anything in the liturgy on his own authority" (*SC,* no. 22).

2. Liturgical reforms must take into account the basic structures of traditional liturgical rites, but be open to the genuine pastoral needs of the individual churches.

3. Tradition is to be respected and the pastoral good of the church must always be safeguarded. The use of scripture in the liturgy

is mandated, and the council authorized the renewal of the liturgical books as soon as possible.

Norms Drawn from the Hierarchic and Communal Nature of the Liturgy (SC, nos. 26–32)

1. "Liturgical services are not private functions, but are celebrations of the Church, which is the 'sacrament of unity,' namely, the holy people united and organized under their bishops" (*SC,* no. 26; also nos. 27, 28, 29, 30, 31, and 32). Liturgy is meant to be celebrated in common; individual or quasi-private celebrations are to be avoided. The more privatized a sacramental liturgy becomes, the less perfect it is (see also can. 837).[55]

2. "In liturgical celebrations...each person [minister or layman] should perform his role by doing solely and totally what the nature of things and liturgical norms require of him" (*SC,* no. 28). All ministers exercise a unique liturgical function, and this ministry must not be disregarded or degraded.

3. To promote active participation, "the people should be encouraged to take part by means of acclamations, responses, psalmody, antiphons, and songs, as well as by actions, gestures, and bodily attitudes. And at the proper times all should observe a reverent silence" (*SC,* no. 30).

4. No special placement should be given to anyone, unless civil law and liturgical law require this, to any person or class of persons (*SC,* no. 32). The stress of this norm is on the equality of all in the presence of God.

Didactic and Pastoral Liturgical Norms (SC, nos. 33–36)

1. Although a sacramental celebration is primarily an act of praising God, there is also a descending aspect: God instructing us. The emphasis in liturgy is not so much on the "effect" or the "minimal elements of validity," but on the reality which the sacrament itself signifies (*SC,* no. 33).

2. "The rites should be distinguished by a noble simplicity; they should be short, clear, and unencumbered by useless repetitions; they should be within the people's powers of comprehension, and normally should not require much explanation" (*SC,* no. 34). The more complicated and repetitive the rituals are, the less liturgical they are.

3. In sacred celebrations a more ample, more varied and more suitable reading from sacred scripture should be restored (*SC,* no. 35). The role of the Word of God is given a greater position and presence in the liturgy. Liturgies with no proclamation of the Word of God are not good liturgies.

4. "A sermon is part of the liturgical service....The sermon should draw its content mainly from scriptural and liturgical sources" (*SC,* no. 35). The homily is a key part for every sacramental liturgy. This is in keeping with other statements from the magisterium indicating that the most important task of the priest is to preach the Word of God.

5. "Bible services should be encouraged, especially on the vigils of the more solemn feasts, on some weekdays of Advent and Lent, and on Sundays and feast days, especially in places where no priest is available" (*SC,* no. 35).

6. A wider use of the vernacular is allowed because of its great advantage for the people (*SC,* no. 36). As regards the vernacular, a decisive role was given by the council to the conferences of bishops.

Norms for Adapting the Liturgy to the Genius and Traditions of Peoples (SC, nos. 37–40)

1. "In the liturgy, the Church has no wish to impose a rigid uniformity in matters which do not involve the faith or the good of the whole community. Rather she respects and fosters the spiritual adornments and gifts of the various races and peoples. Anything in their way of life that is not indissolubly bound up with superstition and error she studies with sympathy and, if possible, preserves intact" (*SC,* no. 37). This is an opening to cultural differences and a clear statement that uniformity is not a major goal. There is a rejection of "europeanization" and the affirmation of the value in other cultures.[56]

2. *SC* (nos. 38–40) provides for cultural revision of the liturgical texts, provided the "substantial unity of the Roman rite is preserved." Preliminary experimentation is allowed and a "more radical revision" in some cases is seen as necessary. There is clearly an openness to liturgical change based on cultural differences. Vatican II clearly entrusted

a major part of this task to the conferences of bishops who have first-hand experience of the situation.

The revised code of canon law echoes these norms, stating that the sacraments are "actions of Christ and the church" (can. 840), underscoring the role of the church community. Moreover, "whenever necessity requires or genuine advantage suggests...it is lawful for the faithful for whom it is physically or morally impossible to approach a Catholic minister, to receive the sacraments of penance, eucharist, and anointing of the sick from non-Catholic ministers in whose churches these sacraments are valid" (can. 844).

Implications

These norms apply to all levels of church leadership and, to the extent that they apply, bishops in their conferences, a bishop in his diocese, or a priest in his parish may not arbitrarily disregard them. Whenever this happens—and at times it has—the people of God are presented with a disregard of the ordinary magisterium by church leaders themselves. In turn, many ask themselves: If church leaders can randomly ignore the magisterium, cannot I when I think it best for me?

Second, none of these criteria is in any way unchangeable. Another council of the church could establish different norms and criteria. Therefore, they cannot be presented as absolute but rather as the official norms for the church's liturgy at this point in time, and as such must be respected.

The Church Is a Basic or Universal Sacrament

In Western thought the church itself as basic sacrament was never part of the magisterium's teaching. Not until the twentieth century was it specifically a part of sacramental theology. Yet at Vatican II the bishops overwhelmingly accepted the role of the church as a basic or universal sacrament. We will return to this theme in detail later. For the moment, let us consider the statements made by the bishops at Vatican II on this matter.

By her relationship with Christ, the Church is a kind of sacrament of intimate union with God, and of the unity of all mankind (*Lumen gentium* [hereafter *LG*], no. 1).

For each and all she [the Church] may be the visible sacrament of this saving unity (*LG*, no. 9).

Christ…through this Spirit has established His body, the Church, as the "universal sacrament of salvation" (*LG*, no. 48).

The Church is the "universal sacrament of salvation," simultaneously manifesting and exercising the mystery of God's love for man (*Gaudium et spes* [hereafter *GS*], no. 45).

The Church is essentially both human and divine, visible but endowed with invisible realities, zealous in action and dedicated to contemplation, present in the world, but as a pilgrim, so constituted that in her the human is directed toward and subordinated to the divine, the visible to the invisible (*SC*, no. 2, equivalently stated).

For it was from the side of Christ as he slept the sleep of death upon the cross that there came forth the wondrous sacrament which is the whole Church (*SC*, no. 5).

Liturgical services are not private functions, but are celebrations of the Church, which is "the sacrament of unity" (*SC*, no. 26).

The Lord…who had received all power in heaven and on earth (cf. Mt. 28:18)…founded his Church as the sacrament of salvation (*Ad gentes* [hereafter *AG*], no. 5).

Implications

The bishops at Vatican II clearly stated that the church is a sacrament, a universal sacrament and, more pointedly, a universal sacrament of salvation. It was left to theologians to determine the connection between the universal sacrament, the church, and the particular sacraments such as baptism, eucharist, and so on, and between universal salvation and particular salvation. Not all theologians have moved in a similar way when formulating this relationship nor has the magisterium been unified in its own statements on this issue.

The Enhanced Role of the Laity

In the documents of Vatican II, the role of the laity in the church was dramatically enhanced. It was decided, in the discussion on *Lumen gentium,* that the section on the people of God should precede the sections on the hierarchy and on lay ministry, thus underlying the common base of all Christians because of their baptism. A list of some conciliar statements makes this enhanced role of the laity abundantly clear.

> All the baptized "share a true equality with regard to the dignity and to the activity common to all the faithful for the building up of the Body of Christ" (*LG,* no. 32).

> All share "in the mission of the whole Christian people with respect to the Church and to the world" (*LG,* no. 31).

> All "have an active part to play in the life and activity of the Church" (*Apostolicam actuositatem* [hereafter *AA*] 10).

> All without exception are called upon by the Lord "to expend all their energy for the growth of the Church and its continuous sanctification" (*LG,* no. 33; cf. *AA,* no. 2).

> All "are commissioned to that apostolate by the Lord Himself" (*LG,* no. 33).

> All the baptized are "made sharers in the priestly, prophetic, and kingly functions of Christ" (*LG,* no. 31; cf. *AA,* nos. 2, 10).

> Christ "gives them a share in His priestly function" (*LG,* no. 34).

> "The great Prophet...fulfills His prophetic office...not only through the hierarchy who teach in His name and with His authority, but also through the laity" (*LG,* no. 35).

Regarding this, Kloppenburg notes, "A generous doctrine indeed on the nature of the laity and its place and role in the Church!"[57]

Implications

Every Christian has a role in the church, externally in the church's mission to the world but also internally in the church's sacramental celebration. Every baptized-eucharistic Christian shares in the kingly, prophetic, and priestly role of Jesus and has received a commission from the Lord himself, not from pope, bishop, or pastor. The attempt by some to restrain the non-ordained Christian from an active role in the sacramental life of the church is a deviant reading of the documents of Vatican II.[58]

The Endorsement of the Ecumenical Movement

At Vatican II, the decree *Unitatis redintegratio* (November 21, 1964) became the charter for modern Roman Catholic participation in the ecumenical movement. Jeffrey Gros, a member of the NCCB Secretariat for Ecumenical and Interreligious Affairs, says that the Roman Catholic Church has committed itself to three ecumenical issues:

1. A spiritual, internal renewal, which includes a biblical, theological, and liturgical renewal;
2. A theological dialogue toward full unity, which includes times of common prayer and worship and a renewal in the education of all Christians in the basics of our common faith;
3. A common mission and witness to the world. Both Paul VI and John Paul II have visited the headquarters of the World Council of Churches in Geneva, thus giving an official recognition of the Roman Catholic Church's relationship to the WCC and its mission.[59]

Implications

The full acceptance of the sacramental life of the Eastern churches by the Roman Catholic Church enhances the role of divergent sacramental theologies. The sacramental theologies of these Eastern churches are markedly different from the traditional sacramental theology of the Roman Catholic Church. By accepting the full sacramentality of the Eastern churches, the Roman Catholic Church must now integrate into its own sacramental theology a much wider acknowledgment of differing theologies.

Second, the acceptance *in principle* of ecumenism has raised the question of the meaning of church to a much more complex level. The bishops at Vatican II stated in *Lumen gentium* that the church subsists in the Roman Catholic Church:

> This is the sole Church of Christ which in the Creed we avow as one, holy, catholic, and apostolic. After His Resurrection, our Saviour, handed her over to Peter to be shepherded (Jn. 21:17), commissioning him and the other apostles to propagate and govern her (cf. Mt. 28:18ff.). Her He erected for all ages as "the pillar and mainstay of the truth" (1 Tim. 3:15). This Church, constituted and organized in the world as a society, subsists in the Catholic Church, which is governed by the successor of Peter and by the bishops in union with that successor (*LG,* no. 8).

Much has been written on this passage since Vatican II. A. Grillmeier, a *peritus* at the council, noted in his commentary, which appeared only a short time after the close of Vatican II, that two major points must be emphasized when one compares the final text with the 1963 draft of this chapter of *Lumen gentium,* and with various *vota* submitted by diverse bishops. First of all, Grillmeier says, "the true and unique church of Christ exists as a concrete fact of history."[60] Although a mystery and a spiritual creation, the church must be recognizable within our human history.

Second, the concrete form of this church is the Catholic Church, but "it is no longer said that it 'is' the 'Roman' Church. This means that the Roman Church as a local church is only part of the whole church, though its bishop is head of all the bishops of the Catholic Church."[61] "Ecclesiality," he goes on to say, "does not simply coincide with the Catholic Church, because ecclesial elements of sanctification and truth can be found outside it."[62] In a footnote he notes that the 1963 draft had read:

> This Church, therefore, truly the mother and teacher of all, constituted and ordained as a society in this world, is the Catholic Church, directed by the Roman Pontiff and by the Bishops in union with him.[63]

This 1963 formulation was not retained. Thirteen bishops had demanded that "est" [is] be retained, and "subsistit" be removed. This was ultimately not accepted by the plenary group of bishops, nor was the request of nineteen bishops who wanted the text to read: "subsistit integro modo in Ecclesia catholica" (it subsists in an integral way in the Catholic Church). The commission rejected a request of twenty-five bishops who wanted the definitive text to read: "Iure divino subsistit" (by divine right it subsists in the Roman Catholic Church). The wording, *subsistit in,* received final approval, "thereby deliberately leaving open the question of the relation of the one church to the many churches."[64]

This entire discussion on the existential locus of church and of ecclesiality outside the Catholic Church has enormous implications for a theological understanding of the church as foundational sacrament, and the hermeneutics involved in this discussion tend to become both complex and dense. This issue will be taken up in chapter 5.

1966–2000

From 1966, roughly the end of Vatican II, to the year 2000, a number of very significant issues affected the renewal of sacramental theology. Ten of these issues deserve special mention:

1. The revised rituals
2. Liberation theology of Latin America
3. The ecumenical dialogues
4. The influence of feminist theology
5. The role of the lay person
6. The renewal of the permanent diaconate
7. The *Catechism of the Catholic Church*
8. Traditional Roman Catholic movements
9. The influence of contemporary philosophy
10. The emergence of the multicultural church

The Revised Rituals

During this period of time, all of the sacramental rituals in the Roman Catholic Church were substantially revised. Some of these revised rituals have proven quite successful, namely, the revised baptismal rituals. Some of the revised rituals have not been very successful, namely, the revised ritual of reconciliation and the revised ritual of confirmation.

The actual formulation of the revised rites was entrusted to a post-conciliar committee called *Concilium.* The members of the *Concilium* reworked the former rituals according to the general norms outlined above. However, as Anscar Chupungco notes:

> In effect the legitimate variations proposed by the present *editio typica* of the sacramental rites represent the work of the *Concilium*

and subsequently of the Congregation for Divine Worship. This implies that the kind of changes allowed by the *editio typica* is often determined by their perception of what is essential to the substantiality of the Roman rite, and what can be dispensed with. It is evident that in the world of liturgical scholarship the perception will differ from one school of thought to another.[65]

The revised rituals were intended to include adaptations and accommodations required by a multicultural world, but since those who revised these rituals had their own stance, and even bias, on this matter, the revised rituals have both strong points and weak points. They are not ideal manifestations of liturgical insight.

At times, the revised rites were brought into the dioceses and parishes too quickly and without much preliminary catechesis, while at other times, though less frequently, there were strong efforts by the dioceses for preliminary catechesis. Further modification and adaptation are clearly in order as we move into the third millennium, but two major issues tend to restrict any further revisions. First, given the enormous amount of energy and time the postconciliar revisioning process demanded, there does not appear to be a strong desire to engage in a similar process.

Second, discussions on liturgical practice have in many ways ceased to be focused on liturgical theology itself and have become focused on authority issues. To change the liturgy, even when this might seem necessary, requires Vatican approval; and any change, no matter how beneficial it might be to the people of God locally, when it is done without prior Vatican approval, becomes an authority issue. Even though the decree on the liturgy deliberately included the conferences of regional bishops in the adaptation process, precisely because these church leaders know firsthand what is better suited to a local situation, in practice these same conferences of bishops have little independent responsibility in liturgical matters.[66]

With some influence from the Roman Catholic ritual revisions, the Anglican Church in the United States developed its own revised *Book of Common Prayer* and several major Lutheran Synods published their *Lutheran Book of Worship*. In the eucharistic rituals of both the Anglicans and Lutherans, a deliberate alignment with Roman Catholic eucharistic worship has been made. The cycle of readings for Sundays is now the same in all these churches, and a Eucharistic Prayer based on

Hippolytus (Eucharistic Prayer II in the Roman Ritual) appears in the Lutheran and Anglican rituals. For the ordinary Roman Catholic, Anglican, or Lutheran Christian, the eucharistic liturgy in all three churches can be celebrated basically the same way. Because of the closeness of these liturgies, many couples in mixed marriages have developed a pattern of alternating attendance at Roman Catholic services with Anglican or Lutheran services.

As we move into the third millennium, sacramental liturgy has two major unresolved issues: cultural adaptation that has not been thorough enough; and ecumenical expression, which in theory remains disparate, but in practice has become less of an issue.

Liberation Theology of Latin America

In the last part of the twentieth century, liberation theology has become a powerful part of the renewal both in Roman Catholic and Protestant thought. Although sacramental theology has not been the prime focus of liberation theologians, nonetheless their emphasis on the social and ethical dimension of both life and worship has focused on the sacramental structure of the church. Juan Luis Segundo in particular has addressed sacramental theology directly.[67]

It was during the 1960s that the liberation theology of Latin America became important.[68] It arose primarily as a reaction to the widespread collective suffering of the poor who were dominant in many places throughout Central and South America. It understands that suffering, violence, and human-rights violations inflicted on the poor cannot be God's will. These authors were also critical of church leadership, which frequently but not always meant Roman Catholic Church leadership, since its lack of criticism of oppressive political regimes was regarded as contrary to gospel values. Too often church leadership at its highest levels was hand in glove with oppressive regimes. Nor did it take up the cause of the marginalized, a cause basic to the gospels.

Some effects of liberation theology on church leadership can be seen in *Gaudium et spes:*

> The joys and the hopes, the griefs and the anxieties of the men of
> this age, especially those who are poor or in any way afflicted, these
> too are the joys and hopes, the griefs and anxieties of the followers

of Christ. Indeed, nothing that is genuinely human fails to raise an echo in their hearts (see also no. 1; nos. 69–70).[69]

   In the apostolic exhortation on the renewal of religious life, *Evangelica Testifieatio,* issued by the Sacred Congregation for Religious and Secular Institutes on June 29, 1971, the authors urged those who are consecrated by religious vows to "hear the cry of the poor," and they added: "Was it not in order to respond to their appeal as God's privileged ones that Christ came, even going as far as to identify himself with them?" (no. 17). In the next paragraph, the bishops urge the religious to react to this cry of the poor: "How then will the cry of the poor find an echo in your lives? That cry must, first of all, bar you from whatever would be a compromise with any form of social injustice. It obliges you also to awaken consciences to the drama of misery and to the demands of social justice made by the gospel and the church" (no. 18).

   In the decree *Gravissimum educationis,* on Christian education, the bishops urge educational leaders to admit those who are poor, opening their doors "readily to students of special promise, even though of slender means, especially those who come from young nations" (no. 10). A similar call to serve the poor can be found in the decree *Apostolicam actuositatem,* which urges the lay people to be eager to assist the poor, the sick, and to be involved in alleviating all kinds of human needs (no. 8). Many theologians have done much to raise the consciousness of people to the plight of the marginalized.[70]

   In reference to sacramental theology, perhaps the question that liberation theologians raise is the following: How can "good Christians" participate meaningfully in sacramental events such as baptism, reconciliation, and eucharist and then return to their homes without seeing or hearing more clearly the violence, the oppression, and the cries of the marginalized? Sacramental life should make each of us more intensely Christian, yet how many Christians leave the sacramental event, unattuned to the voice of Christ in the oppressed and impoverished people they see but really do not see, hear but really do not hear.

   The episcopal conferences, *CELAM,* at Medellín and then at Puebla exerted a strong and official emphasis to the basic goals of liberation theology. Because of these conferences, the phrase "preferential option for the poor" became widely used in hierarchical, theological, and pastoral areas of the Roman Catholic Church. At times the phrase may have been used begrudgingly, but by and large it has found a place within Roman Catholic theology and will surely be a major part of the theology of the new millennium.

Sobrino has taken the preferential option for the poor to a different depth. In *Jesus the Liberator* he speaks of the poor as a *locus theologicus,* noting that the gospels themselves place the poor in this position of source for theological thought.[71] Now it is one thing to say that there should be a preferential option for the poor; it is another to say that the poor are to be seen as a *locus theologicus.*[72] What would happen, for instance, if one were to describe the standard *loci theologici* as follows:

1. a preferential option for scripture
2. a preferential option for the Church Fathers
3. a preferential option for the magisterium
4. a preferential option for tradition?

It is obvious that these "sources of theology" cannot be placed in the same category as a mere "preferential option"—they have a much more authoritative position within Roman Catholic theology. However, if one says that the "poor are also a *locus theologicus,*" then one is saying much more than "preferential option." Just as one cannot develop anything in a theological way that does not take into account the *loci theologici* mentioned above, so too, in the third millennium there will be increasing pressure to see the role of the poor as a true *locus theologicus,* in keeping with the gospel itself, and not merely as an "option for the poor." Strength for such an inclusion for the poor was heard in the statements of the magisterium just cited.

These kinds of statements, made by the magisterium of the church, indicate much more than a "preferential option." They are talking about the reason for the incarnation itself, the very identity of Jesus, the prohibition of any compromise with any form of social injustice, the fundamental obligation to respond to the "cry of the poor." In the third millennium, theologians will increasingly consider the role of the marginalized in theology as much more than a mere option.

The Ecumenical Dialogues

In 1961, Roman Catholics officially participated in the Third Plenary Assembly of the World Council of Churches and, with this, the hesitations of the Roman Curia vis-à-vis ecumenical meetings was, at least in principle, overcome. Only forty-two years earlier, in 1919, a decree of the Holy Office had forbidden Catholics to participate in any such meetings unless the Holy See gave permission. In that same year, Benedict XV had responded to an invitation to the conference of Faith and Order as follows:

> The teaching and practice of the Roman Catholic Church in regard to the unity of the visible Church of Christ are well known to everyone, and so it is not possible for the Catholic Church to participate in a congress like the one proposed. However, His Holiness wishes under no circumstances to disapprove the congress in question for those who are not united with the See of Peter.[73]

Ecumenical dialogues, both national and international, have taken place, and often the themes for these dialogues focused directly on sacramental theology. The Lutheran-Catholic dialogues in the United States have dealt with baptism, eucharist, and ministry. The WCC publication *Baptism, Eucharist and Ministry,* was developed over a long period of time with many drafts and revisions. The Anglican-Roman Catholic dialogues are perhaps the series of ecumenical Western dialogues with the highest authoritative standing. The series of dialogues between the Roman Catholic Church and the Orthodox churches are of similar standing. Other ecumenical dialogues also have taken place.

In the Roman Catholic Church, there is openness to the mutual reception of eucharist, reconciliation, and the anointing of the sick between Roman Catholics and Orthodox. In allowing this, the Roman Catholic Church has acknowledged the full sacramentality of the Eastern churches. Moreover, there has been an openness, under certain circumstances, for Anglicans and Protestants to receive the eucharist at Roman Catholic celebrations. From a theological standpoint, one must admit in principle that the barrier for Anglicans and Protestants receiving communion at a Roman Catholic liturgy has been formally removed.

Today, when one speaks of "church," it is more and more difficult to exclude the total church, the Church Catholic, as it is sometimes called. To speak of the church as a basic sacrament, one is speaking about the total church, the church in all its fragmentations. Thus, theologically, no one church by itself is the sacrament of Jesus. Every church shares in the sacramentality of the church. The term "church" includes more than the Roman Catholic Church. The ecumenical dialogues and liturgies have been a major part of this reflection, and in the third millennium, the full meaning of "church" will be the Church Catholic.

The Influence of Feminist Theology

Feminist theology is a major factor in the theological discussions in North America and in Europe, and is growing throughout the world. The role of women both in society and in the church has become a major theme of discussion, one that has occupied the interest of the Vatican. Time and again in official statements from Rome, the basic equality, dignity, and freedom of all human beings—women and men—has been acknowledged.[74] In the Christian Catholic Church, there can be no inequality based on gender, no position of lesser dignity based on gender, no curtailed freedom based on gender. In *Lumen gentium* one reads:

> Therefore, the chosen People of God is one: "one Lord, one faith, one baptism" (Eph. 4:5). As members, they share a common dignity from their rebirth in Christ. They have the same filial grace and the same vocation to perfection. They possess in common one salvation, one hope, and one undivided charity. Hence, there is in Christ and in the Church no inequality on the basis of race or nationality, social condition or sex, because "there is neither Jew nor Greek; there is neither slave nor freeman; there is neither male nor female. For you are all 'one' in Christ Jesus" (Gal. 3:28, Greek text; cf. Col. 3:11) (no. 32).

Ferdinand Klostermann, in his commentary on this section of *Lumen gentium*, states:

> Even inequalities which exist in the Church by reason of the different lives Catholics lead, the different positions they occupy as teachers, dispensers of the mysteries of God and pastors, seem to become strangely unimportant in view of a deeper "true equality" *(vera aequalitas)* in the vocation to holiness, in the same faith by the righteousness of God, the same dignity, the same labour in building up the body of Christ.[75]

Whether these inequalities in the church have truly become "strangely unimportant" as we enter into the third millennium remains moot. Still, what the bishops said in this section of *The Dogmatic Constitution on the Church* is indeed a major statement on the equality of all.

Feminist theology, as it has developed since the council, is clearly not primarily a reflection on feminist themes, nor is it a subcategory of theology that is relevant only to women. One must, as Rosemary Radford Ruether carefully reminds us, understand the historical roots of feminist theology.[76] By and large during the last two millennia, women have not been allowed to participate in the theological academy. Three women have been declared Doctors of the Church, but they are exceptions. Because of this, theology has been understood by males, argued by males, written by males, and adopted by males. Moreover, these men have been basically from a dominant class as well, whether the aristocracy or a highly educated class.[77]

There are enough examples of this male-dominated theology to indicate the depreciation of women, at least to some degree. Women in these theological presentations are considered second-class Christians and, at times, even second-class humans. Since the history of women speaking out against their second-rate position goes far back into the second millennium, one can rightfully speak of a "tradition." However, only in recent times is this becoming an approved "tradition" in the church.

In the Roman Catholic Church the voices of women showed a new strength from 1968 onward. Scholars Kari Børresen and Mary Daly began publishing at that time. The movement has grown in strength and in publications. With this growth one can also notice the development of different emphases and different approaches, so that at the end of the twentieth century one cannot honestly say that there is a single feminist theology; rather, there is a wide umbrella under which several forms of feminist theology find a home.

It is, however, one thing to say that women and men have a common equality, dignity, and freedom. It is another thing to put this into practice. The role of women in the sacramental liturgy has been and will remain a very controversial issue. A more visible presence of women in Roman Catholic liturgical celebrations has already taken place, and even though the Vatican has called for a moratorium on the issue of women's ordination, this will remain a topic of continued discussion in the new millennium.

The Role of the Lay Person

From 1966 to 2000, the lay person, both male and female, has become more and more integral to sacramental worship. New ministries have been officially developed—for example, the ministry of lector and the ministry of the eucharist—but other ministerial services have also entered into liturgical celebrations in a strong way. In the absence of a priest, the role of a lay person in celebrating a communion service has been officially approved. In 1898 in Burundi, a celebration of a Sunday assembly at which lay catechists presided was introduced. In 1943, the practice was made obligatory in areas not frequented by missionaries. From that time on, the practice of lay people presiding at a Sunday assembly spread rapidly throughout Africa, South America, Central America, and Asia. "Today it is not an exclusive missionary phenomenon. Several countries in Europe have known it for a good number of years,"[78]

There is nothing at the end of the twentieth century that indicates that this anomaly of Sunday celebrations by Christians without eucharist will end. The leadership of the Roman Catholic Church has done little to provide these communities with eucharistic Sunday celebration. As these communities increase in number and in geographical diversity, a major crisis will clearly emerge. The entire Christian tradition of Sunday liturgy, from earliest times down to the present, has been focused on eucharist. Not to provide eucharistic liturgy for large numbers of Catholic communities means that the magisterium has other issues of higher priority (an all-male and celibate clergy). This kind of prioritization is a scandal, and if it continues, can only lead to disaster.

Since most catechetical preparation for sacraments is done by lay women and, to some degree, lay men, the influence of lay people on sacraments has also grown. Textbooks for sacramental preparation according to the post–Vatican II renewal format abound, and various emphases, different from the pre–Vatican II catechesis, have been used. The *Catechism of the Catholic Church* provides a reference for catechists, and the various commentaries on the *Catechism* outline its strengths and the weaknesses. In the third millennium, sacramental preparation will continue to be the province of lay leadership, and, as these lay teachers become more theologically sophisticated, the actual material and the manner of expounding sacramental preparation will become far more nuanced and better in quality. The very teaching on sacraments by lay women and men, as both children and adults prepare for sacramental reception, will reshape sacramental life and thought. Official books may indeed be provided by the hierarchy for sacramental preparation, but in the actual preparation, many other issues and details will enter into the discussion. These will nuance the way that the sacraments are understood and celebrated.

The general theological level of the laity is rising and this means that lay men and women will call for better liturgical celebrations, better homilies, and better sacramental service. Lay people will know when the shortage of priests is straining eucharistic celebrations and causing a disservice rather than a service to the people of God. Bishops will hear this discontent and will be constrained to bring about changes. At the end of the twentieth century there is a legitimate demand for adequate liturgical services in the church. This demand must be met honestly and effectively.

The Renewal of the Permanent Diaconate

At the urging of many bishops at Vatican II, the diaconate, as a permanent ordained ministry, was reinstituted in the Roman Catholic Church (*LG,* no. 29).[79] The bishops from developing parts of the world were especially eager for this renewal. However, from the contemporary standpoint one notices that the diaconate is more prominent in the traditionally Anglo-Euro-American nations than in the developing countries. In a way, the dream of some bishops at Vatican II has not taken place. Vatican II speaks of a "restoration" of the diaconate. The bishops of the United States have also used the word "restoration" when they considered the permanent diaconate.[80] This restoration or renewal, however, cannot be tied to the past. The role of the deacon in the church today must be viewed creatively and based on the pastoral needs of the church. In 1988, the Bishops Conference of the Netherlands published the results of one of its study committees, a document entitled *The Platform Diaconal Ecclesiology.* After a short theological introduction on the mission of the church, the documents then presented an analysis of society and church in seventeen pages—almost one-half of the entire document. Only after such a sociological and anthropological analysis did the authors speak about the diaconal church ministry.

Among the many areas of diaconal ministry, but certainly not the only area, is the diaconal liturgical ministry. The role of deacons in the celebration of the sacraments has moved slowly and not always universally. There are dioceses and even bishops' conferences that have not implemented the restoration of the permanent diaconate. There are dioceses that have only a few permanent deacons. There are other dioceses that have developed lengthy formation programs for permanent deacons and utilize this ministry throughout their parishes. Sacramental worship in baptism, eucharist, reconciliation, and marriage has been enhanced by the presence of deacons. Para-sacramental liturgy has also been enriched by diaconal ministry. Individual pastors are on some occasions very open and affirming of this diaconal ministry; on other occasions pastors have been to some degree begrudging in their support of diaconal ministry. Even with these varying degrees of episcopal and presbyteral encouragement, the deacon's presence in sacramental liturgy has been a major factor in the renewal of contemporary sacramental theology and sacramental liturgiology. The role of the deacon will be a major element in the sacramental life of the church in the third millennium.[81]

The *Catechism of the Catholic Church*

The publication of the *Catechism of the Catholic Church* is in some ways a mirror of the effort after the Council of Trent in its publication of the *Catechism of the Council of Trent*. The reaction to the *Catechism of the Catholic Church* has, however, been varied. There are those who make exaggerated claims for its value, practically making it the benchmark of every activity.[82] There are others who find it "helpful," or "in need of explanation," or a "reference book." One of the problems with the *Catechism* is that in its early and middle stages it was conceived as a "bishops' book," and only in the later stages was it reoriented to be for everyone. When such a redirection in readership was made, it would have been wise to have started with a new first draft. It is one thing to write for bishops, who have enormous ecclesiastical background; it is a different thing to write for Catholics generally.

Second, this volume, among some Catholics, appears to have more weight than the documents of Vatican II. This totally skews the meaning of magisterial documents. The *Catechism* must be read from, within, and against the hermeneutic of the documents of Vatican II. The documents of Vatican II cannot be read from, within, or against the hermeneutic of the *Catechism of the Catholic Church.*

The pages on the sacraments form a fairly lengthy part of the *Catechism.* This material is divided into two sections: the first deals with broad issues on sacramental theology; the second deals with the seven ritual sacraments. However, as we noted above, the two sections show little integration. Because of this disconnectedness, the *Catechism* offers some excellent material on contemporary sacramental theology, but it also brings ambiguity and mixed signals. The influence of the *Catechism* will, no doubt, continue, but in the early part of the third millennium this material on sacramental theology will become overall less and less influential, because future writings by theologians will move beyond it.

Traditional Roman Catholic Movements

In the wake of Vatican II a number of traditional movements have appeared in the Roman Catholic Church. The most conspicuous movement was and is that of Bishop Marcel Lefebvre, which became a schismatic group within the Roman tradition. A more widespread group includes those who celebrate, or demand the right to celebrate, the Tridentine Mass. In 1984, John Paul II permitted the celebration of the Tridentine Mass under strictly controlled circumstances. Some theological and ecclesiastical leaders in the church believe that this permission was a concession to ultraconservative Catholics who questioned, and at times even repudiated, the liturgical reforms of Vatican II. It is a mixed signal on sacramental theology. Are the liturgical and sacramental changes in the church the official teaching of the church, or are they only one way for Catholics to understand the official Catholic teaching? Even more disconcerting is the dichotomy in the magisterium itself: Which is more important, the magisterium of the Vatican Council or the magisterium of John Paul II? Roman Catholics should never be placed in a situation in which competing voices of the magisterium ask for, and even demand, allegiance. That there are traditional or conservative groups in the church, especially after a major council, is to be expected. The same situation has occurred in the wake of all other major church councils.[83]

John Paul II himself says that the council unleashed aspirations to renewal, and in the very word "renewal" there is included something "new," an element of "novelty." Excess might take place, but an opposition to the "new" can also lead to "another deviation" that opposes growth in the church. What John Paul II proposes is, of course, a balance. There is clearly room for a conservative stance in a comprehensive profile of Christian men and women, but this must be a balanced conservative stance, not a one-sided, obstinate, "ours only," and therefore deviant conservatism.[84]

The Influence of Contemporary Philosophy

The influence of contemporary philosophies has already begun to reshape the way Western people view sacramental life. First and foremost, of course, is the continuing influence of Karl Rahner's understanding of sacrament and symbol, which is strongly influenced by M. Heidegger.[85] E. Schillebeeckx was also clearly influenced by phenomenology, especially by Maurice Merleau-Ponty.[86] Louis-Marie Chauvet's *Symbole et Sacrement: Une relecture sacramentelle de l'existence chrétienne* reflects the thought of M. Heidegger, J. Derrida, C. Geffré, F. A. Isambert, J. Lacan, E. Lévinas, C. Lévy-Strauss, E. Ortigues, P. Ricoeur, and A. Vergote.[87] David Power, in *Unsearchable Riches: The Symbolic Nature of Liturgy,* has used the thought of Paul Ricoeur in a creative way as he assesses the meaning of symbol.[88] Regis Duffy, in his writings on sacraments, has incorporated phenomenology into his approach to the sacred.[89] R. Sokolowski's *Eucharistic Presence: A Study in the Theology of Disclosure* shows a strong influence from E. Husserl.[90] Bernard Lee has brought Whiteheadian process philosophy into the area of sacramental theology.[91] A Heideggerian influence through Rahner can be seen in the writings of E. Kilmartin.[92] P. Lakeland has discussed at length postmodern thought and Christian identity.[93]

What these authors have started will continue into the third millennium, with many other scholars adding to the rethinking of the philosophical basis within sacramental theology. The depth and breadth of their philosophical directions will continue to develop, not only in the sphere of sacrament and symbol, but in the entire sphere of the sacred. Since this particular issue of contemporary Western philosophical thought and sacramental theology is a major focus of this volume, further discussion here is not necessary. What needs to be noted at this juncture is the strong entrance of this contemporary philosophical discourse into sacramental discussion.

The Emergence of a Multicultural Church

The emergence of a multicultural church has become a central issue and will characterize the church of the third millennium in a major way. There is also the critical issue of the Christian Church in relationship to other major world religions. Often this latter relationship is found precisely in those areas where a totally different culture other than Euro-Anglo-American prevails. Thus, there is the emergence of a multicultural church within the framework of a multi-religion world.

The Vatican, because of prior missionary activity, is still seen today as one of the colonial powers, which brought so much misery and shame to the peoples in these other cultures. For political and social, and not merely religious reasons, the interfacing of the Roman Catholic Church with other cultures and other religions will not be a simple issue in the third millennium.

The demographics of the Roman Catholic Church has shifted noticeably. The majority of Roman Catholics are now in the southern hemisphere, not the northern. Still, the northern hemisphere Catholic minority dominates the southern hemisphere Catholic majority. This imbalance will play a major role in the third millennium. Sacramental liturgy has become a lightning rod for this clash. Aylward Shorter is correct when he notes that

> the ardent desire for liturgical inculturation—a new liturgical creation—has to compete with the view of liturgy as a field for the exercise of hierarchical power. In so far as the bishop sees his role as the principal guarantor of an authentic liturgy circumscribed by Church Law, inculturation cannot fail to be discouraged."[94]

What Shorter says will become a more telling factor in the third millennium. The question of liturgy, particularly sacramental liturgy, has unfortunately become a "field of exercise of hierarchical power." It is almost impossible to have a discussion on sacramental theology or sacramental liturgy per se. Time and again, the authority card is played. In fact, the authority card on many occasions dominates over the sacramental card or the liturgical card. The focus of the discussion centers on hierarchical power. This is an unstable position and will, with many collisions, be a part of the sacramental and liturgical world in the first part of the third millennium.

Regis Duffy, in an essay on the sacraments, has a section on the future of sacrament. In this forward glance to the third millennium, he indicates that there are three major unresolved issues for the mission of the church:

1. The cultural context of evangelization and sacrament;
2. the role of the Holy Spirit and its ecumenical corollaries;
3. symbolic competence in a post-industrial age and its corollary, the responsible reception of sacraments.[95]

It is noteworthy that Duffy places the cultural context first. Whether this issue offers a sacramental priority or not is moot. When combined with the other issues—the presence of the Holy Spirit in sacramental life and its ecumenical implications as well as the competence of symbolism in contemporary Western life—clearly the cultural issue raises the prospects of a profound relativization of the standard theological approaches to sacraments and liturgy that one finds in the Roman Catholic Church, in the Anglican Church, in the various Protestant churches, and in the Eastern Orthodox churches.

Much could be said about the stress on multicultural issues that permeate Christian theology at the end of the twentieth century. Indeed, it is one of the major themes in Christian theology, not only in the Western world but also globally. Many issues affecting culture will come up in the following pages and, therefore, this short statement suffices to bring this central issue onto the table of sacramental discourse.

All of the issues described above are key issues that have, in one way or another, both occasioned and affected the revolution in the contemporary church's understanding of sacrament. One should note that this sacramental revolution is not violent or virulent. Nonetheless, it is a revolution and not merely a renewal. Paraphrasing Nietszche, one might say it is a "re-evaluation of all sacramental values." It is obvious that these issues are not all of one piece. Some of the above issues are seriously conflictual, and this has produced a state of deep tension in many areas of the church today. Nor are all the issues deemed acceptable either by certain groups of the magisterium or by certain groups of the theological academy. Nonetheless, acceptable or not, the issues are

currently operative in major ways, and a mere statement of nonacceptance will not make them disappear. Sacramental theology, at the end of
the second millennium, is clearly multidimensional, and the formation
of an organic interconnection of all these elements remains impossible.
The purpose of this first chapter is to place on the table all the major
factors that, during the course of the twentieth century, have become
incisive and operative as regards sacramental theology.

These issues and factors are the twentieth-century legacy of theology to those who now move into the third millennium. Given the array of
such issues and factors, it is clear that not only elements of a *renewal,* but
also of a *revolution,* have taken place in sacramental theology. Some may
shy away from the strength of the word "revolution," but when one
calmly considers the breadth and depth of the many factors pinpointed in
this chapter and their implications already at work in sacramental theology, then "renewal" is too timid; "revolution" is far more accurate. The
presence of a revolutionary change in sacramental theology is even more
apparent when one considers the antagonism that some of these factors
have engendered. There would be no such intensity if all the innovations
were simply a renewal; there is, however, clear evidence of revolution,
precisely because of the periodic intense antagonism both in the theological and the ecclesiastical arenas. To think that we Christians are moving
into the third millennium with a serene sacramental theology is a
Pollyanna dream. As these diverse issues become slowly more integrated
into third-millennium theology, at least to some degree, major changes
cannot help but take place in the way the Christian churches in their ecumenical and cultural totality will of necessity not only consider but also
celebrate a sacramental dimension present in the world, present in the
humanity of Jesus, and present in the church.

I have selected simply one aspect for the remainder of this volume, but it is an aspect that undergirds all the other issues. This focus is
the hermeneutic question, or better, the onto-hermeneutic question.
How do we understand? How do we understand human life? How do
we understand the very term "sacrament"?

2

Methodology and the Point of Departure

Every scientific study requires a careful methodology, and a study of the Christian sacraments is no exception to this rule. Indeed, to understand a religious phenomenon in any of its manifestations, methodology is of the utmost importance. No one method, however, is ever exclusively at play in a given study of a phenomenon. For the sacraments, this multi-methodological aspect is also a given, since sacramental reality is itself a highly complex issue involving a number of dynamics from various dimensions of both human and divine life.

Sacramental complexity is further emphasized by G. van der Leeuw in his book *Sakramentstheologie.*[1] Van der Leeuw states that sacraments have too often been discussed as a specifically Christian phenomenon, ignoring the many connections that the Christian sacraments have, not only with other religious but also human phenomena. Christian sacraments, he argues, cannot be presented as accidental to human life, a sort of secondary layer of phenomena or a sort of "epiphenomena." Instead, they are anchored deep within human nature, within the phenomenon of the *humanum* itself. The separation of sacraments from human life, whether one is considering baptism and eucharist in Anglican and Protestant theology or the seven-sacrament format of Roman Catholic theology or the celebration of the divine mysteries in the Eastern churches, has indeed made the Christian sacraments epiphenomenal to human life.

In the light of Van der Leeuw's comments, let us briefly review some of the major points of departure and subsequent methodologies that one finds in twentieth-century sacramental and liturgical theology.

41

In many ways, the point of departure one selects for any scientific study governs the types of methodologies one can then use. Methodologies and the point of departure are united in a mutually intrinsic way.

FIRST POINT OF DEPARTURE: BIBLICAL DATA:
SOLA SCRIPTURA

The phrase *sola scriptura* (scripture alone) is a hallowed and profound treasure of the Reformation churches, but it is also a profound treasure of any and every Christian church. God's Word nourishes, transforms and makes holy all human life. Without the active presence of God's Word in our life, we are not truly Christian. Without the Word of God, sacraments have no meaning. There can be no doubt that a fundamental part of sacramental methodology must be the Word of God, a Word that stands in both affirmation and judgment on all other Christian realities.

In the reading of scripture, however, both textual and contextual issues have developed. Consequently, methods are needed to gather and interpret available written data on sacraments as found in key Christian sacred books. This means that the Bible, in particular the New Testament, needs to be carefully studied. A careful study involves linguistics, textual criticism, form criticism, and redaction criticism. The contemporary use of these textual and contextual methodologies has, at times, not been well received by sacramental or liturgical theologians, since, in the past, some theologians have misused biblical texts and contexts regarding the sacraments. This misuse has resulted in an "eisegetical" understanding on their part of several biblical passages and these same New Testament passages with their eisegetical misinterpretation were then used as key passages for the teachings on the existence, meaning, institution, and effect of sacramental action in the Christian community. One finds this eisegetical use of scriptural passages by Anglican and Protestant theologians who have a rather narrow understanding of *sola scriptura* and by Roman Catholic theologians who, with dogmatic presuppositions, find sacramental indices in New Testament passages where, in the light of critical analysis, such indices simply do not and cannot exist. A major change in the understanding of these sacred texts means a reevaluation of certain theological positions.

If the phrase *sola scriptura* is narrowly interpreted, the New Testament passages and their relationship to the sacramental action of the church will also rest on this interpretation. However, no church experiences the sacramental actions of baptism and eucharist only through the lens of scripture passages. During the five hundred years since the Protestant Reformation, there has developed a way of celebrating baptism and eucharist in the Protestant churches that includes a development of liturgies and spiritualities. Indeed, there is something spiritual and sacred in these baptismal and eucharistic moments that comes from the liturgy, prayers, and spiritual preparation found in Lutheran, Presbyterian, and Baptist life. These liturgical and spiritual sacramental celebrations have a foundation that though based on *sola scriptura,* also include symbolic and phenomenological issues.[2]

In ecumenical dialogues on the sacraments, the final document has usually been a consensus document tabulating the issues on which all the participants can agree. A second reading of these documents, however, shows that actual baptism in a church community involves much more than these "common denominator" elements.[3] They provide us with only some aspects of sacramental theology and liturgy. The "much more" dimensions come from the liturgical celebration and the spiritual inheritance within which Lutheran, Presbyterian, Baptist, and other communities celebrate.

In neo-scholastic Roman Catholic theology, New Testament statements have been used as the basis for the institution, meaning, and causality of the sacraments. The sacrament of reconciliation was based on Matthew 16:16, 18:18, and John 20:22–23. John's passage reads: "Whose sins you shall forgive are forgiven them" (NAB).[4] In spite of overwhelming evidence presented by contemporary biblical scholars, there are Roman Catholic sacramental theologians who continue to consider these three New Testament passages as the biblical bases of the institution and the effect of reconciliation.[5] However, no important contemporary New Testament scholar holds such a view. Both the text and the context provide a far different and more comprehensive interpretation of these same biblical texts. A similar eisegetical interpretation of New Testament passages can be found in past scholars as regards the beginnings of the sacraments of confirmation, marriage, and holy orders.[6]

Sola scriptura in both Protestant and Catholic theology has on too many occasions meant a single way of biblical interpretation as well, usually called a fundamentalist interpretation. Thus, scripture alone, without some interpretation, is not a strong point of departure for contemporary sacramental theology.

SECOND POINT OF DEPARTURE:
THE SEVEN RITUAL SACRAMENTS

For the past several centuries this point of departure has been a standard approach for Roman Catholic sacramental theology, and it has been continued by theologians into the twentieth century. This generally begins with a discussion of the physical and metaphysical definition of sacrament and then moves to a detailed consideration of the seven sacraments. The physical definition of sacrament means that one takes into account the physical elements that are involved in such ritualizations; namely, the use of both words and material objects. When one moves to a "metaphysical definition," one is faced with an intrinsic definition of sacrament that makes it intrinsically distinct from all other metaphysical realities.[7] After a discussion of the existence of sacraments and their physical and metaphysical essences, these authors immediately turn to a presentation on each of the seven sacraments.

This point of departure and its methodology make the seven sacraments epiphenomenal to human life and the human environment. There are phenomenological issues that unite a given Christian sacrament to something human: a human meal (eucharist), human washing (baptism). Prior to all these symbolic and phenomenological human aspects, one is told to consider the metaphysical and physical realities of a Christian sacrament. Metaphysically considered sacraments are no longer part of the natural order. A change has taken place in the essence of the sacrament, in the *res metaphysica.* A change has also taken place in the physical aspects of sacramental matter, the *res physica.* These changes range from the use of words and material objects in an instrumental and causal way by a transcendent God to a total transubstantiation of the substance, *res metaphysica.* In the eucharist even the appearances or *res physica* are fundamentally changed since they no longer adhere in a natural form. In holy orders the priest undergoes, so this theology states, an ontological change; he is no longer the same human person.

When one segregates out the seven ritual sacraments and provides them with some sort of metaphysical definition, there is a clear move toward the epiphenomenal. There is an onto-theological[8] approach in all of this that fits in well with other dimensions of past Roman Catholic theology, namely, with the two-storied universe of nature and grace, and with the church itself as perfect society alongside the secular realm, which in its own way is itself a perfect society, albeit a natural one. Without this other epiphenomenal dimension, the human person cannot be saved.[9]

For third-millennium sacramental theology, this point of departure with its philosophical methodologies cannot be sustained. The *Catechism of the Catholic Church* attempts to avoid this by beginning its section on sacraments with a lengthy discussion called "The Sacramental Economy,"[10] but in its description of the seven sacraments the *Catechism*'s initial presentation of the sacramental economy plays no operative role.[11] This point of departure and the onto-theological methodologies that flow from it cannot help but continue to make the seven sacraments of the Roman Catholic Church epiphenomenal to human life generally. In doing this, the individual sacraments cease to speak to the very people for whom the sacraments might be spiritually helpful, as Juan Segundo has indicated.[12]

THIRD POINT OF DEPARTURE:
THE HISTORY OF THE SACRAMENTS

Contemporary sacramental theology for the first time in the entire history of the Christian Catholic Church has a scholarly grasp of the history of each of the ritual sacraments. This is surely one of the superb accomplishments of twentieth-century study on the Christian sacraments. To attain this comprehensive historical understanding, scholars have employed the methodological factors that all historians must use. The composite image of the Christian sacraments that these historians have developed is, on many occasions, at odds with the academic and deductive composite image of sacraments that the neo-Thomist theologians of the post-Tridentine period developed, as well as with the image of sacraments found in the works of some Anglican and Protestant theologians. Historical data on the sacraments and the hermeneutical tools of these methodologies are likewise unavoidable for a sound theology, but the historical approach by itself may not be the ideal starting point.

History is vitally important. There is a clear dialectic between the historical data and the Christian doctrine on sacraments. In the contemporary world, one without the other—history eschewing doctrine or doctrine eschewing history—cannot be considered valid. There is clearly a correlation between these two dimensions of Christian life. Nonetheless, history does not of itself create church doctrine; on the other hand, church doctrine cannot present an image of a sacrament for which the historical data offers no validity. If, on the one hand, there is over a long period of time a historical silence on a doctrinal issue, then the doctrinal issue might possibly be maintained. If, on the other hand, the historical data over a long period of time moves in an opposite direction from the current, standard, church approach, then the church approach needs to be radically reconsidered.

An example might help. Prior to 215 C.E. there is no uncontested historical data on *ordination* to Christian ministry. Prior to this, how a person was accepted into a given role of Christian ministry is not known with any certainty, and any and every view remains conjectural. In other words, a dogmatic view that from New Testament times onward, those who were *episkopoi, presbyteroi,* or *diakonoi* were "ordained," is simply a matter of conjecture. Historical data during this time is silent or inconclusive on the question. Consequently, every position—they were not ordained, or they were ordained, or some were ordained, or in some churches there was ordination—can be maintained or denied, but only on a conjectural basis. Dogmatically, some might argue such ministers had to be ordained, but this position, too, remains conjectural.[13]

Another example is the early historical data on apostolic succession of bishops. Historical data does not substantiate the standard presentation that "bishops" succeed the apostles. During the entire second century, there is major historical data that indicates that *presbyteroi,* not *episkopoi,* were considered the successors of the apostles.[14] Nowhere in the gospels is there any indication that the apostles were ordained, nor, with the exception of Luke, are the twelve and the apostles seen as identical.[15] Theologians have continually raised the issue whether the phrase "bishops are the successors of the apostles" can really be held up as a doctrine of the church.[16]

Historical data will continually raise such questions about individual positions, and this is healthy. Without a sound historical basis, sacramental theology cannot help but be considered epiphenomenal, or even a form of religious ideology. Theological positions are seemingly superimposed on history to provide a certain ecclesial and ecclesiastical verification.[17] In all of this, historical studies are important, but they cannot be seen as the point of departure for sacramental thought in the third millennium.

FOURTH POINT OF DEPARTURE:
JESUS AS THE PRIMORDIAL SACRAMENT—
THE CHURCH AS THE FOUNDATIONAL SACRAMENT

Jesus in his humanity as the primordial sacrament, and the church as the foundational sacrament, became a point of departure for many Catholic theologians once the writings of Semmelroth, Rahner, and Schillebeeckx became popular. This provided a much-needed balance to sacramental theology, since it moved away from a "two-and-two-only sacrament" approach, on the one hand, and from a "seven-and-only-seven sacrament" approach, on the other. Reaching beyond both scholasticism and neo-scholasticism to the patristic period of both East and West, these authors presented an approach to Christian sacramentality that was old and yet new. Sacramentality was seen by these authors as a more profound aspect of the Christian Church with a primordial base in the Incarnation itself and a foundational base in the church. Sacramental thought was more closely tied to Jesus, since, in the limited two or seven views of sacraments, the tie to Jesus was basically that sacraments were instituted by Christ. An intrinsic connection to the very Incarnation was never involved, either in the metaphysical or the physical definitions of sacraments, and the New Testament connection was understood only through the causal institution by Jesus of the sacraments.

Moreover, the intrinsic connection to the church provisioned the ritual sacraments with a profound ecclesial quality: they are the actions of the church. Indeed, Vatican II documents on several occasions indicate that in the eucharist one finds the source and summit of the church's being (*SC,* nos. 6, 7; *LG,* nos. 3, 7). One finds this same relationship of sacrament and church in the writings of Henri de Lubac and John Zizioulas.[18] Louis-Marie Chauvet, in *Symbole et Sacrement,* likewise uses this approach but enriches it with a deeper philosophical foundation.[19]

In third millennium sacramental theology, the primordial relationship between the ritual sacraments and the Incarnation and the foundational relationship between ritual sacraments and the church, must be continued and developed. It is a major step away from the epiphenomenal approach of the past and a strong development of an organic sacramental hermeneutic. A danger remains, since it is possible to see the Incarnation itself as epiphenomenal to the world, namely, through a purely accidental relationship between creation and Incarnation. If one's christology is epiphenomenal, stemming from an onto-theological basis that views Jesus only as a remedy for fallen nature, then the sacraments will likewise be epiphenomenal and onto-theological.

The same caution can be raised regarding ecclesiology. The church can be theologically presented as epiphenomenal to the world, namely, as a second ark of salvation, a *Deus ex machina* redemptive mediation, a haven only for the elite. If the church is in this way seen as epiphenomenal and if the church, at the same time, is to be considered a foundational sacrament, then the ritual sacraments as actions of this foundationally sacramental church are likewise onto-theological epiphenomena. These two caveats indicate that one must do more than merely relate the sacraments to the church as a foundational sacrament and to Jesus as primordial sacrament. The very fabric of one's ecclesiology and the very fabric of one's christology must also be considered in their own sacramental quality.

Nonetheless, Jesus in his humanity as primordial sacrament and the church in its interrelatedness of living Christians will remain a part of the third millennium sacramental life, but the understanding of these ideas of primordiality and foundationality needs to be readdressed and rethought within a different hermeneutic.

FIFTH POINT OF DEPARTURE: A CRITIQUE OF THE ONTO-THEOLOGICAL PRESUPPOSITIONS OF CLASSICAL SACRAMENTAL THEOLOGY AND AN OVERCOMING OF ONTO-THEOLOGICAL THOUGHT

The title of this section is rather long, but it represents the wording of Chauvet's position in *Symbole et Sacrement*. Needless to say, this book by Chauvet represents a postmodern approach to Christian sacramental theology. For that very reason, it should stand as one of the significant approaches for those who will study sacramental theology in the third millennium.

In his first chapter, Chauvet presents a lengthy description and analysis of the sacramental thought of Thomas Aquinas. His *foci* are grace and cause, and he studies both the similarities and differences of Thomas's sacramental thought as found in *Commentary on the Sentences* and the treatise on the sacraments within the *Summa Theologica* (Pars III). Sign, sacrament, grace, and cause are the issues Chauvet uses to show the nuancing of thought in the writings of Thomas. But Chauvet does more; he also points out the implications these ideas and changes bring to bear on sacramental theology.

In his second chapter, which deals with the overcoming of onto-theology, Chauvet enters into the enterprise of postmodern philosophical thought. He cites Heidegger, Lacan, Lévinas, Derrida, Habermas, Bachelard, and Ricoeur. Chauvet is providing readers with a point of departure, not only for sacramental theology but for the entire enterprise of Christian theology. Thus, what he argues and presents in this chapter has implications for a theological treatise on God, the Trinity, the Incarnation, redemption, the church, and morality. Postmodern philosophical thought turns the onto-theology of classical theology into a different kind of thinking.

Because we in the West think in such a Greek way, our metaphysical approach centers on being, as it has been understood in the West until postmodernism began to develop. The only way we understand God is through an onto-theology. This "onto-" aspect of the correlation has been seriously questioned, and indeed a new paradigm has been established in the West so that Westerners find themselves at this threshold to the third millennium wondering if the "onto-" aspect of their onto-theology has any currency left.

The following pages will make use of Chauvet's insights, as well as those of Heidegger, Habermas, and Ricoeur. A younger generation in the Western world has no doubt already abandoned the "onto-" aspect of classical Western thought and assimilated many aspects of postmodernity. To continue speaking on the basis of a philosophy that is for the most part unintelligible and meaningless to new generations may be a fruitless task. If scholastic onto-theology is the form in which sacramental life is presented to the new generations, sacramental life will be seen as meaningless.

Regis Duffy offers the reader a look ahead as he describes "The Future of Sacrament"[20] at the end of his lengthy essay. "Sacramental theology," he writes in *Systematic Theology,* "if it is to be effective for the mission of the Church, must take into account some unresolved issues."[21] One of these issues is "symbolic competence in a post-industrial age and its corollary, the responsible reception of sacraments."[22] This rethinking of symbolic competence in a postindustrial and postmodern age corresponds very well with the direction Chauvet is taking. Duffy enumerates two other issues for effective sacramental theology in this same time period: "(1) The cultural context of evangelization and sacrament; and (2) the role of the Holy Spirit and its ecumenical corollaries."[23] However, these two issues, in my view, are better related to the next and final point of departure.

SIXTH POINT OF DEPARTURE:
THE SACRAMENTALITY OF THE UNIVERSE

No one point of departure is adequate for any theological endeavor, and so the selection of the sacramentality of the world might be seen alongside of and complementary to Jesus as primordial sacrament and the church as a foundational sacrament. It might also be seen as a part of the demise of onto-theology and the reprise of certain aspects of postmodernity. Still, there is another issue that today urges this aspect as an integral part of any sacramental point of departure. This issue has various components of which the following are perhaps the most significant: the globalization that is taking place in our contemporary world; multicultural sensitivity that questions the hegemony of the West; and dialogues among world religions, all of which are involved in a journey to the sacred. Even the issue of the church as sacrament needs to make use of the possible sacramentality of the entire world, since the church *as the foundational sacrament* is the entire church. No one church and no individual denomination, not even the Roman Catholic Church, can claim to be the totality of the church as basic sacrament. In this sense, ecclesiality and sacramentality cannot be divided.

E. Kilmartin, in his essay "Theology of the Sacraments: Toward a New Understanding of the Chief Rites of the Church of Jesus Christ,"[24] entitles a section "Sacramental Nature of the Cosmos." He notes that in the patristic and in the early Middle Ages, many theologians considered that salvation history began with creation itself. Therefore <u>all creation</u> bears the mark of God's <u>love for humanity</u>. The Christian ritual sacraments, Kilmartin argues, "were valued as particular concentrations of the sacramental nature of all creation. They were interpreted as the highest manifestations of God's presence in the whole of the cosmos."[25] Kilmartin notes that the systematic theologians of the twelfth and thirteenth centuries have the same basic outlook, affirming that created realities, when used in the sacraments, attain their full meaning. Notice that he does not say a *new* meaning; he says a "full" meaning. In the sacraments, as in the cosmos, he writes, there is a *sacrum commercium*. This approach was changed, Kilmartin notes, with the post-Reformation development of a secular sphere of philosophy, in which "stress was placed on the power of human reason to reconstruct reality and to manipulate and change it."[26] This new view of reality could only produce both major problems as well as a profound disconnectedness within the Christian framework of sacramentality itself.

> The attempt to establish the institution of sacraments by a positive divine decree, without reference to the sacramental nature of all reality, does not correspond to the teaching of the early and high Scholastics, although they also held for the institution of sacraments by Christ. It is indicative of a lack of ability to maintain an integrated view of the real world. In a word, with the loss of a sacramental understanding of all reality, the doctrine of analogy is deprived of its grounds.[27]

The modern technological way of thinking does indeed make it difficult to experience the cosmos as open to transcendence or the cosmos as reflecting the mystery of God's grandeur. Contemporary Western people live within a worldview that is closed in on reason and science itself. Duffy focuses on this issue in a detailed way.[28]

Neither van der Leeuw nor Kilmartin develops to any extent the sacramentality of the world. The same lack of development can be seen in the *Catechism of the Catholic Church*. Section one of its sacramental presentation (nos. 1076–1209) is called "The Sacramental Economy," and the authors state that "it is therefore important to explain this 'sacramental dispensation' *(chapter one)*. The nature and essential features of liturgical expression will then appear more clearly *(chapter two)*" (no. 1076). The difficulty is, as we noted above, that the material presented in this first section of the *Catechism* on the sacramental dispensation does not play any major operative role when the *Catechism* moves to section two, a far longer section, on the seven sacraments of the church (nos. 1113–1690). The material in chapter one is totally ignored in chapter two. The world-encompassing sacramental economy, which is touched on in the first section of the *Catechism,* loses all significance when the individual sacraments are presented in the same *Catechism.* However, it is helpful to see in the *Catechism* a brief description of the sacramental economy beginning with creation itself (nos. 1077–1109) and also a discussion of signs and symbols (nos. 1145–52), which ranges far beyond the liturgical sphere of Christian thought.

In the late patristic and early medieval discussion of the sacramentality of the entire world, probably Rupert of Deutz and Bonaventure had the greatest influence. Both of these scholars had as their task the tracing of the presence of the Trinity throughout creation, since all created beings have been created by a triune God.[29]

At the end of his volume, Chauvet says: "Creation is itself charged with sacramentality."[30] He goes on to explain that sacramentality, including Christian sacramentality, arises "only at the intersection of these two dimensions, cosmic and historic."[31] It would have been intriguing had this element of creation been more expressly stated throughout his book.

I wish to make Chauvet's thesis far more explicit in my presentation on sacramentality. Therefore, this volume begins (in chapter 3) with the world and its possible forms of sacramentality. From there I move to the Incarnation, which means Jesus, in his humanness, as the primordial sacrament (chapter 4). I turn next to the church as a foundational sacrament (chapter 5). Next I attempt to form a synthesis of contemporary sacramentality and postmodern thought (chapter 6). Finally, I consider solemn statements of the magisterium and their meaning within this postmodern framework (chapter 7).

Before beginning the next chapter, however, two important observations must be made. In this litany of various points of departure, the reader may have noticed that I did not include as a point of departure the statements of the magisterium of the church. This in no way is intended to deprecate the value and necessity of these magisterial statements for Roman Catholic theology. Indeed, references to these magisterial documents will be made throughout this volume. The majority of official and defined statements of the magisterium on sacraments is expressed in the documents of the Council of Trent. Almost all the defined statements are expressed negatively: "If anyone says…then, let that person be anathematized." In other words, the view stated is *not* a point of departure for Roman Catholics. These negative statements make a constructive point of departure difficult. A point of departure, in most instances, does not effectively begin with something negative, a statement that says not to go in this or that direction. Such negative statements are not points of departure, but points of non-departure, and for this reason I have not listed magisterial statements as an operative point of departure.

Second, transcendental Thomism was not mentioned as a point of departure. This may appear strange, since a number of major scholars can be listed as transcendental Thomists: Pierre Rousselot, Joseph Maréchal, Maurice Blondel, Gustav Siewerth, Johann Baptist Lotz, Max Müller, Bernhard Welte, Karl Rahner, and Bernard Lonergan. To some degree or another, all of these scholars focus on the issue of human subjectivity, particularly in the way in which Kant and Schleiermacher had presented it. Heidegger has been used, again in varying degrees, by many of these scholars. In the sense that the discussion focuses on the issue of subjectivity and the epistemology this involves, transcendental Thomistic thought can be allied, at least to some degree, to the efforts of Chauvet.

In sacramental theology one finds this transcendental Thomistic approach in Rahner's *The Church and the Sacraments,* and in Schillebeeckx's *Christ the Sacrament of Encounter with God.* In both of these volumes the sections the respective authors devote to Jesus as sacrament and the church as sacrament echo with Heideggerian and phenomenological overtones. However, when Rahner discusses individual sacraments,[32] and when Schillebeeckx considers such themes as sacramental character, *ex opere operato* and *ex opere operantis,* the revival of the sacrament, matter and form,[33] both authors revert to a neo-Thomistic, onto-theological framework. In sacramental theology neither author satisfactorily unites the Heideggerian and phenomenological side with the scholastic side. As a result, I will indicate instances in which transcendental Thomism has been of help for sacramental theology, and instances in which it has been unhelpful.

3

Sacramental Structures in the World at Large

Roman Catholic, Anglican, and Protestant theologians and church officials have generally used the word "sacrament" with hermeneutical ease. These authors, both remote and recent, have stated with an apodictic fierceness either that there are two and only two sacraments, or that there are seven and only seven sacraments. With a similar ease, these same theologians and church officials have declared that this or that sacramental act was or was not a valid sacrament; they have declared that this or that denomination's baptism, eucharist, ordination, was or was not acceptable as a valid sacrament by their own denomination and, therefore, such an action was not a sacrament at all.

Around the mid-twentieth century, when certain Roman Catholic theologians began to describe the church as a foundational sacrament, they also used the term "sacrament" with hermeneutical ease. In the documents of Vatican II, the bishops officially described the church as a sacrament with little explanation of the precise meaning of "sacrament" used in this new context. Theologians who were opposed to this line of thinking argued their opposition by calling the church a "sacrament" but *only through an analogical use* of the term. Nonetheless, in calling the church a sacrament only in an analogical sense, the *clarifying* hermeneutical term is presumably "analogical," while the term "sacrament" itself is presupposed to be hermeneutically clear. It is the facile use of the terms, "analogical" and "sacrament," that I wish to emphasize, noting that in these contexts neither term is clear.

The theme of this chapter is sacramental structures of the world at large. First, I address the hermeneutical and onto-hermeneutical shift in

Western thought today; second, I consider some basic theological positions on the sacraments today; third, I indicate a possible meaning for the phrase "the sacramental structures of the world at large."

THE HERMENEUTICAL AND
ONTO-HERMENEUTICAL PROBLEM

Gary B. Madison's comment on Husserl provides a clear basis for the contemporary questioning of a facile hermeneutic:

> A pivotal moment in the unfolding of Husserl's phenomenology occurred in 1907 with a series of five lectures delivered in Göttingen. In these lectures Husserl introduced his celebrated "phenomenological reduction," the express purpose of which was to achieve a decisive overcoming of what the French translator of this work, Alexandre Lowit, has called "la situation phénoménale du clivage," in other words, the subject/object split which presides over the origin and subsequent unfolding of modern philosophy from Descartes onwards. To speak in contemporary terms, what Husserl was seeking to accomplish by means of the "reduction" was a thoroughgoing "deconstruction" of the central problematic of modern philosophy itself, namely, the "epistemological" problem of how an isolated subjectivity, closed in upon itself, can none the less manage to "transcend" itself in such a way as to achieve a "knowledge" of the "external world."[1]

In this lengthy but important observation, Madison points out one of the key philosophical issues that emerged in the twentieth century: the "deconstruction" and "reconstruction"[2] of the subject/object way of thinking that had dominated Western thought, including theological thought, from the Middle Ages to the twentieth century. Husserl addressed this issue at the beginning of the century, and as the decades went by, the issue of this split was more and more deeply challenged by major philosophers, not merely in epistemological terms, but increasingly in onto-epistemological terms.[3]

The widespread subject/object way of Western thinking and the consequent hermeneutical ease with which Roman Catholic, Anglican, and Protestant theologians and church officials have used a subject/object linguistic base are exemplified whenever these same leaders have spoken about sacraments generally, or whenever they have invalidated or validated either their own sacraments or those of other churches. One finds in their declarations a presupposed certitude as they proclaim a given sacramental celebration valid or invalid. Their very certitude gives evidence of their hermeneutical ease. They know in objective ways what a sacrament is and what it is not.

This entire manner of thinking and speaking has been questioned by twentieth-century Western philosophers. Of course, the issue of sacraments was by no means the focus of this rejection. Rather, the focus was on the entire pattern of Western thought and hermeneutic. Discourse on the sacraments is but one consequent arena, *which I am choosing* in order to exhibit an instance in which this fundamental questioning has challenged and continues to challenge theological discourse. I have selected the *hermeneutical ease* that these leaders and writers have used when they present material on the sacraments as a clear illustration of the urgency of this deconstruction of Western thought patterns. For the vast majority of the people in the Western world today, the presumed hermeneutic of these church and theological leaders, a hermeneutic based on the now seriously challenged subject-object onto-epistemology, has no meaning whatsoever. In other words, the hermeneutic that these church people use as a tool for meaning has become, for a large part of the third-millennium population of this world, meaningless.[4]

Today's world is multicultural, and since globalization does not mean exclusively a Westernization of the world, it is correct to say that the total world is being inculturated in and through a multicultural fusion of horizons. Cultural ways of thinking and cultural meaning structures are currently interactive. Thus, to speak of the world as a sacrament may have little meaning for a culture in which the very word "sacrament" is missing. Nor can theologians argue that most cultures have a unique symbol system in and through which the term "sacrament" becomes meaningful. When the word "sacrament" in the framework of these same theological traditions means only two rituals or only seven rituals, or the term "sacrament" refers only to the Roman Catholic Church or only to the Christian Church, or the term is applied only to a Jewish individual, namely Jesus, then "sacrament" has no facile entree into a non-Western culture simply on the basis of a given culture's symbolic framework. The exclusivity inherent in the term "sacrament," when used in this way, precludes any meaningful relationship to the symbol system of a non-Christian culture.

There is, moreover, in all of this discussion, a presumed Archimedean place that the Western authors mentioned above use to judge what is and what is not a sacrament. Such authors *know* what is correctly and validly a sacrament and what is not. But, one might legitimately ask, what is this Archimedean point? What is this view *sub specie aeternitatis?* The search for an Archimedean point is the Achilles' heel of the traditional subject/object dichotomy and its concomitant way of knowing and being. It is also the Achilles' heel when it comes to multicultural thought. Why is the Western Archimedean point the benchmark from which one can adjudicate all validity and invalidity? What warranty does this Western positioning claim to have over different thought structures? In theological thought, but not only there, whenever there are instances of hermeneutical ease in the context of multicultural issues, a suspicion of Western theological imperialism cannot help but arise. Even without this suspicion of Western hegemony, the very implication of an Archimedean point finds absolutely no resonance in postmodern thinking. Such a claim is hermeneutically meaningless.

In *Les Mots et les choses*, Michel Foucault speaks of a discursive practice, namely, a whole set of common themes or ideas produced within a broad period of time and throughout a wide variety of various disciplines and multiple areas of human endeavor. Such a conceptual unity is called by Foucault an *episteme*. A particular episteme is marked by a certain dominance.

> The origin of a particular tradition is not the radical beginning of the tradition. A particular tradition is marked by a certain dominance. The space and time when the particular tradition begins to dominate constitutes its place of origin. So, too the demise of a particular tradition is not the final moment of its life. Rather, the space and time where and when a particular tradition loses its dominance is the time and place of its demise.[5]

In this view the Western subject/object thought pattern had its origin only when it came into dominance, but it had had a long development prior to that period of origin through dominance. During that development time it was at best an embryonic episteme. So, too, its demise is taking place before our eyes as it loses its position of dominance. This does not mean it has disappeared; it simply means that it has ended as a meaningful episteme. To continue to filter one's theology through a dying episteme is meaningless.

Yet another factor plays a disconcerting role in the field of sacraments. What we have just treated above might be seen as the *phenomenological* factor, and what we take up now is the *existential* factor. These two factors complement one another. Both have characterized twentieth-century Western philosophy in a major way. Later postmodern philosophers are, in central ways, postexistential phenomenologists as well.

Let us consider the existential factor. Theologians and church officials speak freely of baptism and of eucharist. Baptism, they say, is this or that. Eucharist, they say, is this or that. However, baptism is not a replication, a verbal phrase emphasizing an action, nor is baptism a replicated clone, a substantive phrase emphasizing a thing. Each baptism is not a duplication of a rote activity, nor is each baptism the enfleshing of a duplicative reality. Rather, each baptism is an existential event, an existential action, an existential *Ereignis*.[6] Each baptism is an individualized, historically discrete, temporally unrepeatable moment in the life of an individual, of a particular community of Christians, and of the temporal-historical presence of an active God. There is no such thing as generic baptism, just as there is no such thing as generic eucharist.[7] Each baptism is a unique event; each eucharist is equally a unique event. To use a Scotistic term, there is an *Haecceitas*—a "thisness"—about each sacramental celebration. There is, then, a fundamental sacramental *Haecceitas* that cannot, with any hermeneutical ease, be relegated to non-importance by an overarching generic term such as "baptism" or "eucharist." As an existential event, as an Ereignis in the Heideggerian sense of this term, there exists an interplay of many subjectivities and an interfacing of commingled intentionalities. There exists, as Paul Ricoeur would say, a fusion of horizons.[8] The uniqueness of each and every baptism or eucharist bears eloquent witness to sacramental *Haecceitas*. No actual baptism can ever be repeated; no actual eucharist can ever be repeated. The reality of baptism can only be found in the singularized happenings of these existential baptisms and eucharists. Outside of these actualized and singularized baptismal and eucharistic events, the very terms baptism and eucharist have at best some generic, nonrealistic, linguistically conventional meaning. Multiple unique factors in an existential sacramental event, including its non-repeatability, its *Haecceitas,* if you will, make a ritualized action an event that can be called a sacramental baptism or a sacramental eucharist. The individuality and the singularity of each discrete sacramental act is not peripheral or accidental to what baptism and eucharist are. There is no baptism except in the very existential action and event of a given baptism. There is no eucharist except in the very existential action and event of eucharist. There is, therefore, no "essence" of either baptism or eucharist that is replicated or cloned in the celebration of a given sacrament and thereby constitutes it as a sacrament. Nor is there any essence of a thing called sacrament that is replicated or cloned in the celebration of a given rite at a given time by given people and, thereby, constitutes this individual action a sacrament.

If we consider the actual baptism of a specific individual named "X," we find the presence of specific ministers, of specific family members, and of specific friends. We find the celebration occurring at a specific and unrepeatable moment of time, at a specific and unrepeatable place within the cosmos. The personal, physical, temporal, spatial coordinates for this actual moment of baptism will never occur again. Generic baptism is a figment of the imagination.

The implications of this sacramental *Haecceitas* are obviously intense. Any theology of baptism is only a theology *about* baptism, descriptive rather than prescriptive, since every theology of baptism deals with some generic baptism but not with the actual reality of an existential moment of baptism. It is in this latter event that one experiences the reality of baptism; in books we learn only some things about baptism.

Canonical and liturgical regulations are no different. These regulations speak about baptism or eucharist generically, and thus they too are more descriptive than prescriptive, since laws or canons are meant for general situations, not for individualized, unrepeatable situations. Frederick McManus writes:

> The liturgical celebrations of sacraments and other services are actions implicating the whole person of each member of the Christian assembly; they are matters of the most intimate faith and piety, which are articulated communally. The norms that govern them are more aesthetic and artistic than juridic or canonical.[9]

McManus indicates that the flexibility of current liturgical law and an openness to adaptation reflect the pastoral situation itself. He notes that sacraments are ultimately celebrations of the mysteries in the Spirit, and so not easily governed. He reminds us that there is indeed a legitimate openness, a permitted recognition of the religious value of diversity, and even an invitation to greater cultural adaptations. Having noted all of this, McManus comments that in liturgical celebrations there is an expression of true Christian faith and there are "recurring forms and patterns that are evidently subject to canonical discipline and normative custom."[10] But what are these "recurring forms and patterns" except abstractions and generalizations? Is it some recurring form and pattern that makes a given sacrament valid and acceptable? If so, then we clearly have some reiterated cloning going on. We are once again back to the world of objective essences, and it is precisely such a world that contemporary Western postmodern philosophy denies. McManus writes with a certain hermeneutical ease, but for the majority of the world the very hermeneutic he is using is without meaning.[11]

The reason for emphasizing sacramental *Haecceitas* is this: one only experiences a sacrament in the existential, particular doing of a unique sacramental action. It is in this unique action alone that sacrament has meaning. General statements on sacraments have their place, but it is secondary not foundational, ancillary not controlling. Twentieth-century philosophers say that "totalizing Archimedean principles are renounced"[12] as basic principles of onto-hermeneutics.

One might argue against this form of discourse by saying: Is this not putting the cart before the horse? Is this not letting a contemporary philosophy determine one's theology or a church's dogma? Why should some current philosophy dictate one's theology? This is not my point at all, to put philosophy before theology, to put the cart before the horse.

When McManus speaks about "recurring forms and patterns that are evidently subject to canonical discipline and normative custom," a postmodern thinker would immediately recall some of the key passages from Habermas, particularly in *Logik der Sozialwissenschaften.*[13] Or, as Ricoeur describes it, "the conception of historical consciousness and the provocative rehabilitation of the three connected concepts of prejudice, authority and tradition."[14] This text of Habermas is by no means marginal, for it goes to the central issue, the *Brennpunkt,*

> to the place from which this hermeneutics speaks and upon which it raises its claim to universality. This experience is the scandal constituted, on the level of modern consciousness, by the sort of alienating distanciation—*Verfremdung*—which is not merely a feeling or a mood, but rather the ontological presupposition which sustains the objective conduct of the human sciences. The methodology of these sciences ineluctably implies an assumption

of distance; and this, in turn, presupposes the destruction of the primordial relation of belonging—*Zugehörigkeit*—without which there would be no relation to the historical as such.[15]

There is clearly a hermeneutic of tradition that engenders a set of prejudices, a set of authorities, and a set of traditions. The question that lies at the center of this debate is the derived place of an unsurpassable claim to universality. McManus evidences one of these hermeneutics of tradition with his call for obligatory recurring forms and patterns as also normative customs. There is indeed a positive way of considering prejudice, tradition, and authority, which Gadamer attempts to validate against the pejorative appraisal by the *Aufklärung* of these three phenomena. *Wahrheit und Methode* specifically deals with this rehabilitation.[16] Postmodern thinking asks a serious question about any unsurpassable claim to universality in two ways: first, on the basis of hermeneutics, there is a clear questioning of any hermeneutical ease; second, on the basis of some sort of onto-hermeneutics, there is a clear affirmation of the return to the subject on the one hand and of structural temporality on the other. We will return to this approach later in greater detail. For now we note that McManus—and with him so many other Christian authors who write on sacraments, whether canonists, theologians, or members of the hierarchical magisterium—employs a certain hermeneutical ease, and in the claim for universality and atemporality, faces a severe and far-reaching challenge from postmodern thinkers.

To clarify my position, let us take another serious look at the way in which traditional theology and dogma are defended against these inroads of contemporary philosophy. The manner in which theologians and church officials have considered sacraments in the past embodies a philosophical framework, namely, the subject/object philosophy that twentieth-century Western philosophy has radically questioned. If there is a cart before the horse in what is said above—that is, using contemporary philosophy to determine theology and doctrine—there is clearly a cart before the horse in what has been said on sacraments from the twelfth century to today. Language and hermeneutics are twinned. The epistemological and onto-epistemological hermeneutic in which the language on sacraments has been traditionally couched has its own dialectic practice, its own *episteme*. As a result, the very same critique that one might make of this current radical questioning of traditional Western thought can be brought to bear on the "scholastic," the "neo-scholastic," and the "transcendental-Thomistic" approach as well. What the current philosophy has brought and brings into question is precisely the hermeneutical ease that these three forms of Western theology employ whenever they speak of sacraments. All three are speaking about a "generic" sacrament, an objective "essence" of sacrament, that one finds replicated in the individual celebrations of sacraments, thereby constituting them as valid sacraments. It is this essentialism that is at the very nub of the problem:

1. Is sacrament something generic, essential, trans-temporal, and trans-historical, and the actual sacramental celebrations mere instances or cases of a given sacrament?

2. Or is sacrament only a reality when it takes place in a highly individualized existential moment of space and time with highly individualized subjectivities and their interfacing of divergent intentionalities, and are all generalized presentations on sacrament only abstract, unreal, generalized statements?

In my view, today position one is unintelligible. It is not only unintelligible insofar as it has its own epistemological framework; it has its own onto-epistemological framework as well, since it deals with something nonexistent, a generalized and abstract idea of sacrament, as though it has some essential reality. This is why there is a question about the *hermeneutic* ease that one finds in so much sacramental presentation. The use of the term "sacrament" is easily understood, so the argument goes, since it refers to this overarching essential reality called baptism or eucharist, which transcends any single, individual, existential moment of either baptism or eucharist. It is precisely this essential reality of baptism, present in each and every "case" of baptism, which makes baptism truly baptism. The hermeneutics behind this kind of phrasing is what is questioned, this over-validation of a so-called objective approach to the minimizing of the existential and subjective situation.

A significant step was made when Semmelroth, Rahner, and Schillebeeckx began to speak about the church itself as a foundational sacrament. The ritual sacraments, with their individual distinctness, were placed within a foundational framework, namely, an understanding of the sacraments as actions of the church itself.

The new *Code of Canon Law* continues this direction of sacramental thought:

> Liturgical actions are not private actions but celebrations of the Church itself, which is "the sacrament of unity," namely a holy people, assembled and ordered under the bishops (can. 837).

The *Catechism of the Catholic Church,* for its part, states:

> Liturgy is an "action": of the *whole Christ (Christus totus)* [cf. 1136]. It is the whole *community,* the Body of Christ united with its Head that celebrates [cf. 1140].

In both of these official church statements we see that sacraments are fundamentally actions and, even more, actions of the church. This is another way of saying that the church is a foundational sacrament.[17] In all of this, however, there is a hermeneutical ease in which the theologians, as well as the writers of these official statements, have used the word "sacrament." The phrase, "the church is a foundational sacrament," is presented as self-evident. But is it? The phrase, "the liturgy is an action," is stated as if it is self-evident, but is it? Questions immediately arise. When one says that the church is a foundational sacrament, is this the universal church, the local church, or both? Is the universal church some sort of "essence" overarching all the local churches, and, if so, is the universal church an "invisible church essence," a position that frequently has been rejected by Roman Catholic Church leadership? Or is the universal church a "visible essence," which then involves all the issues surrounding the papacy? This position finds little acceptance in what one calls the Church Catholic or the wider ecumenical church. Are local churches at heart simply cloned replications of this universal church, an action emphasis, or a replicated clone of a universal church, a substantive emphasis? In either case, to what does sacrament refer? An essence? A grand plan? An overarching Archimedean point? Or, more philosophically, an object beyond our subjectivity, and therefore real because it is not tainted by personal subjectivity? Is this subject/object framework for speaking at all viable today? In the West there is growing agreement that such an onto-epistemological framework is untenable and, therefore, a way of sacramental thought and action that is filtered through this form of subject/object onto-epistemology is equally untenable and, as a result, hermeneutically questionable or even meaningless.

When one says that liturgies are "actions of the church," it is not clear what is meant, since only a concrete, individual, existential action, a baptizing, is taking place. Clearly an action is occurring. An individual is being baptized. A very definite, existential church community is part of this baptizing event. Where does the "church's action" enter in? Are people who are not there at that precise point of space and time actually there as agents and even more as primary agents? What kind of hermeneutic is being used when we hear that liturgical actions are "celebrations" of the church itself; "actions" of the church itself? How can one have meaningful actions that are not made concrete in time and space and in persons? What objective entity do the authors of this kind of statement have in mind, and what kind of onto-hermeneutic are they using when they make this kind of statement? The same can be said of the phrase, "liturgy is an action of the whole Christ." Merely translating "whole Christ" into Latin, *Christus totus,* as the *Catechism* does, does not clarify anything. The hermeneutic and the onto-hermeneutic behind these kinds of statements have been called into question, and the challenge of this questioning cannot be set aside as irrelevant.

When one moves to an even more delicate issue, namely, Jesus in his humanness as the primordial sacrament, several issues immediately arise:

1. How can something finite, the humanness of Jesus with all its own spatial, temporal, and personal coordinates, be raised to an Archimedean position of primordial? Is something radically finite being made into something non-finite; some individual being made into something primordial, into an archetypal being, and therefore no longer a finite, individual being?

2. If Jesus' humanness is primordial, is Jesus truly human *(alethos anthropos),* perfectly human *(teleios en anthropoteti),* and consubstantial with us *(homoousios hemin)?* This is the teaching of the Council of Chalcedon. Is Jesus no longer human, as we understand ourselves, since we do not experience ourselves in any form of primordiality?

3. If this "primordial Jesus" is the primordial sacrament, is this not setting up some sort of "grand plan" or Archimedean point in a finite world, a world that is radically experienced as historical, temporal, and limited? On what hermeneutical base is such a primordial Jesus understandable, since our human hermeneutic is intrinsically historical, temporal, spatial, and finite?

It is not self-evident that the theologians who use this phrase, "Jesus, the primordial sacrament," have avoided a facile hermeneutic. In each of the three cases mentioned above, the case of existential sacraments, the case of the church as foundational sacrament, and the case of Jesus in his humanness as primordial sacrament, something is being said about a very particular element or reality of the historical, temporal, and finite world, which nonetheless appears to predicate something ahistorical, atemporal, and non-finite.

The precise word that bespeaks this ahistoricality, atemporality, and non-finitude is "sacrament," because the word not only overarches time, space, and finitude, but at the same time focuses on individual and specific realities, which alone are or can be qualified as sacraments. In other words, why can only two or seven rituals be called and actually be sacraments? Why is the church, and it alone, a foundational sacrament—and no other religious group is or can be so designated? Why is Jesus in his specific humanness, and he alone, called, and in truth is the primordial sacrament, and no other person in his or her specific humanness is called or can be called primordial sacrament?

I am not, at this moment, denying the validity of the Catholic Church or its claim to uniqueness, nor am I denying the validity of Jesus as central to the Christian faith. These are, indeed, legitimate issues that have arisen in a very strong way in the twentieth century and will continue to be discussed into the new millennium.[18] They are not, however, my focus here. My focus here is a hermeneutical one, which centers on the ease with which one employs the term "sacrament" and thereby presupposes a self-evident meaning. Nor is the hermeneutical issue I focus on simply an epistemological issue; rather, it is an onto-epistemological issue, since the very term "sacrament" involves both an intellectual recognition of the symbolic dynamism of an action, the epistemological dimension, and also the reality or "being" to which the symbol points, the ontological dimension.

One might ask: Where is the connection between all of this and the sacramental structure of the world, which is the theme of this chapter? If "sacrament" has its basic meaning only with two or seven ritual sacraments and nothing else, then clearly there is something epiphenomenal taking place. In this framework of discussing "sacrament," one is hermeneutically unable to understand sacramentality outside the dimension of these two or seven areas. These two or seven areas stand out *(ek-stasis)* from ordinary human phenomena in an exclusive way and, as a result, they transcend ordinary human hermeneutics and transcend ordinary human phenomena.

One speaks of transubstantiation only in the case of the eucharist, and this is clearly a transcending of human and physical phenomena. One speaks in theological discussion of an ontological change in the humanness of one ordained, and this is a transcending of human and physical phenomena. One speaks of an instrumental efficient causality ascribed to sacramental material *(materia et forma),* which is an instrumentality and effectiveness of the instrument far beyond any understandable human phenomena. One speaks of an imprinting of character that has nothing correlative to it within the ambit of human phenomena—and character has meaning and being only within the dimensions of three sacraments. When one speaks of sacrament in any of the above ways, the whole tenor of the discourse presents both hermeneutical and onto-hermeneutical issues that are today totally unintelligible except to a small group of people. The esotericism of this language and the hermeneutics involved in an understanding of this language is the issue on which I am presently focusing.

When we consider the church as foundational sacrament and Jesus as primordial sacrament, the selection of this particular religious body alone as sacramentally symbolic, and this particular human being alone as sacramentally symbolic plays a role in the relationship of sacrament and world. But the terms "foundational" and "primordial" only intensify the problem, since it is the exclusivity of these two religious entities that removes them from the ordinary dimensions of human discourse and from the dimensions of our lived world. The very foundational and primordial sacramentality of these two realities, Jesus and church, gives them a uniqueness that deprives them of the temporality, historicality, and finiteness that is our fundamental human experience, and endows them with a super-spatial, super-temporal, super-finite qualification. It is precisely this super-qualification, so it is argued, that allows them to be seen as foundational and primordial. But is this entire discussion meaningful or meaningless? The problem has to do with hermeneutics and onto-hermeneutics.

All these issues lead to the question of the lived world, the framework in which the ordinary human person lives and moves. In the last chapter mention was made of the framework of the world at large as a point of departure and certain authors were cited, but once more we find that even these authors say rather casually that the world is a sacrament, "the sacramental nature of all reality" (Kilmartin) and "creation itself is charged with sacramentality" ("Ainsi la confession de la création est-elle chargée de sacramentalité") (Chauvet).

Chauvet clarifies his position in an excellent way, however, when he writes:

> The "profane" (that is, the natural) state of the world and of history is thus recognized as the possible sacramental place of a sacred history.[19]

It is this tentativeness, the *"possible* sacramental place," which should be noted. One cannot simply say that the world itself is a sacrament. There is no basis for such an assertion and thus, such a use of the word "sacrament" is facile and, because of this, hermeneutically unintelligible. To say that the world is a "possible sacramental place" is at least intelligible to some degree. No apodictic assertion is made, but simply one of possibility, and not a totally illogical one at that.

On the basis of what has been said, the argument or thesis of this present chapter, and the remainder of the book as well, is this:

> **The world we live in and experience through human perception, and in this way alone (Merleau-Ponty), is possibly a sacramental place (Chauvet), but this depends on an analysis of our human self, our *Dasein*, and its relationship to others and to the ecosystem, thus an analysis of an *In-der-Welt-mit-Anderen-Dasein* (Heidegger). But this also includes an onto-hermeneutical understanding of the human person, both in his or her conscious and his or her unconscious dimension (Ricoeur), and also in a decentering of the subject dispersed through language (Lacan).**

> **From there, I want to say that were we totally theonomous, then the world indeed would be sacramental and the need for "special sacraments" would be negated (Tillich). But this at least implies that there are moments of worldness, *Weltlichkeit*, in which any person experiences, or can experience, sacramentality, and it is only because of these human moments, open to every human phenomenon per se, that it is possible to speak meaningfully of a person, of a church, or of a ritual as**

sacramental. The possible place of sacramentality in the lived world at large provides a hermeneutical key, or better, an onto-hermeneutical key, for those involved in the sacramental actions of church life and, thereby, produces a meaningful self-understanding of sacramental *Haecceitas*.

Such a descriptive thesis cannot help but be controversial. Even when we have finished discussing all the issues contained in the above thesis, it will necessarily be admitted that the end result is not the final answer. Just as there can never be a definition of postmodernism, since postmodernism itself eschews definitions, so too a postmodern approach to sacramentality cannot be a final definition.

The entire discourse is Western through and through. Were I to attempt an understanding of sacramentality by means of Chinese philosophy, it would be developed in a totally different way. This, too, is in keeping with postmodernist thought patterns, which are open to a diversity of hermeneutical and onto-hermeneutical programs. No one way of thinking exhibits the "grand plan" of all reality.

A Basic Theological Position on Sacraments

One further preliminary step needs to be taken, however, before we move into the thesis of this volume. This step is a theological one, not a philosophical one. In the theological world today, a few key issues on sacramentality have arisen that will guide us in our further discussion. The first of these key issues has been officially brought into theological discourse by the *Catechism* itself.

The *Catechism of the Catholic Church* begins its discussion on sacraments with a section on the sacramental economy (1076–1209). This section is divided into two parts:

- Chapter 1 (1077–1134) explains the sacramental dispensation or basis of sacramental action.

- Chapter 2 (1135–1209) explains the nature and essential features of liturgical celebrations, which appear "more clearly" because of the foundation on sacramental dispensation.

What is the basic sacramental dispensation that provides the foundation for all sacramental discussion and clarifies the liturgical celebrations? The authors of the *Catechism* make this basic sacramental dispensation crystal clear when they place their presentation within a trinitarian framework:

- The Father: Source and Goal of All Liturgy (1077–83);

- Christ's Work in the Liturgy (1084–90);

- The Holy Spirit and the Church in the Liturgy (1091–1109).

In all of this material, it is clear that the action of God is established as the foundation of all sacramentality.

Sacramental primordiality belongs to the action of God rather than to anything finite, even to the humanness of Jesus. Foundationality belongs to the action of God rather than to anything finite, such as the church. As we read above, God is the source and goal of all liturgy, sacramental and nonsacramental. God's action is both the primary, primordial, foundational source and the ultimate goal of all sacramentality.

In the section on the Father,[20] the authors have produced one of the best parts of the entire *Catechism*. What is this action of God the Father? The authors are very clear. In each paragraph we read that God blesses.[21]

> *Blessing* is a divine and life-giving action (no. 1078).
> The whole of God's work is a *blessing* (no. 1079).
> From the beginning, God *blessed* all living beings, especially man and woman (no. 1080).
> God *blessed* us through Abraham (no. 1080);
>   through the birth of Isaac;
>   through the escape from Egypt;
>   through the gift of the promised land;
>   through the election of David;
>   through the presence of God in the temple;
>   through the exile (all of these in no. 1081).
> God *blessed* us through the Church's liturgy (no. 1082).
> God *blesses;* we respond (no. 1083).

The meaning of these paragraphs is crystal clear. The Father is the source of all liturgy because, first and foremost, God *blesses* us. Two things, therefore, enter into the very meaning of the word "sacrament":

1. A sacrament is a celebration of God's action, God's blessing.

2. It is the one God who blesses us, even though in the *Catechism* this is predicated of the Father.

To paraphrase the Athanasian Creed, the Father blesses, the Word blesses, the Spirit blesses. But there are not three who bless. Only One blesses. In other words, the very foundation of sacraments, from a theological standpoint, is the *action of God.* This is, theologically speaking, what primordially and foundationally makes a sacrament a sacrament. God is not some "entity," who says from his eternal throne, "I am blessing! I am blessing!" The God who blesses cannot be understood apart from the ones God is blessing: God's entire creation (no. 1079); all living beings, especially men and women (no. 1080); God's people from Abraham to Christ (nos. 1080–81); God's gathered people in the church (nos. 1082–83). This blessing-action of God is specifically described in its "dual dimension," the primordial blessing from God and the subsequent "response" to the blessing by individualized people (no. 1083).

Sacramentality, therefore, is not a thing; nor is it a created thing, a *materia,* a *forma;* nor is it a human action. It is basically an action of God. There is, therefore, no created "thing," as such, that is a sacrament. There is no "human action," as such, that is a sacrament. Rather, there is an action of God, a blessing, and a subsequent human response. But notice the words: an action of God and a human response. These are generalizing words; they are abstracting words. God's action, blessing, is not a generalized action/blessing, nor is it an abstract action/blessing. The subsequent human response is likewise not a generalized or abstract response by generalized and abstract human beings. God's blessing/action is an action that occurs at a specific moment in time and in a specific instance of space to and for some specific human beings. From our human standpoint, we can say that God's blessings are thoroughly existential. To formulate God's blessing abstractly and in generalized terms is to miss what this action of God is all about, and what the subsequent response-action of human beings is all about. A sacramental action of God only occurs in sacramental *Haecceitas.* There is no "essential" general sacramentality, sacramental *generalitas.* Sacramentality is profoundly temporal, profoundly spatial, and profoundly relative. God's blessing/action is a unique blessing/action at a unique time and in a unique space for unique people. Moreover, the human response to this divine blessing is a unique response at a unique time and in a unique space by a unique person. All other generic descriptions of blessing/response are *entia rationis,* constructs of the mind.

In the second part of this trinitarian section of the *Catechism* on *Christ's Work in the Liturgy* (nos. 1084–90), there is, unfortunately, a basic ambiguity. The format that the writers use is clearly trinitarian, but in this section on Christ there is a constant move from the divinity of Jesus, the trinitarian focus, to the humanity of Jesus, the incarnational focus. Nonetheless, since the context is Trinity, and not Incarnation, we are again focused on the action of God, not on the actions of the humanity of Jesus.

The *Catechism* (no. 1085) reads: "In the liturgy of the Church, it is *principally* his own Paschal mystery that Christ signifies and makes present" (italics added). What is this "principal" action that one finds in all liturgy and, for our present focus, in all sacramental liturgy? It is principally the action of the Logos who makes present the paschal mystery. It is the action and presence of the Logos in sacraments that are stressed, in spite of the authors' continual mixing of Trinity and Incarnation.[22]

In this section of the *Catechism* on the Logos, sacramentality is fundamentally and principally the action of God, and secondarily the subsequent response of people to this primordial action of God. What is written here is, of course, generalized and abstract; for example, God is present in the mass or present in the minister (no. 1088). In actuality, however, God/Christ is present only in an actual celebration of an actual, existential eucharist; God/Christ is present only in actual, existential ministers with personal names and identities. God/Christ can be called and in actuality can be present only within sacramental *Haecceitas.* All other generalized and abstract descriptions of the presence of the Logos/Christ are constructs of the mind. Real sacramental presence is "real" only in actualized, existential, sacramental situations, not in some generalized "real" presence.

In the paragraphs on the Holy Spirit we are presented with the lengthiest part of this trinitarian chapter (nos. 1091–1109). For God the Father, one page sufficed. For the Logos/Christ, two pages sufficed. For the Holy Spirit we have almost five pages. Whether this imbalance is meant to emphasize a particular issue is unclear; the imbalance, however, is noticeable. In these paragraphs we hear such key phrases as:

The Spirit encounters in us the response of
Faith which he has aroused in us (no. 1091);

In this sacramental dispensation, the Holy
Spirit acts in the same way as at other times
in the economy of salvation (no. 1092);

In the sacramental economy, the Holy Spirit
fulfills what was prefigured (no. 1093);

Every liturgical action is an encounter between
Christ and the Church—a Church communion
which the Holy Spirit gathers (no. 1097);

The Holy Spirit recalls the meaning of
salvation (no. 1100);

The Holy Spirit gives a spiritual understanding
of the Word of God (no. 1101);

The Holy Spirit gives the grace of faith (no. 1102);

The Holy Spirit makes the unique mystery
present (no. 1104);

The Holy Spirit comes to the community so
that the offerings may become the body and
blood of Christ (the Epiclesis) (no. 1105);

The Epiclesis is the heart of each sacramental
celebration (no. 1105);

The Holy Spirit transforms us (no. 1107);

The Holy Spirit brings us into communion
with the divine (no. 1108).

These are but some of the statements we read in this section, but
once more it is clear that the emphasis is on the action of the Holy
Spirit, the action of God. One cannot possibly miss the kind of statements the *Catechism* is making: the Holy Spirit brings, transforms, is,
comes, makes, forms, and so on. As these action words convey, sacraments are *actions* of God, whether one considers Father, Logos, or
Holy Spirit.

The implications of this basic theological position regarding sacramentality—that primordially sacramentality is God's own action—are profound. God, who is absolutely free, cannot be bound by any human, ecclesial, or ecclesiastical regulations. No creature restricts the actions of an absolutely free God. Nor can an absolutely free God be bound by any human, created, or finite conditions. In other words, there can be no *a priori* limitation on an absolutely free God who acts in an absolutely free way. Even the sources of revelation must be interpreted against the primordial freedom of God.

In the section on the Holy Spirit mentioned above, one statement should not be passed over lightly: "In this sacramental dispensation the Holy Spirit acts in the same way as at other times in the economy of salvation" (no. 1092). In this economy of salvation, God blesses his entire creation (no. 1079) and all living beings, especially men and women (no. 1080). This statement already indicates that God can act sacramentally in all creation at any time and in any place and for all men and women. Sacramental action is the prerogative of an absolutely free God; sacramental action is the prerogative neither of a church nor of church ministers.

A second implication in the above material indicates that sacramentality is basically an action and, more specifically, a dual-dimension action; God primordially acts, and we humans respond. Because we are, in our very *Dasein,* existentially concrete, specific, time-and-space-conditioned beings, temporality is also a central and integral part of the sacramental action/reaction. One cannot miss the Heideggerian overtones in such a position.

> The primordial ontological basis for Dasein's existentiality is temporality. In terms of temporality, the articulated structural totality of Dasein's Being as care first becomes existentially intelligible....We must go back and lay bare in their temporal meaning the ontological structures of Dasein which we have previously obtained. Everydayness reveals itself as a mode of temporality....In terms of temporality, it then becomes intelligible why Dasein is, and can be, historical in the basis of its Being and why, *as historical,* it can develop historiology.[23]

Sacramentality cannot be presented in an atemporalized and essentialized way. Whenever this is attempted, sacramentality ceases to be principally and primordially the action of God and becomes a form of intellectual ideology. Every essentialization and objectification of sacramentality has the inner capacity of being manipulated and controlled by finite factors. If, on the other hand, sacramentality is God's action within a thoroughly temporalized and existential event *(Ereignis),* then all essentialized, and therefore abstract and generalized presentations of sacramentality, are seen in their hermeneutical impotence. In these instances no attempt to use the term "sacramentality" with hermeneutical ease can assuage its lack of meaning.

A third implication from the above analysis of sacramentality is the meaningless position in which one finds oneself if sacramentality is reduced to two and only two, or seven and only seven, instances of Christian life. A reduction of foundational sacramentality to only one religious body of human beings is likewise meaningless. A reduction of primordiality to one human being shares the same fate. All such theories of sacramentality, which is primordially an action of an absolutely free God, reduce the absolute freedom of God, indicating that God may act in and only in a given arena. The words of the *Catechism* cited above state that the Holy Spirit acts in the same way as at all other times in the entire economy of salvation and that God blesses all of God's creation, especially all men and women.

Only after all the above lengthy preliminary discussion can one move to the issue of the world as a possible place of sacramentality.

THE WORLD AS A POSSIBLE PLACE OF SACRAMENTALITY

If, from a theological standpoint, sacramentality is primordially the action of the one God, then, and only then, can one speak of a possibility of sacramentality wherever and whenever God acts. This basis allows us to go beyond a two-sacrament framework, a seven-sacrament framework, an only-in-the-Christian/Catholic-Church framework, and even beyond a Jesus framework. Even this kind of statement, however, must be clarified. Sacramentality is possible whenever God acts *and* there is also a subsequent human response to this action of God. Only in such a dual dimension is the sacramentality of the world possible and meaningful.

If one says that every cloud is a sacrament of God, every tree is a sacrament of God, or every river is a sacrament of God, these phrases have no meaning whatsoever. The world by itself is not simply sitting somewhere in space as a cosmic sacrament. A cloud is not just some-where in the sky as a cosmic sacrament. Trees are not just growing in some earthly forest as a worldly sacrament. To speak in this way would be another instance of hermeneutical ease. God's creative action may be in every cloud and tree and river, but the sacramentality aspect takes place only when this action produces a subsequent reaction from some human person. One can see many trees yet see or experience nothing sacramental. One can see many rivers yet see or experience nothing sacramental. Sacramental *Haecceitas* occurs when a human person or human persons begin to react to the blessing *qua blessing* of God in the tree, in the cloud, or in the river. It is this action/reaction on the part of an existential person or existential persons that creates the possibility of the sacramentality of the world. There is not an objective world, unaffected by subjectivity, which one can call sacrament. Only divine action and human reaction in a concrete situation form the basis for possible sacramentality.

If this is the deduction one must make, then there have been and are many, many occasions in the history of human beings when sacra-mentality has taken place. To reserve the meaning and existence of sacramentality to precisely numbered Christian liturgies, to a single religious entity, or to a single, specific human life renders sacramental-ity hermeneutically meaningless, except to the small group of human beings who think in these narrow lines; consequently, what this cadre of human beings wishes to say publicly about sacramentality remains meaningless to the vast majority of Western people at this present time. Even within the Christian communities, since there is a division among those who limit sacrament to two from those who limit sacrament to seven, and a division among those who propose that the church is a foundational sacrament and Jesus's humanness is a primordial sacra-ment while others consider these two instances as only an analogical use of the term "sacrament," it is clear that exclusive limitations only produce hermeneutical chaos.

When subjectivity enters into every hermeneutical framework in a central way, then one can begin to trace and retrace the paths contem-porary Western philosophers, from Descartes through Kant and Fichte, have been taking, and one can see the issues with which these philoso-phers were dealing. With subjectivity as an integral part of the lived world of human beings and of human perception, a first challenge arises when one hears that the human mind is infinitely open. Friedrich Ast once wrote:

> To the mind *[Geist]* there is nothing foreign *as such,* since it con-
> stitutes the higher, infinite unity, the center of all life, that is
> unbounded by any periphery.[24]

Ast goes on to say that unless the mind were this way, it could never ask about unfamiliar perceptions, sensations, and ideas. However, in contemporary thought there simply is no such thing as this open-ended, unbounded, infinite unity called mind.[25] Heidegger is correct when he writes: "In the question about the meaning of Being, what is primarily interrogated is those entities which have the character of *Dasein.*"[26] He goes on to say, however, and this is basic to his methodology: "We are ourselves the entities to be analyzed. The Being of any such entity is *in each case mine.*" "Das Seiende, dessen Analyse zur Aufgabe steht, sind wir je selbst. Das Sein dieses Seienden ist *je meines.*"[27] We ourselves, in our own subjectivity, are the primary locus of our analysis. We do not focus on some generalized, abstract understanding of *Sein,* nor do we say that whatever is has *Sein* and would be the locus of our study, which has in the West even included God as *esse ipsum.*

From Husserl, Heidegger inherited his major concept that inten-tionality is the very structure of consciousness in all its modes.[28] Heidegger moves beyond the epistemological and sees intentionality in its ontico-ontological presence.[29]

Second, Heidegger developed Husserl's understanding of *catego-rial intuition.* For Heidegger, this means that Being is not in any sense a being. Categorial intuition focuses in Heidegger on the difference between *Sein* and *das Seiende.*

Third, Heidegger inherited from Husserl insight into the a priori, especially the a priori that all human consciousness is temporal. This meant, for Husserl, that consciousness has to be of a living present, a present that constantly articulates the retention of what is just past with the anticipation or prehension of what is going to happen.[30] In Heidegger, however, the a priori is far more fundamental; namely, tem-porality is the only horizon within which we are even able to under-stand the meaning of Being.

All of this is merely a description of the subjective side of both human knowledge and human existence. Subjectivity is never an isolated subjectivity but always a subjectivity related to others and to the lived world. The starting point is not with some sort of generic being, a totally objective field since everything has "being." This is rejected because the only being we really know is our own being, our own *Dasein*. As Heidegger notes, we do not know how a tree "trees." This step, a step into the human phenomenal existence, is basic for phenomenology.[31] There is no Archimedean point. We perceive and experience ourselves, others, and the world primarily through our human, personal perception. This human, personal perception is thoroughly temporal.

Although one starts with the analysis of one's own *Dasein,* solipsism is not the ultimate outcome. Heidegger clearly addresses the critical issue of solipsism:

> By "Others" we do not mean everyone else but me—those over against whom the "I" stands out. They are rather those from whom, for the most part, one does *not* distinguish oneself—those among whom one is too. This being there too *(Auch-da-sein)* with them does not have the ontological character of a Being-present-at-hand-along-"with" them within a world. This "with" is something of the character of Dasein; the "too" means a sameness of Being as circumspectively concernful Being-in-the-world.[32]

The other is the one whom I recognize as also in my world. Deep within each human person there is an interrelatedness, not a discreteness. Individuality is more on the surface of human life, while interrelatedness is more at the depth of human life.[33]

Heidegger, however, did not take subjectivity to the fullness that Maurice Merleau-Ponty has. Although Merleau-Ponty is indebted to Heidegger in a very comprehensive way, his major work, *Phenomenology of Perception,* moves beyond Heidegger, just as Heidegger moved beyond Husserl. For Merleau-Ponty, subjectivity remains the point of departure. We perceive all life and all areas of life from a non-objectifiable horizon beyond which we human beings cannot go. There is no unlimited, unbounded, infinite horizon. We are always limited by the horizon of our own non-objectifiable selfhood.

This is different from the way in which the Western world has understood perception. Merleau-Ponty writes:

> Science and philosophy have for centuries been sustained by unquestioning faith in perception. Perception opens a window

onto things. This means that it is directed, quasi-teleologically, towards a truth in itself in which the reason underlying all appearances is to be found.[34]

This philosophy, he says, is collapsing before our eyes.[35] Phenomenology, thus, is a philosophy that puts "essences back into existence and does not expect to arrive at an understanding of man and the world from any starting point other than that of their 'facticity.'"[36] Phenomenology is "a study of the advent of being into consciousness, instead of presuming its possibility as given in advance."[37]

Intentionality and horizon play major roles in the way Merleau-Ponty understands human, lived perception. "The synthesis of horizons is no more than a presumptive synthesis, operating with certainty and precision only in the immediate vicinity of the object."[38] As one moves outward beyond the immediate vicinity of the object, a fusion of horizons becomes more and more problematic, so that one can hardly speak of a synthesis of horizons. In other words, within an immediate horizon the meaning of something might be different from what it is within a larger horizon. Similarly, our perception is always bodily, but we are not "souls" or "minds" existing in some Platonic way within a body, nor are we some Aristotelian animate form entrapped in matter. For Merleau-Ponty, we do not have a body; rather, we are our body.[39] Nor do we have speech; we are speaking entities. "As soon as man uses language to establish a living relation with himself or with his fellow, language is no longer an instrument, no longer a means; it is a manifestation, a revelation of intimate being and of the psychic link which unites us to the world and our fellow men."[40] We think bodily; we speak bodily; we are bodily. This involves all the limitations not only of bodiliness in a generalized way, but in the specificities of one's own distinct bodily frame.

Merleau-Ponty clarifies this even further. Shortly after the publication of *Phenomenology of Perception* (1945), Merleau-Ponty spoke to the *Société française de philosophie* (November 23, 1946). In an open discussion after the formal address, he made the following lengthy statement as a reply to a question:

> If a friend and I are standing before a landscape, and if I attempt to show my friend something which I see and which he does not yet see, we cannot account for the situation by saying that I see something in my own world and that I attempt, by sending verbal

messages, to give rise to an analogous perception in the world of my friend. There are not two numerically distinct worlds plus a mediating language which alone would bring us together. There is—and I know it very well if I become impatient with him—a kind of demand that what I see be seen by him also. And at the same time this communication is required by the very thing which I am looking at, by the reflections of sunlight upon it, by its color, by its sensible evidence. The thing imposes itself not as true for every intellect, but as real for every subject who is standing where I am. I will never know how you see red, and you will never know how I see it; but this separation of consciousnesses is recognized only after a failure of communication, and our first movement is to believe in an undivided being between us.[41]

Each of us is a remarkable unity of body, intellect, spirit, and speech. Each of us is remarkably unique and, at the same time, limited by our own perception, our own horizon, our own intentionalities, and by the horizons and intentionalities that surround us in a particularized and existential way. Each of us is, therefore, a distinct *Haecceitas*.

We are not, thereby, solipsistic, but our intentionalities, our horizons, our speech, our bodies, and our minds continually coexist, not side by side, but intentionally with each other. We are shaped by, and we ourselves shape, our lived world. Language, whether it is the language of literature or the language of art and music, is, for Merleau-Ponty, the entry point in which one finds profound moments of human interrelationships and a fusion of intentionalities.

The implication for sacramentality, which Merleau-Ponty does not make, is as follows. This personal subjectivity, this individual and marvelous *Haecceitas*, allows us to react to a God acting in and through some being with its own intentionality and horizon, and, in so doing, we begin to perceive the constitutive arena of this action/reaction and also the existential action/reaction itself, which we can call sacrament. This does not mean that we end up with some clear idea of God. Rather, it means that in this personal encounter with a pre-acting God, I experience an event that draws me to an immanent presence that is now acting upon me in and through an immediate portion of my lived world. The event itself, the action itself with its reaction, becomes a sacrament of and a sacrament to, but never in any generic or essentialized sense. It is a sacrament *of* a (perhaps) present and acting God *to* me, an individual, at a precise moment of my time, of my space, of my bodiliness, of my speech/silence, of my non-objectifiable horizon, of my present intentionality, of my lived world. In this happening, this event, which we might call sacrament, I experience an incipient fusion of horizons, an incipient interpenetration of intentionalities, a speaking silence and a silent shout, a visible in an invisible, and an invisible in a visible. The way I perceive sacrament and the way you perceive sacrament may never be the same, but I can share with you something of my "happening," something of this action/reaction event with you, and you will on the basis of your own individualized "happening" *(Ereignis)* begin to fuse with my horizon and to co-penetrate my own intentionality.

The world is a possible place for sacrament, but only when I, in the whole of my *In-der-Welt-mit-Anderen-Dasein,* my ecological and interrelational being, share in an action/reaction event in which I can name *qua* event a sacrament *to* me personally *of* what perhaps might be the mystery of God. Only after this primordial event, or only after many such primordial events of the world as possible sacrament, will a hermeneutical discussion on sacraments in a theological field of discourse take on a beginning meaning for me.

What we have said so far clearly moves in different directions. Only if individual human beings experience worldliness in sacramental moments will the dramatic liturgies of religions have any meaning. Only if individual human beings experience worldliness in some sacramental moments will church moments ever be meaningful sacramental moments. Only if individual human beings experience worldly people in some sacramental way will Jesus ever be seen as some sort of sacramental moment himself. To speak meaningfully in this way is hermeneutically difficult, since it means a deconstruction of so many Western thought patterns and a reconstruction of thought on a quite different basis.

On the issue of individuation, Allan Wolter, at the end of his preface on the text and translation of Scotus's early *Oxford Lecture on Individuation,* wrote:

> In the *Ordinatio* revision of this seventh question, Scotus makes an important claim, that where rational beings are concerned it is the person rather than the nature that God primarily desired to create. [42]

Scotus speaks from a different *epistemé,* of course, but the focus of his remarks is similar to the focus of Merleau-Ponty insofar as the existential individual is given priority over a non-existential essence. In her article on Scotus, Rega Wood notes that Scotus "is trying to find not the efficient cause of individuals, but the totality in virtue of which a nature is rendered incommunicable."[43] This does not mean that one cannot speak of essence, but as Merleau-Ponty noted above, essence has meaning only when and to the degree that essence is reinstated into existence. Wolter indicates that for Scotus the individual is primarily intended by God. In a postmodern philosophical approach, one would say that the existential individual reality has a primordial place of preference.

Let us return to Heidegger's thought to make this reality of the individual even clearer. Heidegger writes that phenomenology is a process whereby one lets "that which shows itself be seen from itself in the very way in which it shows itself from itself."[44] He goes on to note that realties we encounter in daily life have a dual aspect: realities do indeed manifest themselves to us at least to some extent, but there is always an extensive area that remains hidden. All phenomena, including the *Dasein*, have a part of their reality that proximally and for the most part does not show itself at all. There is something that lies hidden in contrast to that part of the reality that proximally and for the most part does indeed show itself. The hidden part, however, truly is part of the total phenomenon and, in fact, essentially constitutes its meaning.[45] In one and the same phenomenon there is a proximally and for the most part manifest aspect, a showing itself in itself, but there is as well a proximally and for the most part hidden aspect, a not showing itself in itself, which needs to come out of its hiddenness so that the full meaning of the phenomenon in question can be truly understood. It is obvious that this line of Heidegger's thought fits in well with what he says elsewhere on a pre-Aristotelian understanding of *Aletheia* (truth).

This, too, helps us understand the action/reaction called sacramentality. There always is in the sacramental action/reaction a part that proximally is mostly hidden and a part that proximally is mostly manifest. There is a showing itself in itself and a not showing itself in itself. Sacramentality, therefore, is intrinsically finite. There has never been and there never will be a perfect sacrament, since the disclosure in sacramentality will include some showing itself in itself and, at the same time, include a not showing itself in itself. Particularity is always proximally and, for the most part, a combination of such showing itself from itself and not showing itself from itself.

In the same manner of thinking, but using the realities of the conscious and the unconscious, Paul Ricoeur writes in a most careful but penetrating manner:

> The "consciousness" to which the unconscious is *other* is not self-presence or the apperception of some content, but the *ability to retravel the journey of the figures of the spirit.* The hermeneutics of these figures by way of the symbols in which they were born appears to us as the real partner of regressive hermeneutics, whose meaning is revealed when in its turn it finds its own other in the progressive hermeneutics of the phenomenology of spirit. Now we discover the unconscious as the other of its other, as a destiny, opposed to any progressive history oriented toward the future totality of the spirit. Finally, we have left unanswered the question of the fundamental identity of these two hermeneutics—an identity which leads us to say that a phenomenology of spirit and an archaeology of the unconscious speak not of two halves of man but each one of the whole of man.[46]

Ricoeur cautions us about the standard Western understanding of consciousness. In the Western framework one too easily says, "I think." Ricoeur points out that Marx, Nietzsche, and Freud, each in his own way, raised challenging questions about this approach to consciousness.[47] Ricoeur sees the fairly united and mounting challenge of these three philosophers, since they are all attacking the same illusion, "which bears the hallowed name of self-consciousness. What this challenge demands is not a reduction of all things to consciousness, but a reduction of consciousness itself."[48] He states this in many other places as well.[49]

With this analysis of the archeology of the unconscious, Ricoeur is stating that consciousness is now perceived as symptomatic of something far more important in the human *Dasein*. Consciousness is indeed important, but it is no longer seen as though it and it alone offered the *raison d'être* of human life and, consequently, of any philosophy dealing with human life.

If we apply this archeology of the unconscious and the phenomenology of the spirit to the reality of sacrament, we begin to realize that sacrament, a sign *to* and a sign *of,* addresses far more than consciousness. It is a sacrament *to* the other of its other, *to* the destiny opposed to a history oriented to a future totality of the spirit, and *to* the whole person, who is both archeologically unconscious and phenomenologically spirit. If the archeology of the unconscious is addressing the whole person, then there is a dark side, a silent side, a hidden side to sacrament, a not showing of itself in itself. This raises the question whether any finite sacrament, therefore, can be called primordial, since there will always be a not showing itself in itself. Sacramental primordiality must remain, it would seem, totally with the action of God, a God who is infinitely and freely beyond all revelation. Sacramental events, therefore, speak and do not speak, show and do not show, sign and do not sign.[50]

The world is a possible place for sacrament, but this does not need any facile hermeneutic to make it meaningful. What the various strands of postmodern thought bring to this issue is of profound value, but there is a reevaluation of all values connected to this philosophical enterprise. There is a deconstruction and a reconstruction that clearly challenges the standard forms of Western philosophical thought, forms in which and through which sacramentality in the Western Christian churches has generally been theologically formulated.

It is obvious that to say the world is a sacrament of God is not in any way self-evident, and any facile approach to the world as a locus of sacramentality involves an enormous reformulation of the sphere of discourse. Nonetheless, that the theological and philosophical issues described in this chapter provide a proper point of departure for any and every Christian discussion on sacraments today seems to be, at least for the contemporary Western world, preferred among those mentioned in the preceding chapter. On this basis, then, let us move to the second step, namely, the sacramentality of the humanness of Jesus, which some theologians have presented as the primordial sacrament.

4

Jesus and Primordiality

In this chapter, we will consider three issues. The first is the twentieth-century theological attempt to present Jesus Christ, in his humanness, as the primordial, basic, or root sacrament.[1] Many late-twentieth-century Roman Catholic theologians have made such presentations, and in their various writings the precise naming, either of Jesus or of the church as primordial, basic, root, foundational, and so forth, has never been uniform.[2] A few Orthodox theologians have shown interest is this way of speaking but have done so with serious reservations.[3] Likewise, a few Protestant theologians have reacted favorably to some extent to this kind of sacramental discourse.[4] This theme offers the theological section of this present chapter.

Second, we will consider the issue of primordiality from the standpoint of twentieth-century Western philosophy and indicate that the heremeneutics involved by the above-mentioned theologians seem to be no longer viable and, therefore, the view of Jesus as primordial sacrament cannot be sustained in any solid way. This theme is the philosophical section of this present chapter.

Finally, we will readdress the theme of Jesus, the primordial sacrament, in light of the philosophical material analyzed.

THE PRESENTATION OF JESUS
AS PRIMORDIAL SACRAMENT

There are two key theological passages, one from Karl Rahner and the other from Edward Schillebeeckx, that present the position of

Jesus as primordial sacrament in a most comprehensive and, at the same time, fairly concise way. Although these passages were written several decades ago, they still embody the core of this theme. Both of these men perceived the theologically necessary union between Jesus as sacrament and the church as sacrament and, therefore, in these passages there is a continuous flow from Jesus to church and from church to Jesus. Though somewhat dated, these passages are well worth our deep reconsideration.

In *The Church and the Sacraments* Rahner wrote:

> But now in the Word of God, God's last word is uttered into the visible public history of mankind, a word of grace, reconciliation and eternal life: Jesus Christ....This is what we mean by saying that Christ is the actual historical presence in the world of the eschatologically triumphant mercy of God.... There is the spatio-temporal sign that effects what it points to. Christ in his historical existence is both reality and sign, *sacramentum* and *res sacramenti,* of the redemptive grace of God.[5]

Rahner clearly indicates that Jesus, in his historical human nature, is the sacrament of God, *sacramentum,* but since God is in Jesus through the incarnation of the Word of God, one can also say that in the humanity of Jesus, *sacramentum,* one perceives the very reality of the sacrament, *res sacramenti.* Of notice is a strong Heideggerian influence in Rahner's use of historicity, namely, historicity applied to Jesus, the Word incarnate. Rahner says that Christ "in his historical existence is both reality and sign." Obviously, one has to read these paragraphs carefully to perceive the full emphasis on the humanness of Jesus, which can be somewhat obfuscated by the typical Rahnerian language.

By naming Jesus as the primordial sacrament, Rahner is stating that Jesus has a primordiality vis-à-vis every human person, whether that person is Christian or not. The humanness of Jesus is, consequently, unique. All human beings not only have a certain functional connection to the humanness of Jesus, but they also have an ontological connection, since the perfection of every human life is only realized in and through the primordiality of Jesus precisely as the primordial sacrament.

When it comes to the church as a foundational sacrament, Rahner speaks clearly:

> The Church is the abiding presence of that primal sacramental
> word of definitive grace, which Christ is in the world, effecting
> what is uttered by uttering it in sign....the Church is truly the fun-
> damental sacrament, the well-spring of the sacraments in the strict
> sense. From Christ the Church has an intrinsically sacramental
> structure.[6]

Rahner's choice of words deserves some reflection. Jesus is described as the "primal sacrament," indicating his primordiality for all sacramentality. Jesus and the church are interconnected: "From Christ the Church has an intrinsically sacramental character." The sacramentality of Jesus is the "well-spring of the sacraments in a strict sense."[7] Rahner avoids the term "analogous," but a sacrament called the "well-spring," the *primal sacrament,* and the sacrament that makes the church "intrinsically sacramental" in structure could never be seen as "only analogous" unless it is regarded as the *primary analogue.* We will return to the issue of analogy in a few paragraphs.

One other issue, which in many ways complicates and perhaps compromises Rahner's approach to Jesus as the primordial sacrament, is the issue of bodiliness. Rahner describes a natural symbol as one in which what is symbolized and the symbol itself are intrinsically related, just as the body is the manifestation of the soul.[8] Rahner goes on to apply this concept of the intrinsic body-soul symbol to the sacramental causation he is advocating. In applying this scholastic approach of body and soul to the humanness of Jesus as the primordial sacrament, Rahner seems to say that the bodiliness of Jesus is the natural sign of his human soul. In other words Jesus' body is a sacrament of his human soul. Consequently, it is in all actuality only the soul of Jesus that is the primordial sacrament of the forgiving grace of God. Jesus is primordial sacrament only in his spiritual and soul dimension; indirectly, and only indirectly, would his physical and bodily dimension be a part of this primordiality. This dimension would do so only by being a "bodily sacrament of the soul." Jesus' bodiliness is a sacrament of his soul, and Jesus' soul is the sacrament of God's presence. However, Rahner is alone in making the comments above. Most theologians claim that it is his total humanity, body and soul, that is primordially sacramental, not simply one part of his humanity that is primordially sacramental.

Schillebeeckx is clearer on the issue of Jesus' full humanness as the sacramental focus. Schillebeeckx begins his section on Christ the primordial sacrament with an understanding of the trinitarian God.[9] With the trinitarian God as the foundation, Schillebeeckx says:

> The man Jesus, as the personal visible realization of the divine grace of redemption, is *the* sacrament, the primordial sacrament, because this man, the Son of God himself, is intended by the Father to be in his humanity the only way to the actuality of redemption.[10]

Schillebeeckx is crystal clear, and his exact phrasing should be noted carefully: "the man, Jesus, is *the* sacrament, the primordial sacrament." This focus on the humanness of Jesus is paramount for any clear understanding of the way in which twentieth-century theologians have generally presented Jesus as primordial sacrament.

If the divine Logos, the second Person, is called the primordial sacrament of the Father, the first Person of the Trinity, whether the Trinity is presented through the Augustinian or through the Basilian Eastern approach, then the door is open to subordinationism within the Trinity itself. God the Father is the true reality of God, *res sacramenti*, and the Logos is a reflection of this reality, *sacramentum tantum*. The presence of the Father in the Logos would be, in this scenario, the *res et sacramentum*. Augustine, Basil, Rahner, and Schillebeeckx do not proceed in this fashion, but there are some theologians, as we shall see, whose terminology concerning the second Person causes major ambiguity and concern.

For Rahner and Schillebeeckx, Jesus, in his humanness, is a primordial sacrament, but *of what* is Jesus' humanness a sacrament? Rahner and Schillebeeckx offer the following answers:

Rahner:	grace, reconciliation, eternal life
	the grace of God
	the eschatologically triumphant mercy of God
	the redemptive grace of God
Schillebeeckx:	the divine grace of redemption
	the only way to the actuality of redemption

Jesus' humanity, as a sacrament *of* something/someone, evidently centers around God's loving and redeeming grace for all men and women. The words these two theologians use may differ, but the faith

reality of which each speaks is clearly God's redemptive love for us—
redemptive because it is forgiving, *love* because it is grace. God has
intended this forgiving grace, this redemptive love, as the perfection of
all human beings. Thus, for these authors, Jesus' primordial sacramentality is a sacrament *to/for* all human beings. The uniqueness of the gift,
God's forgiving grace, and the universality to whom and for whom this
forgiving grace is intended are constitutive elements of Jesus as primordial sacrament. No other humanness can be primary to this primordiality, and this primordiality has a universal human comprehension. If
another humanness could be primary beyond Jesus, then Jesus himself
could not be called primordial sacrament. Primordiality excludes any
other primacy. Moreover, if Jesus were primordial only to Christians or
only to a certain percentage of the human race, then his primordial
sacramentality could not be called primordial. There could be in this
scenario another humanness who would be primordial for other people.

When this same line of argument is applied to the Christian
Church as foundational sacrament, similar challenges arise. No other
religious group can be the channel of God's forgiving love and all
extra-Christian-ecclesial elements are in some way foundationally
Christian. The phrase most often used is "ecclesial elements." These
elements are found outside the Catholic Church, but they are claimed
by the Catholic Church to be ecclesial. Once again, this kind of statement and claim is considered by non-Christian religious groups as
hermeneutically meaningless.

The response of the Christian Church to the rejection of these
claims cannot be merely pious or theological. For instance, one cannot
say that these people, if they really understood God's economy—imply-
ing, "as we Christians certainly do"—would acknowledge the veracity
of the Christian claims. In this kind of answer the philosophical challenge is disregarded. The challenges and the rejections are not made on
faith or theological bases. Rather, the challenges and rejections are
made, more often than not, on hermeneutical grounds; namely, that what
is said has no meaning in human discourse. If the message is hermeneutically meaningless, then there is necessarily a prior step in the counter-
argument, to make the message hermeneutically meaningful. This needs
to be done before any theological explanation is made.

Chauvet indicates that the scholastic theologians also began their
understanding of the liturgical sacraments from the hypostatic union as

the point of departure. In chapter twelve of his volume, *Symbol and Sacrament,* he writes:

> The present chapter aims at showing that the relation between God and humankind in the sacraments is best understood starting not from the hypostatic union, as the Scholastic theologians did, but from the Pasch of Christ.[11]

In the first part of his chapter, Chauvet presents at great length the view of Thomas Aquinas on sacramental theology (453–76). Chauvet does mention other authors, Isidore of Seville, Venerable Bede, Paschasius Radbertus, Peter Lombard, and Albert the Great, when speaking of the role of the Holy Spirit in the eucharist.[12] When speaking of the break, or "deadly dichotomy," between the eucharistic body and the ecclesial body of Christ, Chauvet mentions Hugh of St. Victor, Alger of Liege, the school of Anselm of Laon, Peter Lombard, and Rupert of Deutz.[13] Nonetheless, what he presents is basically an analysis of the sacramental theology of Thomas Aquinas, and his sacramental theology has as its point of departure the hypostatic union. Chauvet's main objection throughout his presentation is twofold: first, Thomas, who in other areas of his writings has a strong and rich pneumatology, presents in his sacramental writings a "pneumatical weakness."[14] Second, Chauvet notes that there is in Thomas a "sacramental theology excessively separated from ecclesiology."[15]

> Hence, what is surprising in both Thomas' ecclesiology and sacramental theology is not that there are such evocative expressions about the action of the Spirit [which Chauvet had just cited in detail]; it is rather that compared with those concerning Christ, there are *so few.*[16]

I have mentioned Chauvet's lengthy critique of the Thomistic approach to sacrament, because Chauvet offers us a profound theological hermeneutic of this Christo/sacramental approach that not only he himself but other scholars find theologically wanting. Moreover, Chauvet's critique utilizes twentieth-century philosophical and hermeneutical considerations that challenge, in a foundational way, this Thomistic approach to sacraments.

Chauvet lists clearly his objections and, in his text, indicates their interrelationship. Drawing from his chapter, we can list his objections as follows:

1. The lack of pneumatology;
2. A Christo-monistic tendency;
3. A separation of sacramental theology from ecclesiology;
4. The "deadly dichotomy" between the eucharistic body of Christ and the ecclesial body of Christ;
5. The emphasis of Christ as head of the body to the exclusion of the Holy Spirit;
6. The rare mention of the local church community, the concrete liturgical assembly;
7. A sacramental theology of a strongly institutional kind;
8. The development of the power of orders and the power of jurisdiction;
9. The one-sided valorization of the priesthood as the power to consecrate *in persona Christi;*
10. The eucharistic prayer narrowly focused on the words of institution;
11. An instrumental efficient causality understood in such a way that every supplication is deemed insufficient;
12. The connection to the hypostatic union, which largely erases the mediation of the church.

I have spent time on Chauvet's analysis to indicate that when one says that Jesus is the primordial sacrament, understood in connection to the church as a foundational sacrament, a host of difficulties arise. The focus on the Incarnation, which Rahner and Schillebeeckx stress, is clearly within the Thomistic tradition, and both of these authors are avowedly Thomistic. Some of the objections that Chauvet raises regarding the position of Thomas, therefore, can be legitimately raised when one considers the views of Rahner and Schillebeeckx as well.

Chauvet does not eliminate the Incarnation from his own approach to sacramentality. He writes:

> We believe that the dogmatic affirmation, according to which the sacraments are events of grace, is inseparable, on the theological plane, from the humanity of God and, on the economic plane, from the sacramentality of history and world.[17]

From beginning to end, Chauvet continually emphasizes the bodiliness, the worldness, the temporality and historicity of human life,
and therefore the wide gamut in which sacramentality is meaningful.
Even his stress on the Holy Spirit includes this vast materiality, since
the Spirit operates far beyond church boundaries.

Another voice on this issue is that of the Benedictine Raphael
Schulte, as found in his essay "Die Einzelsakramente als Ausgliederung
des Wurzelsakraments" (The Individual Sacraments as an Outgrowth of
the Root Sacrament).[18] This essay attempts to reintegrate sacramental
theology into the entire theological enterprise.[19] He relies heavily on the
work of Otto Semmelroth.[20] Schulte states that the term "sacramentality"
is applied to the church and to Jesus only *analogously*.[21] Schulte writes:

> When Jesus Christ is described as the original sacrament of our
> salvation, one is actually thinking on him in a personal way, in his
> Person, which united the divine and human nature, in the meaning
> described elsewhere as hypostatic union and [in the meaning
> described elsewhere] of the redemptive action on our behalf.[22]

In this approach, the very Person of the Logos is specifically mentioned and "sacramentality" can only be attributed to the Person of the
Logos analogously. It is my view that Schulte is theologically incorrect
when he tries to apply sacramentality, even analogously, to the divine
Person of the Logos. In Rahner and Schillebeeckx, it is the "man" Jesus
who is seen as primordial sacrament, and in their view primordiality is
not analogous. Rather, the humanness of Jesus is the *primary analogue,*
the basis of primordiality, whereby one can then speak of the church as
sacrament and also of the liturgical celebrations as sacraments.

Semmelroth also speaks of sacrament as analogous when applied
to Jesus and the church:

> Of course, if the church today takes up this term, "sacrament,"
> in order to describe itself, it means this in an analogous sense;
> not all the elements in the concept of sacrament which were
> developed for the seven individual sacraments, and which were
> unified since the eleventh century, are realized in the sacrament
> Church in simply the same way. However, the constitutive ele-
> ments of the sacrament are indeed realized in the Church *[aber
> die konstitutiven Elemente des Sakramentes sind doch in ihr
> verwirklicht].*[23]

Semmelroth is not very clear in his argument. The church as sacrament is so by an analogous use of the term "sacrament," but the church as sacrament realizes all the constitutive elements of sacrament. One does not generally speak about similar constitutive elements being the same in two realities, and then state that these realities, though constitutively the same, are so only analogously. If all the constitutive elements are found in both realities, one would logically deduce that there is a univocal use of the phrase "all the constitutive elements."

When Schulte, for his part, describes the church as a root sacrament, he writes:

> The Church, seen from the *one* God-Man, Jesus Christ, as the original sacrament of salvation, is a *root sacrament* in *participation* with the being of its head and lord, *in such a way* that it is not presented as *another* person along side or beneath Christ, but just that what in this context body of Christ or people of God means: the community of many persons (of course understood as mystery) as members of this Church, which itself has to fulfill *together with* Christ its life-task, the further developing of that which was done (already) by the Lord.[24]

Schulte's approach to the church as a sacrament clearly emphasizes that the church is only a sacrament insofar as the church is united to Christ. Christ as sacrament and church as sacrament are constitutively united. However, when Schulte says that the church is not another person alongside or beneath Jesus—meaning Jesus as Person, for otherwise the term *andere* would have no meaning—we are once more called on to understand Jesus as sacrament in the sense that Jesus, as the second Person of the Trinity, is the "primordial sacrament." For Schulte, such a relationship between the Person in the God-Man and the church must once again be analogous. To speak of the second Person of the Trinity as even analogously sacramental easily leads to a form of adoptionism, and for this reason such theological presentations should be avoided.

Later in his essay Schulte attempts to describe a sacrament as follows:

> To this end one can in the following way describe provisionally sacrament in a Christian understanding, without it being thereby a full expression of *all* its essential moments: In sacraments one is

dealing with an interpersonal, personal-ecclesial event occurring
through a significatory use of things, symbols, gestures and words
in which the inner meaning of the components is so made manifest
and announces that the media thus employed allow the resolution
of the will and heart constituents [in the event] to come to expression in a personal and life-giving way.[25]

Schulte clearly sees a sacramental moment as an event,
Geschehen. He also brings in the interrelationships of many individuals,
and he addresses the use of physical elements. A deeper meaning of
one's life and existence is thereby made manifest. He goes on to explain
why he calls this an understanding of Christian sacraments. The persons
involved are *Gott und Mensch,* God and human beings.[26] Temporality,
however, is missing; nor is historicity cited. We see here a generic
description of sacramentality that has no reference to sacramental temporality and historicity, no reference to sacramental *Haecceitas.* Schulte
is operating from a subject/object onto-hermeneutic, and he is clearly
moving in the direction of some essence of sacrament that does not
exist.

In all of this, one sees that there is certainly not unanimity among
recognized scholars on the meaning of primordial and original sacrament, whether this is applied to Jesus or to the church. However, these
issues cannot become clear until we have considered the philosophical
section of this present chapter.

THE ISSUE OF PRIMORDIALITY FROM THE STANDPOINT
OF CONTEMPORARY WESTERN PHILOSOPHY

In contemporary Western philosophy the understanding of
Dasein, the human phenomenon, has radically changed from the prevailing Aristotelian-Cartesian model. In the first place, as we saw
above in the citation from Ast, the human mind is not an unbounded
center for knowledge. Kant's *Critiques* have sharply moved intellection into a form of subjectivity, and since Kant's time, numerous
philosophers have upheld and developed the intrinsic limitations of
human cognizance. In these limitations, it was not simply a question of
finiteness, a limitedness due to one's post-lapsarian ontological status.[27]
The human mind itself has intrinsic limitations for which there is no
exit. One does not know the phenomena outside of one's own self in

themselves. One only knows the *noumena* of external objects, and these *noumena* are known via intrinsic categories of the mind itself. Merleau-Ponty and Ricoeur have both gone far beyond Kant and deepened this study of limited human intellection. Heidegger limits the possibility of knowing being to the analysis of one's own *Dasein*. Any other methodological analysis of an extrinsic being, *ein Seiendes,* is *negated* from the start. Objects, in Heidegger's framework, do not exist; *Existenz* is only attributed to *Dasein*. Objects are either *Zuhanden* or *Vorhanden*. The customary Western subject/object approach to human life plays no role in this kind of contemporary philosophical thought.

Max Horkheimer's *Critique of Instrumental Reason* continued the insights of Weber in which reason, freed from anything mythic and religious, was seen as purposive and centered on means rather than on ultimate ends. Weber's term *Zweckrationalität* does not mean a "reason seeking revelation" (Tillich), but only a reason that was called instrumental reason. The grand scheme of the Enlightenment, with its belief that human reason could eventually comprehend the very principle of both history and society, was rejected. Together with Adorno, Horkheimer published *Dialectic of Enlightenment,* in which these authors not only critiqued Homer, "the basic text of Western civilization," but also the Enlightenment itself:

> The system the Enlightenment has in mind is the form of knowledge which copes most proficiently with the facts and supports the individual most effectively in the mastery of nature. Its principles are the principles of self-preservation.[28]

Through an untiring barrage of criticism, scholar after scholar during the twentieth century hammered at the theory of knowledge that had gained ascendancy in the West. A counter-description of an adequate epistemological framework of human thought is, perhaps, the initial characteristic of contemporary postmodern philosophy.

However, there is more than epistemology at stake. There is also the consideration of human life itself, which is the basis of all thought processes. One hesitates to say the "ontology" or "essence" or "nature" of human life, since all of these terms have received diverse criticisms by postmodern philosophers. *Lebenswelt* has often been preferred. Still, beyond a merely epistemological reevaluation, there has been an onto-epistemological reconsideration. As his basic purpose for the elaborate analysis of the fundamental structures of *Dasein,* Heidegger took up the forgotten *What is Being?* Gadamer and Ricoeur, along with many others, have distanced themselves from this Heideggerian purpose. Gadamer states his own position clearly: "What man needs is not only a persistent asking of ultimate questions, but the sense of what is feasible, what is possible, what is correct, here and now."[29] Or again, "I bypass Heidegger's philosophic intent, the revival of the 'problem of Being.'"[30] In the thinking of several of these twentieth-century philosophers, ultimate questions yield to more basic and urgent human existential questions. Philosophically, then, the human person is not only limited within his or her own perceptive horizon, but the structure of a human person is also limited in a much more inward, constitutive way. The return to the subjective is not merely epistemological but is onto-epistemological as well.

Perhaps it is Ricoeur who has said this most clearly:

> At the end of this itinerary, which has led us from a problematic of language to a problematic of reflection, I should like to show how we can, by retracing our steps, join a problematic of existence. The ontology of understanding which Heidegger sets up directly by a sudden reversal of the problem, substituting the consideration of a mode of being for that of a mode of knowing, can be, for us who proceed indirectly and by degrees, only a horizon, an aim rather than a given fact. A separate ontology is beyond our grasp: it is only with the movement of interpretation that we apperceive the being we interpret.[31]

The return to the subjective has been a progressive return. When Descartes, in his careful, methodological way, moved to the final *Cogito, ergo sum,* there was an unspoken presupposition. Similarly, when Kant moved in a careful, methodological way to his own analysis of pure and practical reason, there was an unspoken presupposition. When Heidegger painstakingly moved through his analysis of *Dasein,* there was also an unspoken presupposition. This unspoken presupposition is the ever-present pre-understanding that all human minds operate on the *cogito* model; all human minds operate on the pure reason model; all human structures operate on the *Dasein* model. In all of these earlier stages of the return to the subjective, there was the presupposition that all human beings in a foundational way functioned in a similar pattern, and therefore "ontologically" all were cut from a similar mold.

Later in the twentieth century some Western philosophers emphasized and clarified far deeper strands of the subjective, which involved, more and more, not only the subjective but also the individual. Heidegger's analysis of temporality as constitutive of *Dasein* clearly provided the impetus for this directionality. Human thinking is constitutively drenched in temporality; human *Dasein* is thoroughly and "ontologically" conditioned by temporality. To be human is to be temporal. Time, however, more profoundly as ontological time *(kairos)* rather than chronological time *(chronos),* suffuses human existence. As the temporality of *Dasein* was more carefully brought into the philosophical discourse of contemporary Western thought, individuality also became more dominant. Merleau-Ponty wanted to bring essences back into existence, and the existentiality of thought and being echoed ever more strongly the temporality of thought and being.

Gadamer himself wrote:

> Understanding is not to be thought of so much as an action of one's subjectivity, but as the placing of oneself within a process of tradition, in which past and present are constantly fused.[32]

Individuality as subjectivity is not an isolated, atemporal subject; one exists not in some sort of methodological solipsism, a locus to which the *cogito* and the Kantian pure reason lead. Individuality and subjectivity are not private dimensions of human life. Temporality precludes this. There is no present time without a past. We see this in Gadamer's discussion of tradition and authority, his *wirkungsgeschichtliche Bewußtsein,* and in Ricoeur's archeology of the unconscious. Nor is there a present time without a future. We see this in Gadamer's conclusion that understanding is never simply and merely "a reproductive attitude but always a productive attitude as well,"[33] and in Ricoeur's "eschatology of the spirit."

Temporality in this approach is clearly a temporality of an *In-der-Welt-mit-Anderen-Dasein,* even if in this phrase Heidegger's ontological overtones would be muted. Gadamer himself speaks about this intertwining of temporality in his discussion on the fusion of horizons, *Horizontsverschmelzung,*[34] and his ideas have given rise to a discussion on universal commensurability, on the one hand, and the incommensurability of all value systems, on the other.[35] Is there an unbridled particularism with its correlate of a total rejection of universalism, or, is there some basic universal commensurability with its own intrinsic hierarchy of standards? Probably there can be no such either-or situation, and this open-ended dichotomy may be precisely what Gadamer intended. Still, there are indeed unique or individualized and personalized horizons, and one person's horizon is not *necessarily* the benchmark for the horizons of other people. In this entire line of argument, temporality involves a foundational limitedness, a primordial finiteness, and a personal uniqueness from which the structures of human life do not escape. Personal uniqueness, however, is found only in an equally individualized historical and traditional time, only in an individualized eschatology of the spirit. Atemporal human thinking is meaningless thought, and atemporal human existence is meaningless existence.

Ricoeur moves in a similar direction when he writes:

This [fusion of horizons] is a dialectical concept which results from the rejection of two alternatives: objectivism, whereby the objectification of the other is premised on the forgetting of oneself; and absolute knowledge, according to which universal history can be articulated within a single horizon. We exist neither in closed horizons, nor within an horizon that is unique. No horizon is closed, since it is possible to place oneself in another point of view and in another culture....But no horizon is unique, since the tension between the other and oneself is unsurpassable.[36]

Subjectivity, individuality, temporality, and fusion of horizons are all key issues, and they mutually affect one another. One can see why these issues present a challenge, especially to the selection of one individual (Jesus) and one community (church) to serve as a primordial or foundational horizon against which and through which all sacramentality is to be understood. The uniqueness of Jesus is important, but because he is a unique human being, he too is limited and finite. This very limitation and finitude precludes per se the attribution of something primordial and universal. Nor can one community be raised to a stage of special incommensurability. There is clearly a connection to this philosophical discussion with the thesis of this chapter.

Throughout the twentieth century, linguistics has been an issue of enormous philosophical discussion. Linguistics, however, cannot be understood apart from some of the anthropological issues mentioned above. Language is not some sort of accidental appendage attached to human life. Both Friedrich Ast and Friedrich August Wolf influenced Friedrich Schleiermacher, to whom the modern use of the term "hermeneutics" can be traced.[37] The theory of hermeneutics, which Schleiermacher developed, subordinates his theory of understanding *language* to the goal of *understanding* itself, namely, the reconstruction of an author's mentality at the time of writing. One might say that Schleiermacher's approach is overtly psychologistic in tone, since the goal of hermeneutics for him was to understand the original meaning of the author as he or she wrote a particular text. It was Schleiermacher himself who wrote that the goal of hermeneutics was "to understand the discourse just as well as and even better than its creator."[38]

Wilhelm Dilthey furthered the work of Schleiermacher. Dilthey opposed the anti-Hegelian positivism of his times and encouraged the provisioning of a philosophical methodological foundation to the human sciences, *Geisteswißenschaften,* which would be as solid as the foundation provided by the methodology for the natural sciences, *Naturwißenschaften.* For Dilthey, this involved the need to secure an objective basis for lived experience, *Erlebnis,* to reconstruct historical events and objects. Dilthey attempted to avoid the psychologism of Schleiermacher and did so by widening the perimeters of the hermeneutic circle to include issues that Schleiermacher had for the most part ignored: historical background, social customs, cultural and political institutions.

Contemporary understanding of language and hermeneutics continued to develop. Gayle Ormiston and Alan Schrift state clearly the major change in hermeneutics that took place in the twentieth century:

> But with Heidegger a fundamental shift in the approach to and discourse of hermeneutics takes place. To overcome the epistemological limitations and methodological prohibitions which emerge in the works of Schleiermacher and Dilthey, Heidegger turns hermeneutic analysis toward the question of Being. Hermeneutics is no longer directed toward discovering the epistemological foundations of the human sciences or the methodological principles which lead to objective knowledge in *Geisteswißenschaten.* Instead emphasis is placed on the disclosure of the ontological conditions which underlie such knowledge or claims to knowledge.[39]

This is the move described above from epistemology to onto-epistemology. For his part, Gadamer, in opposing this move of Heidegger that included a form of ultimate ontology, stressed history and tradition. Thus he could conclude:

> Language constitutes the hermeneutical event proper not as language, whether as grammar or as lexicon, but in the coming into language of that which has been said in the tradition: an event that is at once assimilation and interpretation.[40]

Ricoeur is no less hesitant to espouse Heidegger's approach to language and hermeneutics.[41] Passages from Merleau-Ponty, Habermas, Lévinas, and Derrida could also be cited to indicate this distancing from Heidegger. Aside from the proponents of some linguistic philosophies, the issue of an "objective" reality as the center of language and hermeneutics and its objectivity alone is not the focus of these phenomenological studies on language. Discourse itself is much deeper than the mere denotative communication of clear ideas about some "objective" reality, which linguistic analysts make central.

The human person is a speaking person; he or she is not someone who simply has speech in a utilitarian way. The conveyance of objective knowledge is not even the main goal of speech, much less its only goal. Ricoeur makes some important comments on this matter, which have direct bearing on language and symbolism and, therefore, language and sacramental theology.

> Symbolism marks the breakthrough of language toward something other than itself—what I call its opening. This breakthrough is saying: and saying is showing. Rival hermeneutics conflict not over the structure of double meaning but over the mode of its opening, over the finality of showing.[42]

Ricoeur speaks often in this direction.[43] When a human person uses human language in discourse, he or she opens an area of multivalent meaning and an equivocalness in the being of the subject, in the discourse itself, and in the realities about which it speaks and shows. There is also a concealment aspect, since no language or symbol opens, says, and shows a fullness of any kind beyond which there is no recourse. Language and symbols thoroughly belong to the arena of finitude. There is no human language, human discourse, or human symbolization of something infinite or of something total. Language is a constitutive element of a finite and limited person and, as such, is itself limited and finite. Moreover, language not only opens, says, and shows a multivalent meaning of the equivocalness of being; it is also an opening, saying, and showing of a multivalent opener, sayer, and shower, and this self-disclosure also shares in the equivocalness of being.

Contemporary hermeneutics finds every appeal to eternal and unchanging verities an impossibility. Contemporary hermeneutics finds such language meaningless. This is not to say that twentieth-century Western hermeneutics is the last word on the issue of semiology and the phenomenology of language. Within the hermeneutical circle of these philosophers, a return to the point for reevaluation is always present, but the circle itself is finite, even though its perimeters can be enlarged and its very structure changed. Just as the issue of subjectivity led to individuality in society, the issue of language leads to subjectivity, not to pure objectivity; to individuality in society, not to essentialized constructs beyond the sphere of the individual in society; to a multivalent equivocalness of being, not to a connotatively clear and singular referent.

The above sketch of contemporary Western philosophy was not intended to be a comprehensive study of postmodern philosophy. Rather, the point of the above material was simply to highlight some basic issues that these philosophers of the West have brought to bear on human understanding. Does this material have repercussions on theological thought, and, for our purposes, on the theology of the sacraments? To consider this issue, let us move to part three of the present chapter.

JESUS AS PRIMORDIAL SACRAMENT IN THE LIGHT OF TWENTIETH-CENTURY PHILOSOPHY

If primordiality has any meaning for Western people today, it can apply, perhaps, only to the action of God, either in a creating event or in a revelatory and/or sacramental event. Such a statement is, of course, theologically based and not philosophically based. To say this, one would already need to believe in God and, even more precisely, in a God who is believed to be intrinsically capable of creating and subsequently able to reveal something to human beings. Constitutive of such a creating/revealing God is the aspect of primordiality, because, in this creating and revelatory/sacramental event, it is God who has primacy of place and action. It is God who primordially acts and, then and only then, is there even a question of a human response.

We have seen in the first part of this chapter that this understanding of divine primordiality was clearly expressed in the *Catechism of the Catholic Church,* which spoke about God, more specifically about the trinitarian God, as *the source and goal of all liturgy.* "Source and goal" indicate, in this context, a primordial source as well as an ultimate goal. This is not to say that God is the primordial sacrament. As we saw above, God in no way is, or can be, a sacrament. Rather, if one needs to speak of primordiality in a sacramental event, such primordiality is constitutive because of a free primordial action of an absolutely free God. Primordiality is not an element of this discourse because of any postulated "primordiality" in the finite, limited, and individuated response of a human person, or human persons, to the revealing action of God. In our relationship to God, God is always the primordial agent, the primordial source. Human response, by nature, is always derived, secondary, and responding, and this response is finite, limited, time-conditioned, and individuated.

With the acknowledgment of divine primordiality in the sphere of sacramental discourse, let us discuss three issues that arise when we consider the statement that Jesus, in his humanness, is the primordial sacrament.

The World as a Possible Place of Sacramentality

We have already noted that not even the universe or cosmos, in itself or in any part of itself, can be called or considered sacramental per se, much less primordially sacramental. Some aspect or aspects of the world can indeed be a place of sacramentality, but this does not say that one such locus is in itself primordial or has any preferred position above another possible locus in the world of sacramentality. The event in which a moment and a space of this world becomes a moment and space of sacramentality remains an existential and individualized event alongside other equally existential sacramental events. In virtue of its temporality and historicity, no one individual moment serves as a primordial benchmark or standard for any other moment. Aspects of the world can indeed be possible places of sacramentality; by themselves they can never be places of *primordial* sacramentality.

Contemporary Western philosophy upholds this position since we humans really do not know the "being" of things, other than ourselves, nor do we know them except in and through our human perception and from the horizon of our perception. The involvement of subjectivity in all our perception and knowledge disallows stating in any categorical way that an individual aspect of the world enjoys primordiality.

Moreover, contemporary Western philosophy has challenged the very basis for such an attribution, since it has challenged a previous way of thinking that was predicated on an Archimedean foundation. In order to identify anything as primordial, it is necessary to situate oneself in an Archimedean location and, from this place, *sub specie aeternitatis,* identify a given created reality as primordial. The onto-hermeneutical understanding today precludes any and all such designation of primordiality to any and all perceived and apperceived phenomena.

Jesus in His Humanness as Primordial Sacrament

If the above judgment is true regarding the manifold creatures that constitute our humanized world, then a legitimate question arises when one speaks of the humanness of Jesus as primordial sacrament, since the humanness of Jesus is one of these finite, limited, individualized creatures in our perceived and apperceived world.

Prior to the creature issue, however, we should note that primordiality, when applied to Jesus, affects some very serious theological and doctrinal matters as well, particularly, the doctrine of the Incarnation, which has been expressed by such phrases as "Logos became flesh," or "God became human." Doctrinally, when we speak about the *incarnate* Word or God who became *human,* what is at stake is the humanity of Jesus itself. When one attributes primordiality to the humanness of Jesus, is the full humanness of Jesus clearly maintained? This is the doctrinal question.

The Council of Chalcedon was most clear on what this union of the divine and the human *was not.* In parallel passages the bishops at Chalcedon first described the relationship between the divine nature and the human nature of Jesus by stating something about each nature. They did this in a very balanced framework as we see in the following citations:

Jesus was of one nature, *homoousios,* with God, and
Jesus was of one nature, *homoousios,* with us.

Jesus was truly, *alethos,* God and
Jesus was truly, *alethos,* human.

Jesus was perfect, *teleios,* in his Godhead and
Jesus was perfect, *teleios,* in his humanity.

Jesus was *begotten* of the Father from all ages, and
Jesus was *[begotten]* of Mary in time.

These Chalcedonian statements indicate that Jesus was fully God on the one hand and fully human on the other. Therefore, the humanness of Jesus remains in itself created, finite, and limited, since being human means being finite, limited, and created. No explanation of the humanness of Jesus can be constructed that would make Jesus less than "of one substance with us," "truly human," "perfectly human," and "a human individual born of a woman." If the Word of God became human in a way constitutively different from all other human beings, the Christian meaning of the Incarnation would be seriously compromised, if not thoroughly denigrated.

The bishops at Chalcedon went on to explain the ways in which the union between the divine and human in Jesus *cannot* be construed:

asunchutos	not mixed, i.e., one does not mix the divine and the human together into a *tertium quid.*
atreptos	not changed, i.e., after the union neither the divine nor the human has been essentially changed.
adiairetos	not separated but only distinguished.
achoristos	not divided.[44]

Without any doubt, as the Council of Chalcedon affirms, one must speak of a unity in the Word made flesh, but this unity cannot be at the expense of either the humanity or the divinity. Jesus, in his humanness, must be presented constitutively in the same kind of humanness all other men and women share. To do anything else would render his humanness different from ours and would make the Christian doctrine of the Incarnation a meaningless statement and a meaningless reality.

Can one say, then, that any human being at all could be primordial? The answer is no, because primordiality is not a constitutive part of human nature. Can one say that any creature at all can be primordial? The answer again is no, because, as we have seen above, primordiality goes far beyond human epistemological capabilities and beyond our onto-epistemological world. With both answers negative, there is once more a serious concern about the validity of, the meaning of, and the reality behind the phrase "Jesus, the primordial sacrament."

In "Christology within an Evolutionary View of the World," Rahner went to great pains to maintain the full humanness of Jesus and to offer a basis for the primordiality of Jesus beyond, but not unrelated to, the hypostatic union.[45] He stated that the hypostatic union is a union in the genre of grace and further noted that this union of grace between God and the humanness of Jesus is in the same genre as the union of God through grace that all men and women also have.[46] Rahner realized that the union of grace cannot be an area that grounds primordiality. He goes on to say that if there is a primordiality to Jesus, it is not precisely because of the hypostatic union, a union of grace common to all human beings, but because Jesus enjoys a primacy and a unique causality dependent on God's pledge to us.[47]

In many ways Rahner sounds very much like Scotus in this line of argument, although it is unclear whether it is God's pledging to us or a pledge that is inherent in the human nature of Jesus. The latter would make no sense, so the first seems to be Rahner's approach. Consequently, once more, primordiality is predicated of God. God pledges to all of us what God has also given to Jesus. According to Rahner, from this divine pledge, which is the basis of primordiality, there is both primacy and causality. Both elements are essential. For Rahner, Jesus, as human, must enjoy a "firstness," and because of this "firstness," he is a "cause" for all others. However, it is difficult to say that the firstness is in any way due to something "first" in the finite, human Jesus. Firstness arises only from God's primordial pledging.

The theological question remains, however. Can one speak of Jesus, in his humanness, as the primordial sacrament for all human beings and still retain the Chalcedonian faith statement that Jesus was and is truly, perfectly human, of one nature *(homoousios)* with all of us? To answer this question, let us first consider more carefully issues of postmodern philosophy.

Contemporary Anthropology

Although the issues of contemporary philosophy on the understanding of the human person were sketched above, let us review them step by step. In the Christian doctrine of Incarnation, not only Jesus but human life is celebrated. Christians maintain that in an amazing way God became human, just as we are human. For thirty years, more or less, Jesus lived in the small village of Nazareth and was seen by many people, spoke with many people, and ate with many people. All of these people saw Jesus as simply another human person like themselves. The Christian tradition has been so taken up with the divinity of Jesus that the "humbling" to become human has almost been placed to one side. The "humbling" is seen as an act of divine majesty, the *kenosis,* and the "to what" the divine majesty humbles itself becomes dwarfed by the splendor of "divine humility." What is needed is to reconsider more closely the splendor of the "humble" in the presence of the divine. What it means to be human is clearly key to a complete insight into the mystery of the Incarnation. Jesus, in his humanity, enjoys, as do all other human beings, a human *Haecceitas.*

Various cultures and various periods in such cultures have formulated and reformulated the meaning of the human, and these meanings and lived understandings have been called anthropology. Throughout the world today, there are diverse anthropologies, and none has an edge over the other. In the West, as we move into the twenty-first century, the dominant philosophy has reanalyzed and reexpressed some of the basic components of human life. As we have seen above, four issues were the specific foci of this investigation: return to subjectivity, individuality or *Haecceitas,* temporality, and language.

Return to Subjectivity

The human person has no possibility of knowing things objectively. In all knowledge there is a primacy of human perception, and this primacy involves a return to subjectivity. Our knowledge of ourselves and of our world is, and remains, a basically human knowledge, that is, our own personal view of it. We cannot escape from our own categorical horizon, nor from our own categorical fusion of horizons. Merleau-Ponty states this position clearly:

> Perception is thus paradoxical. The perceived thing itself is paradox-
> ical; it exists only in so far as someone can perceive it. I cannot even
> for an instant imagine an object in itself....Thus there is a paradox of
> immanence and transcendence in perception. Immanence, because
> the perceived object cannot be foreign to him who perceives; tran-
> scendence, because it always contains something more than what is
> actually given.[48]

Jesus, in his humanness, saw the world from his own standpoint and categorical horizon, and with a certain subjectivity. His knowledge was not from the standpoint of an Archimedean panorama.[49] Therefore, his self-understanding was never that of a person who is, in himself and of himself, primordial. His preaching and healing was that of someone who has a part of his reality that proximally and for the most part does not show itself of itself; and who has a part of his reality which, proxi-mally and for only some part, shows itself of itself. Given this imma-nence of showing itself of itself and this limited transcendence of not showing itself of itself, we can only say that the perception of Jesus was limited and, to some degree, subjective; his self-understanding was limited and, to some degree, subjective; his message was, therefore, itself limited and, to some degree, subjective. In all of this he was won-drously human, fully human, perfectly human, of one being *(homoousios)* with us, an individual, human *Haecceitas.*

Individuality or Haecceitas

Modern psychology has provided us with an enormous amount of material on what it means to be a human person. Primarily, this includes what it means to be an individuated human person. The very word "person," in Western thought, has been readdressed in such a way that hermeneutically it engenders a different meaning than that which theologians intend when they use the term "person" for the Trinity or for the one "person" in Jesus. In fact, the widespread contemporary use of "person" in its psychological analysis today renders the continued theological use of the same term hermeneutically meaningless.[50]

The emphasis of the Christian doctrine of the Incarnation is not that God became a "rational animal" or that God became an "essential human." Rather, the emphasis of the Christian doctrine of the Incarnation has been and remains that God became an individual human being who has the name Jesus. Whenever the *terminus ad quem* of the incarnational action of the triune God is seen only as an essentialized human nature and not a specifically individualized and existential human being, then the very meaning of the Incarnation becomes theologically questionable.

In contemporary Western philosophy the return to the subjective has, at least with many of these philosophers, moved more and more to a particularization and to an individualization, to *Haecceitas*. Heidegger's analysis of the *Dasein* still retains an essentializing aspect, since he was so preoccupied with the question of Being. However, philosophers who followed Heidegger did not, as we have seen above, continue this ontological and metaphysical quest for the issue of being. With this break from the ontological, understood in Heidegger's terms and even in Graeco-scholastic terms, the focus has more and more centered on the issue of personal individuation.

From a theological standpoint, it was perhaps Schoonenberg, more than any other contemporary theologian, who posed the question so incisively: *Jesus is truly human. Can he also be God?* The standard theological question has been: *Jesus is truly God. Can he also be human?*[51]

As an individuated creature, and therefore limited, finite, and particular, the issue of primordiality becomes constitutively difficult. Highly individualized creatures, which concomitantly are finite and limited, can never be considered primordial. If these same creatures have a part of their own reality that, proximally and for the most part, does not show itself from itself, then the very non-showing precludes any possibility of acknowledged primordiality, since the reality in question remains partially and proximally unknown. It is not possible to speak of primordiality if part of the very primordial reality remains unknown.

On the other hand, the mystery of the Christian doctrine of the Incarnation rests clearly on the issue that God became a particular human person. To remove individuality from a presentation of the Incarnation removes the very basis of the mystery of God's grace in the incarnational action of the triune God. It is the particular, individual, human Jesus who is created, limited, and finite, who is also the one who is "truly human," "perfectly human" "of one being *(homoousios)* with us," "born of a woman." Only when one focuses on the particularized, existential, human Jesus can the words of Chalcedon and the New Testament be understood. Only in this way is the splendor of the "humble" clearly perceived.

Temporality

The Christian doctrine of Incarnation teaches us that God became human at a definite moment of time. In the theological explanations of this temporality of the Incarnation, the philosophical base for time that Western theologians have generally used has been the spatial under-standing of time current in the Aristotelian and Platonic framework and readvanced by the scholastic theologians. In the Cartesian *cogito* approach, neither a specific time nor space was needed by Descartes for his thinking subject. An atemporal *cogito* was envisioned. With the analysis of time and being by Heidegger, contemporary Western philo-sophical thought has abandoned this space-time approach. Temporality is constitutive of human life, and to think anything human in an atem-poral way is an a priori denial of humanness in itself.

Jesus is not, therefore, some atemporal humanity; rather, Jesus is embedded in history. Jesus has a history, which means that Jesus him-self changes temporally. Heidegger notes:

> Because temporality is ecstatico-horizonally constitutive for the clearedness of the "there," temporality is always primordially interpretable in the "there" and is accordingly familiar to us.[52]

In this approach, temporality is crucial to understanding the mean-ing of both the life and the death of Jesus, how Jesus "takes time" in the sense of an *In-der-Welt-mit-Anderen-Dasein,* and how Jesus "loses time" in the sense of a *Sein zum Tode,* a being that moves ineluctably toward death. On occasion, Jesus' life is presented as something atemporal and cosmic; more than occasionally, his death is presented as something atem-poral and cosmic. This occurs when one atemporalizes the very meaning of Jesus' life and death and a Cosmic Christ theology is elaborated. Through this Cosmic Christ theology, an Archimedean point is posited through which and from which the mystery of creation and salvation is then seen. The mystery of the Christian doctrine of the Incarnation, with its emphasis on the full, perfect, and true humanness of Jesus, requires that Jesus be as temporally constitutive as every other human being and that both his life and death are also experienced as intrinsically and constitu-tively temporal. Atemporality of any sort removes Jesus from the world of *Dasein.* Atemporality prevents Jesus from being "truly human," "per-fectly human," of one substance *(homoousios)* with us, a specific child "born of a specific woman, Mary."

Language

The hermeneutical circle is mentioned in detail by both Heidegger and Ricoeur, although clearly in different ways. Heidegger observes: "When one talks of the 'circle' in understanding, one expresses a failure to recognize two things: (1) that understanding as such makes up a basic kind of *Dasein's* Being, and (2) that this Being is constituted by care."[53] Ricoeur mentions the circle in terms of opening, saying, and showing, which then produces a new opening, a new saying, and a new showing. In other words, language is always disclosive of the archeology of the subject and prehensive of the eschatology of the spirit. Language continually moves in a circular and continuing way.

A sacrament, like all major symbols, is tensive;[54] that is, it is multivalent. Like much of language, a sacrament is revelatory of many things, of an equivocalness of being, not simply of a single monolithic referent. In other words, a sacrament, like language, reveals and camouflages at one and the same time. If discourse provided the final and ultimate word, no further discourse would ever be necessary; if a sacrament or symbol revealed the totality of the reality to which it refers and which it makes manifest in itself and of itself, then there would be no need of sacrament. If primordiality means unsurpassability in the sense that there can be no pre-primordiality, then the source is clear and no further question can arise. If Jesus, in his humanness as the primordial sacrament, has revealed completely the unsurpassable source of all human life-with-God, then there is no further need of such sacramentality, much less primordial sacramentality

Given the disclosure-constituency in human language, the hermeneutical circle in language, and the non-disclosure factor that is proximally and for the most part inherent in discourse and language, we can say that the humanness of Jesus as a sacrament reveals only "something" of the absolutely free God. Given the fact that Jesus is truly human, perfectly human, of one substance *(homoousios)* with us, a child born of Mary, we can say that Jesus is limited, finite, and created, and therefore, *qua* sacrament, can reveal only a limited aspect of God, a finite vision of God, which means that there is always much more divine life which in each and every revelatory, sacramental event, including that of Jesus, needs to be made manifest of itself and in itself. However, this would mean that there is a progressive revelation in Jesus as sacrament, and, were one to say that Jesus is a primordial sacrament, there would then be a progressive revelation of primordiality. This progressive revelation would continue on and on until a utopian moment in which there would be no need of sacramentality, since the reality of which a sacrament speaks would in that utopian moment be fully manifest. A progressive primordiality is meaningless and hermeneutically useless. With an infinite and absolutely free God, such a moment can never be realized. God will always be infinitely greater and freer than any sacramental manifestation or revelation. In such a case, what is perceived and apperceived today as primordial might and will indeed be surpassed tomorrow, and further surpassed in yet another tomorrow and again in still another and another. In this, the phrase "primordial sacramentality" becomes hermeneutically meaningless.

The unique, finite, limited humanness of Jesus is, in its existential concreteness, a tensive sacrament. It has many references. First of all, Christians might see in Jesus a human life that is God-centered. God is acting in the humanness of Jesus, and Jesus, as a human, is responding in a major way to this presence of God in his life. The first and most important symbolization, then, is to perceive in the humanness of Jesus a credible God. The humanity of Jesus, through his life, his death, and his risen life, reveals to us something of God, not a fullness of God, which is impossible, but something of God that is both *fascinosum et tremendum,* fascinating and yet cautioning. As with any and every "holy" person, it is God's action in that person that is ultimately attractive and ultimately meaningful. In this regard one can say that the Jesus event is foundationally theocentric not christocentric. One can say that if the Jesus event is not theocentric, but only christocentric, the event would have no lasting value. Once again, the stress lies on the primordiality of God and God's action, which alone makes any statement of primordiality in the Jesus event meaningful. At this basic stage we are struck by the splendor of divine humility.

There is a second-level symbolization in the Jesus event, namely, the splendor of the humble creature itself. The presence of God in the humble human "ensplendors" the human itself and we begin to see who we, co-humans with Jesus, might truly be. It is only at this level that the christocentric issues begin to emerge with some clarity. Christians are drawn to Jesus or centered in Jesus first of all because of the fascinating and awesome mystery of God, and second because in the humanness of Jesus they see a splendor of the human itself.

Does this analysis on the basis of twentieth-century Western philosophy mean that Christians cannot believe that Jesus is truly God or that they can only affirm that Jesus is truly human? This is surely not the case. This volume deals with sacramentality and, in this chapter specifically, with the phrase "Jesus in his humanness as the primordial sacrament." An entirely different volume would be needed to study the Christian faith statement "Jesus is God" in conjunction with postmodern hermeneutics and onto-hermeneutics.

Mention has been made in this chapter of the church as a foundational sacrament, but the major focus has been on Jesus. Since there are some extremely volatile theological issues that have an impact on the statement that the church is a foundational sacrament, this theme must be presented in a separate chapter.

5

The Church as Foundational Sacrament

The bishops at Vatican II described the church as a foundational sacrament. For official Roman Catholic documentation, this was a new way of designating the church.[1] What precisely does this phrase entail? In the minds of the bishops at the council, "church," as used in contexts involving foundational sacrament, meant the Roman Catholic Church and probably nothing more. In these documents the bishops did not speak of a primordial sacramental character with any reference to Christian churches other than the Roman Catholic Church; even more striking is the lack of any explicit mention of primordial sacramentality when the documents addressed the ecclesiality of the churches in union with Rome.

However, there are instances in these same conciliar documents when the bishops clearly intended a different understanding of "church," and they made this new understanding clear in the texts themselves. For instance, there is a distinction as regards church in *Orientalium ecclesiarum (Decree on the Catholic Eastern Churches).* The introductory sentences set the stage for this differentiation:

> The Catholic Church values highly the institutions of the Eastern Churches, their liturgical rites, ecclesiastical traditions and their ordering of Christian life. For in those churches, which are distinguished by their venerable antiquity, there is clearly evident the tradition which has come from the apostles through the Fathers and which is part of the divinely revealed, undivided heritage of the Universal Church (no. 1).

The Catholic Church values "the institutions of the Eastern Churches." Through such wording, a distinction is being made, even though, technically speaking, the Eastern churches are an essential part of the Catholic Church. Finally, in this passage, we have the phrase "Universal Church," which is meant to cover both the Catholic Church and the Eastern churches. These variations of the referent to the term "church" play no small role when one attempts, in a theological way, to discern the correct meaning of the phrase "the church as a foundational sacrament."

In the above instances, "church," as used in the documents of Vatican II, refers to the church that is in communion with the papacy. When the discussion moves to the separated Eastern churches, we begin to hear other terms. The title of this section of the decree *Orientalium ecclesiarum* is **"De conversatione cum fratribus Ecclesiarum seiunctarum" (Relations with the Brethren of Separated Churches).**[2] In this title "church" is used of those Christian communities not in union with the papacy but in the body of the text we hear other terms: "Eastern Christians" (nos. 24, 25, 26, 27); or "Eastern brethren" (no. 26); or "separated Eastern Churches" (nos. 26, 27, 28, 29, 30). The bishops at Vatican II clearly modified "church" when they intended anything other than the Roman Catholic Church or the Catholic Eastern Churches in union with Rome.[3] Nonetheless, the very naming of these non-papal Christian communities as church raises a question about the meaning of the phrase "the church as a foundational sacrament."

When we turn to the sections in the documents of Vatican II that are concerned with Western Christian communities, other than the Roman Catholic Church (nos. 19–23), there is again a blurring of boundaries. In the decree on ecumenism, *Unitatis redintegratio* (hereafter UR), the official title of this section is **"De Ecclesiis et Communitatibus ecclesialibus in Occidente seiunctis" (The Separated Churches and Ecclesial Communities in the West).** The distinction continues in the text, "These Churches and ecclesial communities" (no. 19 twice), but more often the phrase "separated brothers" is used. Who are these separated Western churches, *ecclesiae in occidente seiunctae?*

In postconciliar documents, both from Rome and from various bishops' conferences, there has been a slow but progressive use of "church," not only for separated Eastern Christian churches, but also for

Anglican and Protestant churches. In other words, the hesitation that one finds in Vatican II to use "church" for any entity other than the Roman and the Eastern Catholic churches has gradually changed.[4] In these post-conciliar documents, Anglican and some Protestant communities are at times referred to as churches. For example, in the joint declaration on cooperation issued by Paul VI and Michael Ramsey in 1966, we read that there is a new atmosphere "of Christian fellowship between the Roman Catholic church and the Churches of the Anglican Communion."[5]

In 1982, John Paul II and Robert Runcie, the Archbishop of Canterbury, jointly issued a statement, *In the Cathedral Church at Canterbury,* in which we read:

> The bond of our common baptism into Christ led our predecessors
> to inaugurate a serious dialogue between our Churches, a dialogue
> founded on the gospels and the ancient common traditions.[6]

With this fluidity of terms it is remarkable to note that certain Vatican II and post–Vatican II church leaders, both ecclesiastics and theologians, have used the phrase "the church as a foundational sacra-ment" with hermeneutical ease. Usually, no explanations are given either for "sacrament" or for "church." It is assumed that both terms are clear. Nonetheless, there is a lack of clarity in the contemporary phrase "the church as a foundational sacrament," and this stems both from the-ology and from philosophical hermeneutics.

In this chapter we consider the theological issues and problems that lie deep within the terms "church" and "sacrament," when used in "the church as a foundational sacrament." Second, we consider the hermeneutical challenges that such a phrase inevitably engenders when viewed through the philosophical hermeneutic of contemporary Western authors. Third, we consider, as we move into the third millen-nium, the ramifications this philosophical challenge brings to the facile use of such a theological phrase.

THE CHURCH AS FOUNDATIONAL SACRAMENT: THEOLOGICAL ISSUES

In the documents of Vatican II, "church" has a multivalent refer-ence, even though Roman Catholic Church is the basic referent. These many references complicate the hermeneutical import of the phrase "the church as a foundational sacrament." Let us consider the situation from two angles: a consideration of the term "church" and a consideration of the term "sacrament."

"Church"

Regarding "church," we can list the usages in Vatican II that we have described above as follows:

Church
- Roman Catholic Church
- Eastern Catholic churches
- Separated Eastern Christian churches
- Separated Western Christian churches

When focusing on other issues, these same documents provide additional usages of the term "church," and these references complicate the issue even further.

Church
- Church from Abel to the endtime
  There is the "universal Church" "from Abel" to the endtime (*LG*, chap. 2);

- Non–Roman Catholic Church
  There is "church" outside the visible structure of the Roman Catholic Church (*LG*, chaps. 8, 15, 16; *UR*, chap. 3);

- Heavenly Church
  There is a "heavenly Church" (*LG*, chap. 7 passim).

Obviously, a clearer differentiation needs to be made if one claims that there is a church almost from creation onward, a church that will last forever in a heavenly paradise. Are all of these meanings of church included in "the church as a foundational sacrament?" If there is a sacramental church prior to the conception and birth of Jesus, then questions arise: of what is this church a sacrament, and *to whom* is this church a sacrament? If there is a sacramental church in heaven, the eschatological paradise, then another question arises: are sacraments necessary in heaven? Does one not see God "face to face" so that sacraments are unnecessary? Third, if there is church outside the visible structure of the Roman Catholic Church, then what need is there for a Roman Catholic Church?[7]

Even though the passages in the documents of Vatican II on the church as a foundational sacrament are very circumspect, it is clear that the bishops, when they discussed the mystery and essence of the church, wanted their words to indicate that basically, by its very nature, the church is sacramental. Thus, when one discusses a "church" from Abel, this church too will have within it something sacramental, and the same can be said of a "heavenly church." Moreover, the "extra-ecclesial" elements that are still "ecclesial" share in this same sacramental foundationality of church. If sacramentality is foundational to the church and the church is foundationally sacramental, then wherever and whenever there is church, there will be something sacramental. The same can be said when one speaks of "ecclesial elements" outside the visible structures of the Roman Catholic Church. These ecclesial elements will also involve something foundationally sacramental.

Let us begin with the presentation of the heavenly church. In such an eschatological discourse, the final, universal, heavenly church sacramentalizes more fully than any other manifestation of church that which church is of itself and from itself. Indeed, in this view, the heavenly church is the culmination of what church is all about and, therefore, it is the culmination of what the sacramentality of church is all about. This is clearly the intent of chapter seven in *Lumen gentium*.

Semmelroth, in his analysis of this chapter, provides a historical overview of its genesis and eventual incorporation into *Lumen gentium*.[8] He notes that the eschatological nature of the church has two facets. The first consists in the various covenants God has made with God's people over the course of salvation history. This facet, he says, is not addressed by the document. The second facet is described as follows:

> The second facet, with which Chapter VII explicitly deals, consists in the fact that the Church does not fully possess her sacramental form in this world, which is destined to be done away with at the last day, to merge into the heavenly consummation where the Church no longer exists except in an analogical sense, as the Church triumphant.[9]

In the opening paragraphs of chapter 7, "sacrament" is explicitly used, the "universal sacrament of salvation" (no. 48). A few sentences later, we read: The "pilgrim Church, in its sacraments and institutions, which belong to this present age, carries the mark of this world, which will pass" (no. 48). In other words, the church abides, but its sacraments belong only to this worldly period of history. It is important to note two issues mentioned by Semmelroth: first, that the heavenly church differs from the pilgrim church, since the pilgrim church does not *fully possess* its sacramental form; second, the term "church" is only analogously applied to the heavenly church. Both of these statements are the theological interpretations of Semmelroth; the two views are not stated in the documents. Both views are controversial.

This eschatological view provides a sort of Archimedean vantage point from which one is able to see more clearly the meaning of our present ecclesial pilgrimage as well as the meaning of the sacramental nature of the church. The mention of an Archimedean vantage point causes some hermeneutical problems. This will be addressed in the second part of this chapter. From a theological standpoint, the reflection that the sacramental character of the pilgrim church is not a fully possessed sacramental character is significant, that the pilgrim church sacramentalizes *only in an incomplete way* is significant. The pilgrim church, precisely because it is of this world, only partially sacramentalizes. Without some view of a "universal church," a "heavenly church," and an "eschatological church," the meaning of the church as the "universal sacrament of salvation" would be stranded in hopeless ambiguity. It is only from the standpoint of eternity, *sub specie aeternitatis*, that the meaning of the church's sacramentality can be deduced.

However, if the pilgrim church possesses its sacramental character only partly, and in a historical way, then the church can only manifest incrementally what it intends to sacramentalize. This view is further strengthened when one begins to ascertain the meaning of a church "from Abel," which implies a progressive historical manifestation. Even with the incarnation of Jesus and the paschal mystery of his life, death, and resurrection, there remains an incompleteness to the pilgrim church and, with its ecclesial divisions, the elements of both holiness and truth are scattered. A question immediately arises: Is there a shattered sacramentality to the pilgrim church? The disunity of the church itself affects sacramentality so that one must consider whether there is a disunity in the very sacramentality of the church itself, a disunity not only of individual Christians but of corporate groups of Christians as well.[10]

Let us compare two phrases:

1.   The church as a foundational sacrament.
2.   A divided church as a foundational sacrament.

Does a divided church divide sacramentality as well? The standard Roman Catholic answer to this is no, because the church *subsists* in the Roman Catholic Church (*LG,* no. 8). Whatever church essentially means is found in the Roman Catholic Church. The separated Eastern churches, however, argue in a similar way. The church, they maintain, "subsists" in their churches, and therefore their churches are icons of all that church basically and foundationally means. Likewise, Anglican and Protestant churches have the same understanding since, in these churches of the West, the Word of God is truly proclaimed and the sacraments of baptism and eucharist are truly celebrated. Is the phrase "the church as a foundational sacrament" only understood as the Roman Catholic Church? Is only the Roman Catholic Church the true and real foundational sacrament? The answer is clearly no. I suggest that until the ecumenical question is resolved, there will be an inherent and essential incoherence in the phrase, "the church as a foundational sacrament."

In the case of the separated Eastern churches, the Roman Catholic Church's standard theology presents serious aspects of the entire problem. The Roman Catholic Church accepts the apostolicity of these churches; the validity of their ordained bishops, priests, and deacons; their celebration of the sacraments, including eucharist; their liturgies and disciplines; their preaching of the Word of God; and their theological traditions. The one issue that complicates the situation is their nonacceptance of the papacy, except in some way as *primus inter pares.* Even more than this verbal acceptance, there is pastoral acceptance. Roman Catholics in serious need who have no recourse to a Roman Catholic priest or deacon can receive the sacraments of reconciliation, eucharist, and the anointing of the sick from ministers of the separated Eastern churches, if these same ministers are willing to do so. Members of these same Eastern churches, if they are in a similar serious situation, may receive reconciliation, eucharist, and anointing from Roman Catholic ministers. No prior permission from a bishop is needed in these situations. In doing this, we Roman Catholics do not ask of the separated Eastern church members any acceptance of the papacy in any form whatsoever. Since the papal question is irrelevant in these situations, then the issue of "church" has to be considered in a non-papal way. Because of the theological and pastoral stances of the Roman Catholic Church mentioned above, the papacy by itself does not seem to be at the basis of the church's foundational sacramentality. If the papacy were an essential basis for ecclesial foundational sacramentality, the Roman Catholic Church could not acknowledge all of the above mentioned issues, nor could the Roman Catholic Church allow pastoral intersacramental sharing. On the basis of the theological and pastoral relationships of the Roman Catholic Church to the separated Eastern churches, one can only conclude that there is clearly foundational sacramentality outside the Roman Catholic Church or, more accurately stated, outside the churches that are in communion with Rome. Until the ecumenical movement is clarified better, the very meaning of the church as a foundational sacrament will remain inherently incoherent.

Another theological issue that clouds this discussion is the relationship of kingdom and church. In contemporary Roman Catholic theology, the two are not coextensive. This affects the theme mentioned above: the many extra-ecclesial elements of holiness and truth found in communities other than the Roman Catholic Church. What is their relationship to the intra-ecclesial structures?

Whenever Roman Catholic theologians have attempted to provide some independence for these extra-ecclesial structures apart from the Roman Catholic Church, serious tensions have begun to arise. Church leaders clearly state that these extra-ecclesial elements of holiness and truth are really "church." This leads one to ask whether such elements should be described as extra-ecclesial at all, since they are immediately claimed as ecclesial. Once again, the phrase "the church as a foundational sacrament" will probably remain unsettled in meaning and basically incoherent until a better relationship of kingdom/church has been elaborated.

Finally, the church as a finite, created, limited reality is given an unsurpassability when the description "foundational sacrament" is predicated to it. Why is this particular, finite, limited, human reality called the Roman Catholic Church endowed with unsurpassability, since everything finite can be surpassed, everything limited can be surpassed, everything created and human can be surpassed?

"Sacrament"

Let us turn our attention to the theological problems in "sacrament." We have seen above that a sacrament is a happening, an event, an *Ereignis*. David Tracy presents us with the following description of an event in reference to revelation:

> "Event" language in contemporary theology is indicative of the gratuitous or gracious character of divine revelation. The very fact that God reveals Godself *is* grace, event, happening.[11]

Tracy says clearly that sacramental action is primarily the work of the triune God: God's blessing, God's action in the paschal mystery, and the many ways of God acting through and in the Holy Spirit. We analyzed this at length above when we considered the presentation in the *Catechism of the Catholic Church*. In a sacramental event, there is a primordial action of God and, only secondarily, a human response.

Tracy emphasizes that this divine action is an event:

> In modern theologies revelation is primarily construed on an interpersonal or encounter model as an event of divine self-manifestation to humanity. This interpersonal model of revelation further assumes that some person-like characteristics (namely, intelligence and love) must be employed to understand the reality of God as God manifests God's self as Wisdom and Love even if they also employ impersonal models for the Divine Mystery.[12]

The primordial action of God in a sacramental event is a self-manifestation of God as personal and loving. To this primordial action of a personal God, there is a secondary human response. Tracy unites this human reaction with contemporary hermeneutical philosophies.[13] Although Tracy, in these passages, is primarily focused on the issue of revelation, in later pages of this same essay he includes the issue of sacramentality as an instance in this disclosure event of God.[14] Tracy makes the following claim: "Among contemporary philosophies, I continue to believe that hermeneutical philosophy provides the kind of contemporary philosophy needed by a revelational theology."[15] I will return to his insights in the second section of this chapter.

For the moment, it is important is to understand that sacramentality is a disclosure event. God is disclosing, and we humans are responding. When, therefore, one says that the church is a foundational sacrament, this implies that the church is, of its very nature, a disclosure event in which God primordially is manifesting God's own self and Christian human beings are responding to this manifestation of God. Is the church, therefore, a locus in which God continually acts in some form of self-manifestation and disclosure, and in which Christians continually are responding to the divine primordial act? Is this some sort of ongoing activity on the part of God and humans? The answer to this is not easy to resolve. There cannot be some view of God who is simply present within the church locus as if God were there at all times saying: "I am revealing myself. Does anyone hear? I am revealing myself." Sacramentality occurs only when God discloses *and* when humans concomitantly, though secondarily, respond.

The difficulty with this way of considering sacramentality, at least regarding the foundational sacramentality of the church, is this: so much of the theological and ecclesiastical material on this theme is not speaking in an "event" or "disclosure" form of discourse. Rather, these writings use, to some degree, the more traditional Western approach of a subject/object form of discourse. The church is objectively sacramental, and the subjective element is not an essential factor in this objectivity. If the subjective element is essential, then the foundational sacramentality of the church depends on subjective elements and this involves relativity. However, I argue that sacramentality, including foundational sacramentality, is an event and a discourse that occurs only when there is a meeting of the primordial divine disclosing and the secondary human response. There cannot be foundational sacramentality in the church unless both the divine and the human interplay takes place. Is this interplay an ongoing, unchanging situation? I argue that it is not. Only when and to the degree that there is a communication in both a moment (temporality) of a disclosing God and, at the same time, in a moment (temporality) of responding Christians, can one speak of a sacramental event, can one speak of the event called church as a foundational sacrament. Subjectively, not all such moments are the same, and therefore there can be degrees of foundational sacramentality.

Tracy speaks of the divine Word as the divine revelatory moment, central to Christian life.

> Too many of these theological formulations of the dialectic of the Christian revelation as Word have ignored the fact that Jesus Christ as Word *is* both disclosive/Logos and disruptive/Proclamation of

God and humanity, of cosmos and history. Word therefore manifests
both nearness and distance, both participation and interruption.[16]

The church as foundational sacrament is a sacrament *of what?*
Primordially of God, of the *Logos,* of Jesus Christ precisely as disclosive and disruptive, as cosmic and historical *Haecceitas,* as near and distant, as participating in human life and disrupting human life, including
human Christian life. In this sense the church as foundationally sacramental is foundationally theocentric and, in virtue of the Logos made
flesh, christocentric. It is not, foundationally, ecclesiocentric.

Secondly, *to whom* is the church foundationally sacramental? The
usual theological answer is universal: to all human beings including members of the church itself.[17] The message of this primordial God and Logos
is proclaimed to each of us: in a historical, temporality/*Haecceitas* way
and also in a cosmic way; in a near way and also in a distant way; in a par-
ticipative way and also in a disruptive way. Our individual-in-community
response, together with the divine self-disclosure, constitutes the church
as foundationally sacramental.

All of the above is abstract and theoretical. Sacraments, however,
only exist in actual events within the historical and existential space-time
continuum. Where, then, in this actuality of the existential space-time
continuum, can one experience the actuality of the church as foundational
sacramentality? Only one answer seems to be possible—in the actual
interrelationality of concrete, living, existential Christians.

> The profane (that is, the natural) state of the world and of history
> is thus recognized as the *possible* sacramental place of a sacred
> history.[18]

Could we not also say of the church:

> The visible, existential church (that is, in its createdness) is thus
> recognized as the *possible* sacramental place of a sacred history.

This comparison intimates that the church, de facto in its existential, created, finite, visible, limited reality, is, primordially, sacramental
only because of the presence of a disclosing God at a given, concrete,
existential moment of the space-time continuum and, second, is therefore foundationally a sacramental church only when de facto the existential, created, finite, visible, and limited members, *qua* members, are
actually responding to the self-disclosing of God. Since not all members

are responding in the same way, but in a way that belongs to each in virtue of individualized *Haecceitas,* then ecclesial foundational sacramentality is itself historical, temporal, to some degree dependent on subjective elements, and, therefore, relative both in its communication and in its manifestation.

THE CHALLENGES FROM CONTEMPORARY WESTERN PHILOSOPHY

Postmodern Western philosophy has given a great deal of thought to the issue of social structure. Since the church is a communal structure, let us consider this area of social or communal structure as it is presented by various philosophers. In a general way, one might focus on the term *Lebenswelt.* Mara Rainwater states the case as follows:

> Life world *(Lebenswelt)*—a term used in the late work of Husserl *(The Crisis of the European Sciences,* 1937), referring to a shared background of culture, tradition and language that contextualizes subjective experience. The prototype of the life-world can be found in the life-philosophy and hermeneutic work of Wilhelm Dilthey who developed Hegel's concept of life and its domain of internal relations. Dilthey also greatly influenced Heidegger's focus on lived, historical experience in *Being and Time* (1927). Most recently, the term reemerges in Habermas's theory of communicative action.[19]

A second philosophical issue that is relevant here is Gadamer's *Horizontsverschmelzung.* We have already made reference to this phrase and seen how Ricoeur uses and nuances this insight. *Horizontsverschmelzung,* however, implies that each subjectivity interfaces other subjectivities and that there is an area of intersticity that has a foundational and, to some degree, a transformational effect on the subjectivities involved.

Likewise, the term "structuralism" must play a part in our discussion, since structuralism does not refer to an individualized aspect of human reality. Rainwater describes structuralism as follows:

> A movement focusing on internal structural relations rather than content, based on the linguistic method of analysis developed by Ferdinand de Saussure. He suggested that language constituted a

self-contained system, wherein meaning was generated within language itself rather than merely reflecting a "given" reality. This revolutionary claim, and the methodology it entailed, attracted immense interest across a spectrum of intellectual disciplines. Lévi-Strauss applied de Saussure's insights to anthropology, Lacan to psychoanalysis, Althusser to Marxism and Foucault to his wide-ranging social critique. The exponents of structuralism maintained an adversarial relation with existentialists and phenomenologists, whose belief in a transcendentally free human subject was rejected.[20]

Post-structuralists tend to reject the static internal relationality of the early structuralist model. Instead, they are open for multiple possibilities within the event of signifier-signified. Lacan and Barthes began as structuralists, but they can be seen in their later works as post-structuralists.

Yet another aspect of postmodern philosophy is semiotics. Both de Saussure in Europe and C. S. Peirce in the United States of America developed a theory of semiotics. Semiotics restudies and reintegrates the presence of sign in the human condition. To help us have a common understanding of terms, let us consider the description of semiotics that Rainwater offers:

> Semiotics—a "science of signs," also known as semiology…studies the constitutive-relational nature of signs and their communicative properties in society. The linguistic sign is a structural relationship between an acoustic "signifier" and the concept or "signified" it refers to. Much extended by Roland Barthes in his analyses of social semiotics where signification is heavily dependent on the connotation or associative powers of the sign, in popular culture and advertising especially.[21]

In these descriptions we notice issues such as relationality, linguistic communication, shared horizons, signifiers and signifieds, and structured coexistence. The individual *qua* individual is not the primary focus; the collectivity is the clear focus, although individuals do indeed constitute a collectivity. The theological phrase the "church as a foundational sacrament" is likewise dealing with a collectivity and, therefore, with relationality, with linguistic communication, with shared horizons, with signifiers and signifieds, and with structured coexistence. For this reason, it is precisely in this area of postmodern philosophy that one must begin. Let us consider each of the above categories in a more analytical way. We will do this by dividing the material, merely for organizational reasons, into two parts: one on semiotics and the other on *Horizontsverschmelzung*.

Semiotics

With his distinction between *langue* and *parole,* de Saussure indicates that an expression in one language, *parole,* is different from a similar expression in different language, *parole.* For instance, as H. Silverman notes, one could say: "Tall evergreen trees inspire a sense of grandeur." But, according to de Saussure, this is different from saying: "Ces grands arbres verts sont magnifiques." The *parole* in each case is uniquely different.[22] In comparison, we could say in English, "The church is a foundational sacrament"; or we could say in German: *Die Kirche ist Ursakrament.* In a semiotic framework, these two statements are not identical either in their signifying *(un significant)* or in what they signify *(un signifié).* The respective words in English and German are not part of the same sign system; these words are signs only within their respective systems *(parole).* Meaning takes place within a linguistic system; meaning is not something "out there" that each linguistic system makes use of.

Hermeneutics belongs within a linguistic system; there is no hermeneutic that is "out there" in an essentialized, non-linguistic framework. This is why the interpretation of a sentence, such as the English, French, and German sentences above, have a different hermeneutic. There is no common hermeneutic for all languages; meaning comes from within the linguistic system and is not imposed from without. De Saussure himself writes:

> In order to have language, there must be a *community of speakers.* Contrary to what might appear to be the case, a language never exists even for a moment except as a social fact, for it is a semiological phenomenon. Its social nature is one of its internal characteristics.[23]

It is clear that the subject and the collective are distinct but conjoined. When one adds the aspect of temporality, one gains a slightly different perspective, namely, the static element of current time and the evolutionary element of past-present-future. De Saussure is well aware of this. He rejects the term "historical linguistics," favors "evolutionary linguistics," and uses more often the distinction between synchrony and diachrony.[24] Because de Saussure searched for a "claim to universality" in the intersection of synchrony and diachrony, his thought has encountered the most telling opposition. R. Harris notes that, in this Saussurean intersection, the brilliance and the vulnerability of his theoretical acumen is clearly seen.[25] Although the relationship between the *significant* and the *signifié* is, for de Saussure, arbitrary, "it nevertheless cannot in any one *état de langue* vary beyond certain limits." Where does one find a claim for universality so that all speech is not arbitrary? It appears to be in a total network of interrelations, establishing individual connections between *significants* and *signifiés*.[26]

I have spent some time on this issue, because it raises the claim for universality in the area of linguistics. Even more, it raises the claim for universality beyond the area of linguistics, because there is some sort of onto-epistemology at work in every philosophical language analysis. Hermeneutical ease presupposes a claim for universality, and religious leaders, when using language with hermeneutical ease, indirectly make a claim for universality in some way or another. The brilliance of de Saussure is the profound expression of language that, in his view, cries out for some claim of universality. The vulnerability of his thought is that his claim has met with strong defenders and challengers, for example, T. de Mauro, S. Ullmann, and R. Harris, to mention only a few. This vulnerability has raised the issue today why any group using a certain language framework can make a claim to universality. This challenge is made not simply on the basis of subjectivity, but on the basis of linguistic collectivity, involving the forces of both *synchrony* and *diachrony*—in other words, the issue of tradition itself and the issue of relativity to every collective group that shares in the *état de langue*. This, as we shall see later, bears directly on the collective/subjective issue of the church as a foundational sacrament, a linguistic phrase that makes a claim on universality.

Clearly, the Saussurean reduction of meaning to language means that outside of language, both *langue* and *parole,* there is nothing relevant. On this matter de Saussure was challenged by Barthes. In 1964, Barthes published *Elements of Semiology,* in which he linked his previous critical work with the theoretical material of de Saussure. For Barthes, there is a text, and one can read it from the standpoint of the author. He calls this kind of reading *scriptible.* A reader seeks to understand the meaning of the author. This produces very little, according to Barthes. The writerly (scriptible) "is the novelistic without the novel, poetry without the poem, the essay without the dissertation, writing without style, production without product, structuration without structure."[27]

The *lisible* is different. It is a text that is a site, a locus for a reading, a place in which *jouissance* (pleasure) occurs. When we read the text and the text speaks, we are animated by our encounter, filled with *jouissance*. Such a reading is an event in which there clearly is a signifier, *un significant,* and a signified, *un signifié.* The words speak to us and echo through our being, and we respond to this pleasure, to this overflow of meaning.

There is something powerfully subjective in this semiotic approach, and Barthes offers a variety of codes to assist us to read in a lisible manner and not in a scriptible manner. These codes include:

the semic code	—	the elaboration of the signifier;
the hermeneutic code	—	the disclosure of the enigma;
the symbolic code	—	one element stands for another;
the actantial code	—	the action code;
the reference code	—	cultural indicators of the text.[28]

The text speaks and we respond. Only then is the novel a novel, the poem a poem, the structure a structure. There is clearly something subjective about this, but this subjective element lies within a communal linguistic system. There is, then, an interpersonal, interrelational, cultural network as well. *Parole* has meaning only within a community.

Moving the discourse even further, Lacan states his own case. In the phrase "I think therefore I am," the "I" of "I think" is not the same as the "I" of "I am."[29] Lacan is clearly stating that Descartes's identification of the human subject with human consciousness is unsustainable. Once again, we see a postmodern philosopher critiquing the epistemological base for most of Western thought. Let us consider a graph that Lacan suggests:[30]

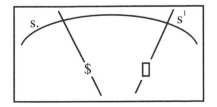

Jürgen Braungardt explains this graph and Lacan's position as follows. In the graph, two counter-currents cross. One arises from the subject in its actuality (= □) to the subject in its consciousness or, as many philosophers call it, the split subject (= $), while the other expresses the movement of language from S to S1.

> These two movements cross each other at two points. Between these two points emerges what philosophers commonly call "consciousness" and which leads ultimately to the constitution of a split subject (=$). In speech the subject of the sentence gets specified further: The statement is complete when the sentence is finished—[the right cross-point]. This would also be the point where the subject encounters the Other, to whom the speech is always oriented. This is the point where the subject receives its identifications and subsequently splits.[31]

The identifications are not, in Lacan's view, self-conscious; rather, they are defined by the place the subject has in relation to the Other. Lacan makes a distinction between "others" and the "Other." This Other is not simply the common denominator of all others, such as family, friends, or co-workers; rather, the Other is the point at which the common denominator merges with language itself. As Braungardt states, "It is the locus of truth, the place where the subject's definition gets generated, where its meaning is completed."[32] There is a split here, according to Lacan, since what one says about one's self is a self-reflected view and not the real self at all. The "I" in the "I think" and the "I" in the "I am" are not identical. This is why Lacan can speak openly about lying.[33]

In all of this, Lacan attempts to challenge the current thinking that a person understands his or her very subjectivity through a false identification of the "I think" and the "I am." With the introduction of the unconscious, Lacan, in ways similar but also dissimilar to Ricoeur, calls for a total rethinking of consciousness, which means a total rethinking of the subjective.[34] Second, it is in and through language, Lacan indicates, that when we speak to the Other we are saying something about ourselves which is ultimately not ourselves. One might draw some parallels between this mode of thinking and the way in which Heidegger spoke about the part of the *Dasein* that proximally and, for the most part, reveals itself and proximally and, for the most part, does not reveal itself. Parallels can also be made between Lacan's mode of thinking and the Heideggerian manner in which we are characterized as *Mit-Anderen-Dasein*.[35] Lacan clearly distances himself from any ontological overtones of Heidegger and moves beyond Heidegger's position in his own explanation of consciousness.

Language takes place in a community, with an Other, but in a way that cannot be absolutized or in a way in which some sort of truth framework detemporalizes the entire field of discourse. The "I am" is continually to be sought, whereas the split "I" is only what we know at a given moment of time in our given communications with given others.

All of this material on language raises a challenge to any easy hermeneutic of the phrase "the church is a primordial sacrament." When various people use this phrase, is it clear to those who use only an English *parole?* Does such an English phrase have any coordinate meaning with those who use a German *parole,* a Chinese *parole,* a Bantu *parole?* On the other hand, is the "I" who speaks and thinks in one instance different from the "I" who is and was at a different instance? There is an "I think/I am" dislinking, so that when "I think" says at one moment, "the church is a primordial sacrament," this may not be the same as when the "I think" says at a different moment, "the church is a primordial sacrament." Much less does this statement have an impact in an identical way on the "I am" who has said at either moment, "I think." The hermeneutical ease that some authors use when they say "the church is a primordial sacrament" suddenly becomes distorted, if not meaningless.

Any rebuttal that is constructed in and through the typical Western subject-object epistemology of an Aristotelian scholasticism or of an Enlightenment understanding regarding both world *[Lebenswelt]* and thinker [I think/I am] dodges the postmodern challenge. We will return to this in part three.

Horizontsverschmelzung

When one speaks of shared horizons or, in the thought of Merleau-Ponty, of the interfacing of intentionalities, a communality of subjectivities—or better, a communality of intersubjectivities—is subliminally, at least, in operation, but usually not central. Postmodern philosophy has clearly turned its attention to the area of communality of intersubjectivities.[36] Gadamer, for instance, has no use for any naive objectivism such as one finds in Western historical sciences and in the so-called self-understanding of the natural sciences. Texts do not contain within themselves a well-defined, unchanging meaning, which hermeneutics has as its task to make clear. Rather, Gadamer is saying something at odds with this naive objectivistic approach. Madison describes Gadamer's position in a clear and succinct way:

> The basic point [in Gadamer's approach] can be stated fairly tersely: what interpretation seeks to understand is not the *intention* of the *author,* but the *meaning* of the *text.* To put the matter yet another way: textual meaning is not reducible to authorial intention. A "good" text is precisely one which has something to say to us, its readers, over and above what its author may (or may not) have intended and willed.[37]

Interpretation is never simply reproduction, and the rejection of authorial intention as the supreme criterion of textual meaning is paramount in Gadamer's approach. But this approach is only understandable on the basis of *Horizontsverschmelzung.* Textual meaning is an *event,* and this event is the act of reading.[38] When one confronts a text, the so-called answers are really answers to questions that we ourselves already pose. There is a basic subjectivity in reading a text that is fundamental to any hermeneutical endeavor. The only "objectivity" here is "the confirmation of a fore-meaning in its being worked out."[39]

This does not mean, however, that we individually insert our own meaning into the text. This would negate what Gadamer calls a conversation. When we enter into a *Horizontsverschmelzung,* we put our own views and presuppositions into a risky situation, and this is fundamental to the "event." Indeed, our own presuppositions and ideas are challenged by this process of event and generally there is a transformation of our own ideas and our own presuppositions. This is what Gadamer means when he writes: "Only through others do we gain true knowledge of ourselves."[40]

Rather than a view of knowledge that sees knowing as a correct representation, Gadamer, in line with many postmodern thinkers, says that all knowing is at the same time a transformation that involves an application into the reader's practical, social situation. Even for those things that one honors and reveres as "tradition," Gadamer says, "the same tradition must always be understood in a different way."[41]

There is clearly a past, there is clearly a tradition, there is clearly a communal past and a communal tradition, but these are horizons we share, not horizons we simply inherit in some unchangeable way.[42] Gadamer clearly moves away from a totally subjective theory of meaning and involves himself in a communal sense of meaning, one in which the subjective still plays a crucial role and the communal plays a social and transformational role, not a reproductive role.

In "Zu Gadamer's Wahrheit und Methode," Habermas focused intensely on Gadamer's vulnerability.[43] Tradition in some ways came to be presented by Gadamer as the structure that holds humankind together. There is a sort of validating and universalizing claim that tradition, in Gadamer's position, involves. As in the case of de Saussure's semiotics, we are once again faced with the issue of universal claim, but, this time, in the area of hermeneutics and *Horizontsverschmelzung*.

A more insightful and penetrating analysis of Gadamer's position was made by Habermas in "Der Universalitätsanspruch der Hermeneutik."[44] Habermas goes to great lengths to indicate that there are limits to hermeneutics. "Hermeneutic consciousness remains incomplete as long as it does not include a reflection upon the limits of hermeneutic understanding. The experience of hermeneutical limitation refers to specifically incomprehensible expressions."[45] He also says: "The experience of the limit of hermeneutics consists of the recognition of systematically generated misunderstanding as such—without at first being able to 'grasp' it."[46] In presenting his own position, Habermas writes:

> To attempt a systematic justification we have to develop the implicit knowledge, that always and already guides the depth-hermeneutical analysis of language, into a theory which would enable us to deduce the principle of rational discourse from the logic of everyday language and read it as the necessary regulative for any actual discourse, however distorted it may be.[47]

Habermas himself has not arrived at the most satisfactory approach to a hermeneutical claim for universality, and his stress on the linguistic usage by mentally challenged individuals has also been criticized. Nonetheless, this debate is extremely important because it highlights once again the postmodern question on any and every claim to universality. The challenge comes precisely from the *Horizontsverschmelzung*, both of co-temporal subjectivities and of historical temporalities.

Ricoeur emphasizes many of the same issues as Gadamer but in a slightly different fashion. In *Hermeneutics and the Human Sciences,* Ricoeur describes the most fundamental hermeneutical problem:

> If we can no longer define hermeneutics in terms of the search for
> the psychological intentions of another person which are con-
> cealed *behind* the text, and if we do not want to reduce interpreta-
> tion to the dismantling of structures [as in the structuralist, purely
> explanatory approach], then what remains to be interpreted? I
> shall say: to interpret is to explicate the type of being-in-the-world
> unfolded *in front* of the text.[48]

The world, in this passage, has clear references to Husserl's
Lebenswelt and to Heidegger's *In-der-Welt-Dasein.* In a given text,
Ricoeur would say, the reader perceives a world in which he or she might
possibly live. "To understand a text is at the same time to light up our
own situation."[49] Ricoeur emphasizes that there is a narrative quality
about our hermeneutical task, but in a narrative the conclusion remains
the "pole of attraction of the whole process." Thus, the conclusion cannot
be either deduced or predicted. A narrative holds a reader's attention by a
thousand contingencies. The conclusion is not at all predictable. Rather,
it must simply be acceptable. Understanding comes only after the event.[50]
Primordiality engenders reproduction, a fait accompli. Teleology engenders a possible and acceptable denouement. Primordiality, the movement
behind the reader, the archeology of the subject, is only a part of the
"event" and offers no prescribed and predictable consequences. The
movement found *in front* of the reader, the eschatology of the spirit,
involves expectation and contingency. There is, for Ricoeur, a productive
imagination, a social imagination, and this means always a challenge to
what is presented as past, as tradition, or as fixed, and moves one into the
unknown telelogical eschatology of the spirit.[51]

The entry of the issue of evil and the concomitant issue of limit that
Ricoeur places in the field of discourse renders the claim for universality
to an even more intense level, particularly because the symbols of evil
cannot be drawn up into *Aufhebung,* an absolute knowledge, a "grand
plan." The symbols of the sacred—and here we should have in mind the
issue of sacrament as one aspect of the symbols of the sacred—lead us to
no absolute knowledge, but only point to a possible eschatology of the
spirit. Ricoeur calls this a double dependence, a dependence of the self on
the unconscious and a dependence on the sacred.[52]

As with all postmodern thinkers, there is no grand synthesis or
plan about which we already have some detailed glimpse. What the
outcome might be remains the exciting part of the human narrative. We

tell our stories together, in a sharing of horizons, without any clear understanding of the ways our stories might end. Primordiality in this sense cannot offer any irreducibility.

Both these sections, the first on *semiotics* and the second on *Horizontsverschmelzung,* have led to a critique of an absolute claim, of a claim for universality. I have not presented the fullness of thought that the authors cited have provided us, but simply pinpointed certain aspects of their thought that challenge the hermeneutical ease with which church leaders and theologians speak about the church as a foundational sacrament. The argument used to challenge such language and its underlying hermeneutic is not theological but philosophical. The challenge is presented on the basis that every collectivity of subjectivities is relational, finite, limited; that every linguistic state, *état de langue,* struggles to make any claim at all for universality. A theological answer to these challenges—God has so chosen—is inadequate. The answer must speak directly to the philosophical issues that are involved in the challenge.

THE RAMIFICATIONS OF THIS PHILOSOPHICAL CHALLENGE TO THE FACILE USE OF THE PHRASE, "THE CHURCH IS A FOUNDATIONAL SACRAMENT"

In the thirty-ninth general session of Vatican II, Bishop Guano of Livorno addressed the plenary group as follows:

> With Christ and through Christ, in itself and by its very presence in the world and by the whole of its life, the Church is a sacrament—the "primordial sacrament" in the words of Cardinal Frings—that is, it is the effective sign both of the redemption and sanctification which Christ brings to men, through her and of the glory which Christ gives to the Father through her."[53]

This address had a profound influence on the bishops at Vatican II and helped them decide to include the sacramentality of the church as a major part of their conciliar documents. Guano eloquently states the way that many ecclesiastical leaders, both bishops and theologians, have described the church as a foundational sacrament. Ecclesiology is clearly connected to christology; the church is an effective sign of God's gift of redemption and sanctification for the entire world.

Is any of the above meaningful? Does it say anything to the third-millennium Western person? In many ways, these sentences are not meaningful. First of all, the use of "church" is abstract. What church is under consideration? In every sacramental action, it is God revealing God's own self. If we say that "church" refers to an overarching universal church, this abstraction from historicity and temporality cannot help but be challenged. Everything we know is individualized, historically positioned in time and space, and thoroughly temporalized. Where is there any meaning for a universal church that is presented as a dehistoricized, detemporalized, despatialized entity? In the referent to the church from Abel to the present, the same objections apply, as in the case of a heavenly church, about which we know very little, if anything. An abstract universalized meaning of church in the phrase "the church is a foundational sacrament" renders the statement meaningless.

If "church" has reference to the Roman Catholic Church and only the Roman Catholic Church, then for a large number of Christians, this phrase has no valid meaning at all, since these Christians see themselves as part of the church, but not members of the Roman Catholic Church.

If "church" refers to all Christian churches, then officials in the Roman Catholic Church would raise objections, because this relativizes, in their view, the role of the Roman Catholic Church, which alone is the one true church. In this approach, Roman Catholic leaders would find the phrase meaningless.

If the term "church" has reference to localized churches, then the sacramentality of the church is really a collage of many sacramentalities, with some local churches more clearly sacramental than others. In the eyes of some, this relativizes the churches in a way that makes the phrase "the church is a foundational sacrament" meaningless. In this instance a small local church might be more foundational than a larger, more prestigious church.

These problems arise specifically because of the theological ambiguity that the many uses of "church" by theologians and church officials have engendered. Postmodern philosophy would find difficulty only in the area in which there is detemporalizing, dehistoricizing, despatializing, definitizing. For our purposes, this postmodern challenge is of paramount importance nonetheless.

Let us approach the issue as believers in God and in revelation, and, with this premise, let us rethink the postmodern challenge indicated above. Every church gathering is localized in a given time and space; it is made up of individuals, that is, of various subjectivities who are also a collectivity. Every temporal, spatial, individual, collective aspect is finite, limited, and relative. The gathering, called church, is finite in respect to all other finite gatherings; is limited in respect to all other limited gatherings; is relative to all other relative gatherings. In all of this, church people, Christians, are no different from any other person or persons on this planet. How, then, can they be called "foundational," if, by this term, one means that the role of the church as sacrament is unsurpassable?

It is necessary to see both the theological and philosophical ambivalence, a dual challenge, in order to see the challenge that a third-millennium person might have with the phrase "the church is a foundational sacrament." Beyond this duality, one should be reminded that, for the vast majority of the third-millennium world, the phrase simply has no meaning. Christians are only about 30 percent of the world's population, and any and every invocation by the church of an unsurpassability is viewed as arrogance and quickly dismissed.

In order to provide some valency to the phrase, I would suggest, first of all, that one must acknowledge that the world itself is a *possible* sacrament, but only with all the caveats already mentioned above. No one finite entity can claim an exclusivity for sacramentality. This already helps preclude any philosophically meaningless exclusivity, since it prevents any one finite, temporal, individualized collectivity from making a universal claim.

Second, and even more important, theologians and church officials should acknowledge that all foundationality, all unsurpassability connected to the phrase "the church is a foundational sacrament," stems from the presence of God, who is revealing God's own self in the sacramental event called church. They should acknowledge that finite, relative, temporal, spatial, individualized, and subjective elements—all the Christians involved—are responding to the foundationality and unsurpassability of God, who is concretely revealing God's own self in a highly individualized collectivity of subjectivities. Christians, of and by themselves, have nothing that can be called foundational and unsurpassable.

This first aspect allows for sacramentality as an event to be present elsewhere in our human world. The same God is the basis for the foundationality and unsurpassability of these sacramental events. The second aspect allows the church to be church in the sense that, in its collectivity, it is responding to the prior act of a revealing God. The criterion for foundationality and unsurpassability lies with the God in whom one believes. The Creed says, "We believe in one church," but all belief is God-directed. When Christians say, "We believe in one church," they are not saying, "We believe in ourselves." Nothing finite is the focus of faith.

The claim to universality (Habermas/Gadamer) in this case remains a claim to a divine universality, not a finite universality. The struggle to find a "universal system" for language (de Saussure/Barthes) moves from center stage. Each church gathering at a given moment of time and space is a moment of sacramental *Haecceitas* and thus is limited and open to further layers of meaning. The symbols of the sacred do not produce any absolute language (Ricoeur), and the symbols of evil render the camouflaging, inherent in every symbol, very apparent and provide an impetus to delve more deeply into the archeology of the person and the eschatology of the spirit.

Perhaps, in all of this, it would be more advantageous to lay aside the phrase "the church is a foundational sacrament," since, from a theological, philosophical, and demographical standpoint, there are too many issues that make the phrase hermeneutically difficult if not meaningless.

This third part of the present chapter is meant only to provide a framework for the possible resolution of the challenges that postmodern thought has brought to this particular theme. In the next chapter, it is my hope to construct a hermeneutically meaningful understanding of sacrament for postmodern, third-millennium people.

6

Postmodern Sacramentality

In this chapter we attempt to draw together the central issues on sacramental theology with the help of postmodern Western thought. As mentioned in the preface, this volume is meant to be an attempt to rethink sacramental theology from the standpoint of contemporary hermeneutics as a possible basis for further discussion. This involves a *Horizontsverschmelzung* between Christian-Catholic theology, on the one hand, and postmodern thought, on the other.

Part of the sacramental and theological legacy of the twentieth century, as we saw in chapter 1, was the influence of contemporary Western postmodern philosophies. These philosophical studies have been widespread throughout the West, highly influential and radically transformative. Three basic approaches to the challenges arising from postmodern thought might be taken by Christian-Catholic theologians. The first is dismissal and rejection. Sacramental theology, in this view, need not bother with these challenges, since one is dealing with theology and not with philosophy. The challenge of postmodern thinkers, as we have already noted, is precisely a challenge at the epistemological and onto-epistemological levels: a challenge to both the Aristotelian-scholastic onto-epistemology and the Cartesian-Enlightenment onto-epistemology. If sacramental theology is to be meaningful in the West today, then, theologians and church officials must seriously consider the hermeneutical issues involved in postmodern onto-epistemology.

A second response is denial of the validity of postmodern thought itself. It should be obvious to the reader that postmodern thought has seriously challenged the very roots of Western self-understanding.

Those who make this kind of response affirm that their own way of thinking is hermeneutically unquestionable, an indication of philosophical arrogance.

A third response is precisely what this chapter attempts to accomplish: a serious effort to unite postmodern ways of thinking and Christian-Catholic sacramental theology. Phenomenology has already influenced such major sacramental thinkers as Rahner, Schillebeeckx, Duffy, and Chauvet. I am indebted to these works, but I want to pursue the efforts already made even more forcibly.

In beginning this task, we should recall what this postmodern effort is fundamentally about. Many authors who have addressed this position might be cited. I select Gadamer, only because he is so straightforward, although Husserl, as we saw above, has written in the same way. In his foreword to the second edition of *Wahrheit und Methode,* Gadamer answers some of his initial critics and rejects their invocation of the Kantian distinction between *quaestio iuris* and *quaestio facti.* Gadamer sees the problematic at a far deeper level. He writes:

> Thus the following investigation also asks a philosophic question. But it does not ask it only of the so-called human sciences (among which precedence would then be accorded to certain traditional disciplines). It does not ask it only of science and its modes of experience, but of all human experience of the world and human living. It asks (to put it in Kantian terms): How is understanding possible? This is a question which precedes any action of understanding on the part of the subjectivity, including the methodical activity of the "understanding sciences" [*verstehende Geisteswissenschaften*] and their norms and rules.[1]

How is understanding possible? This is the lead question of postmodern thought. It is a question about the presuppositions of understanding itself. A language philosopher might stress that understanding comes about when denotatively, not connotatively, language is at its clearest level. To this, a phenomenologist such as Herman van Breda would reply, "But an even deeper question is: what is understanding itself?"

Sacramental theologians can, for their part, speak about Jesus as the primordial sacrament, but a postmodern thinker could easily ask on what basis such a statement is understandable. It is my view that there has been a false hermeneutical ease when such a statement has been made and that this is found when theologians speak about the world or the church as a sacrament. Thus, from philosophy and from theology, the question of understanding arises. What am I asked to understand when I am presented with sacramental statements on world, church, and Jesus? If these kinds of statements are presented with hermeneutical ease, then meaninglessness cannot help but present itself in this discourse. (It might help at this point to reread the thesis of this book found in chapter 3.)

In order to move more carefully in the construction of sacramental theology along the lines mentioned in the thesis, I divide this chapter into the following subdivisions:

1. Theological and philosophical assumptions for each and every sacramental *Ereignis*.
2. The relationship between God's presence in creation and God's presence in a sacramental event.
3. The pan-cosmic possibility of sacramentality.
4. The primacy of human perception or the non-objectifiability of anything beyond human perception.
5. Rituals as celebrations of sacramental *Haecceitas*.

THEOLOGICAL AND PHILOSOPHICAL ASSUMPTIONS FOR EACH AND EVERY SACRAMENTAL *EREIGNIS*

We have analyzed in depth the presentation of a major theological assumption expounded in the *Catechism of the Catholic Church*, namely, that the source and goal of all liturgy, sacramental and nonsacramental, is the action of God: a God who blesses, a God who blesses the world with a paschal mystery, a God who encounters, acts, recalls meaning, gives spiritual understanding, makes present the unique mystery of Christ, transforms and brings us into communion with the divine.[2]

Presented with this primary and originatory divine action, men and women subsequently respond in celebration, awe, thanksgiving, and praise. This is at the heart of each and every sacramental *Ereignis*. It is also a personal moment of disclosure, a revelatory act on the part of God, made at a unique time and in a unique space in union with very unique individuals, and therefore, each and every sacramental *Ereignis* is at the same time sacramental *Haecceitas*.

Sacramentality is primarily, fundamentally, and initially the action of God. Secondarily, it is the concomitant human response of praise and love. This personal, experiential encounter is at the center of sacramental life, and theologically all other issues must flow *from* this revelatory event of sacrament and must flow *back to* this same event. In other words, from a theological perspective this primary action of God and the secondary response of men and women are the controlling issues in all sacramental discourse. Whenever this basic dual-centering of sacramental theology ceases to be the fundamental operative principle in the development of a sacramental theology, sacramental discourse begins to move in an epiphenomenal direction, even an ideological direction, and this gives rise to epistemological meaninglessness.

In speaking of the sacramental event in this fashion, we see that every sacrament is clearly an *Ereignis,* an event, that occurs whenever God is acting in a self-revelatory way and there is a human response to this divine self-revelation. Sacramental events, therefore, indeed involve the human; only when there is a secondary human response to a primary self-revealing act of God can we even begin to speak of sacrament. The world in itself is not a sacrament, but it is a place in which sacramentality is possible. Nonetheless, human perception and response, though secondary, remain an integral ingredient of a sacramental event.

THE RELATIONSHIP BETWEEN GOD'S PRESENCE IN CREATION AND GOD'S PRESENCE IN A SACRAMENTAL EVENT

The action of God and the reaction of men and women are expressed in today's theology in terms of interpersonal presence. Christian theology also teaches that God is the creator of all things and that this creation is not only an original *creatio ex nihilo*—or more precisely *productio rei ex nihilo sui nec subiecti,* as Thomas Aquinas described it[3]—but also an ongoing creation. Paul Tillich was deeply impressed by Thomas Aquinas in this regard, and he incorporates this way of thinking into his understanding of God as the Ground of all being. At each moment, God is grounding the very being of the creature and is, therefore, present in ongoing creation.[4]

Tillich's second formal principle of all theology addresses, in a general way, the question, What does concern us ultimately and unconditionally? Tillich answers that as far as we humans are concerned, our ultimate concern is that which affects our being or nonbeing. The question of being/nonbeing continually confronts us as a question of ongoing creation itself.

> Whether it is a God who is a being besides others (even the highest), or an angel who inhabits a celestial realm (called the realm of the "spirits"), or a man who possesses supranatural powers (even if he is called a god-man)—none of these is an object of theology, for it fails to withstand the criticism of the second criterion of theology, that is if it is not a matter of being or nonbeing for us.[5]

We encounter ultimacy at that dimension when our own nature reaches its final dimension, at the border of our finite being. Beyond that final border of finite being, there are only two alternatives, nonbeing or the Ground of all being. Already in 1928 Tillich had described this boundary situation:

> The human border situation is reached at that place where human possibility is totally placed at finality, where human existence is placed under an unconditioned threat [of nonexistence].[6]

At this boundary, Tillich does not mean that we are standing before two different ways of being. We are in actuality confronted with only *one* way of being, a way in which the structures of freedom can never be avoided and in which freedom unavoidably means decision, a *Ja* or a *Nein*. The boundary situation, then, exhausts all human possibilities. A human person is at the end, the ultimate of his or her being, at the end of the potentialities of his or her being. He or she is at the border of the *Woher* and of the *Wohin*. Beneath or before the *Woher,* or beyond or above the *Wohin,* there is for us only nonbeing. Autonomy, heteronomy, and the demonic all terminate at nonbeing.

Even more than Thomas Aquinas, Bonaventure speaks of the presence of God in all things, calling his position a metaphysics. In the *Collationes in Hexaemeron* he writes:

> This is our whole metaphysics: emanation, exemplarity, consummation, to be illumined by the spiritual rays and to be led back to the highest Reality.[7]

In his volume *Bonaventure and the Coincidence of Opposites,*[8] Ewert Cousins developed this line of thinking in a profound way and, in a more recent article, specifically focused on this passage from Bonaventure. Cousins writes:

> By the coincidence of opposites, then, I mean an organic, interrelated structure of the entire created universe, reflecting the divine archetype of this structure within the inner life of the Trinity.[9]

In the onto-hermeneutic of Thomas, Bonaventure, Tillich, and Cousins, one might easily say that the entire world reflects God and, therefore, the entire world, just by *being* world (metaphysics), is sacrament. However, the theological basis of all sacramentality, as presented by the *Catechism,* would not and could not agree with this position without further clarification. This needed clarification arises from the position that the human response in a sacramental event, even though secondary, is an integral part of the interrelational encounter that constitutes sacramentality. Nonetheless, Thomas, Bonaventure, Tillich, Cousins, and so many others are indeed saying that God is present in all of creation, not only at some unknown chronological beginning, at an original *creatio ex nihilo,* but also in an ongoing way, in a continuing creational act of God, or, as Pierre Teilhard de Chardin calls it, a *création evolutive.* We have then these two issues:

1. God is present in creation.
2. God is present in a sacramental *Ereignis.*

From a theological standpoint there must then be some sort of intrinsic connection between the presence of God in creation and the presence of God in a sacramental event. In both instances, it must be noted, we are primarily speaking about a *personal* presence *of God* to a created entity; we are not primarily speaking about some aspect or quality *of a created thing* that one can then call sacrament. In both instances, presence is clearly expressed in personal terms and not in reified terms. No thing per se is a creature. A creature *is* only in relationship to a creative God. There is also no thing per se that is a sacrament. Sacramental events *are* primarily actions of God and secondarily the human response to this divine action. Sacramentality is an interpersonal event, an *Ereignis,* a revelatory interpersonal disclosure.

It is imperative to distinguish sacramental events from creation events. It is the same God who is *present* in both, but differently. In every sacramental event, there is a presupposition that God has already created the world we live in and that God has created each and every human person. There is a further presupposition that this God is a self-revelatory God who is present in this created world. However, this does not mean that the world *qua* world is "objectively" self-revelatory of God. Rather, it means that the world *qua* world in all its diverse aspects possibly can be a locus of God's own self-revelation to us. This is the point that Chauvet has made. On the one hand, God is present to the world by and through a creative act; on the other hand, God is present to the world in and through a sacramental event. Creation and sacramentality both involve and are identified by the presence of God; however, they are distinct.

This relationship of creation and sacramentality is a case of identity and difference. On the relationship of identity in difference, Heidegger, in my judgment, has offered some of the most incisive contemporary considerations. Not without reason did Heidegger once say that his two most important volumes were: *Sein und Zeit (Being and Time)* and *Identität und Differenz (Identity and Difference)*.[10] In this latter volume, Heidegger begins by saying:

> The usual formulation of the principle of identity reads: A = A. The principle of identity is considered the highest principle of thought.[11]

Later in this work Heidegger probes the relationship of *Dasein* and *Sein,* in which there is both identity and yet difference. *Dasein* is not the total comprehension of *Sein,* and *Sein* is not limited by a particular *Dasein.* He writes:

> Within the framework there prevails a strange ownership and a strange appropriation. We must experience simply this owning in which man and Being are delivered over to each other, that is, we must enter into what we call the event of appropriation.[12]

One should note in this paragraph the two terms "ownership" and "appropriation," *Eignen* and *Zueignen.* Heidegger goes on to say:

> The term event of appropriation here no longer means what we would otherwise call a happening, an occurrence. It now is used as a *singulare tantum.* What it indicates happens only in the singular, no, not in any number, but uniquely.[13]

What the event of appropriation indicates happens only in the singular, not in any plurality, nor as a number in a series (*in einer Zahl*), but uniquely. One might say that Heidegger, in his own terms, is describing *Haecceitas,* a uniqueness constitutive of the appropriation event, a uniqueness also intrinsic to identity. This is the meaning of the principle of identity, A = A.[14] Heidegger's subtle differentiation between "belonging" and "together" is important for our purposes.[15]

In yet another cryptic but important sentence, he says: "The essence of identity is a property of the event of appropriation."[16] In this reference to Heidegger, I do not wish to relate my effort to that of Bultmann or Rahner, who have to some degree "baptized" Heidegger and have identified *Sein* with the Christian God, *esse ipsum.* Such a relationship is not what Heidegger intended. I do not intend to say that Heidegger's *Gehören* is to be identified with creation, and his *Zusammen* is to be identified with sacramentality. All I wish to say is this: in Heidegger A = A is not a tautology, so that A^1 and A^2 are identical. A = A is understood by Heidegger as the event in which *Gehören* and *Zusammen* take place, but neither *Gehören* nor *Zusammen* are totally identical. An event of appropriation, *Zueignen,* includes belonging and identity, *Eignen,* but there is, nonetheless, an overpowering difference. There is, in my view, a proportion between Heidegger's *Gehören/ Zusammen, Eignen/Zueignen,* which is similar to the identity and difference between creation/sacramentality. This is the only connection to Heidegger that I wish to make. Just as A = A does not mean that A^1 is the same as A^2, so also creation (A^1) is not the same as sacrament (A^2).

Heidegger ends his lecture with a summation of the principle of identity:

> The principle of identity means now: a spring demanded by the essence of identity because it needs that spring if the belonging together of man and Being is to attain the essential light of the appropriation.[17]

If we were to exchange the A = A into the personal mode: I = I, then the second I is not a tautology of the first I. "I am I" is a sentence in which "I^1" and "I^2" are identical but different. The same holds for an understanding in postmodern thought of the Cartesian phrase *cogito ergo sum,* in which the *ego* understood in *cogito* and the *ego* understood in *sum* are identical but different, as Lacan points out. My own intent here is to draw from this the following: *In a sacramental* Ereignis, *the creating God and the self-revealing, sacramental God are identical, but distinct; and the created I and the I in the sacramental response are identical but distinct.*

In what we have heard from Heidegger in the above citations, as well as in the discussion of sacraments as primarily actions of God but also secondarily as responses of the human person, this distinction is made on the basis that <u>sacraments are events</u>, just as *Zusammen* is an event in Heidegger. Even more so, they are events that involve *Haecceitas,* the *singulare tantum,* the unique.

> The more fitting formulation of the principle of identity "A = A" would accordingly mean not only that every A is itself the same; but rather that every A is itself the same with itself. Sameness implies the relation of "with," that is, a mediation, a connection, a synthesis: the unification into a unity.[18]

Only when one unites creation and sacramentality somehow as Heidegger unites belonging and together, will both creation and sacramentality be seen as being with, *Zusammen,* the same presence of God, but an actual appropriation, *Gehören,* exists in a way that is an event of appropriation involving, at one and the same time, both *Identität und Differenz.* Sacraments involve created human beings responding to their already creating God in an act of appropriation. This event also includes *Haecceitas.*

<u>Without a relationship between sacramentality and creation</u>, sacramentality becomes epiphenomenal and even magical. It speaks of God's sacramental presence in a way that denigrates God's continuing creational presence. Some profound reflection on both the union and the distinction of creation and sacramentality is requisite. Just as Heidegger profoundly reflected on the very principle of identity, A = A, so, too, we must reflect on creation and sacramentality as united but distinct. What Heidegger accomplished in his meditation on A = A helps us see that creation = sacrament involves identity but also difference, at a very profound onto-epistemological level.

THE PAN-COSMIC POSSIBILITY OF SACRAMENTALITY

There is an implication in all this reflection on identity and difference that radically takes us beyond the standard approach to sacramental thought within the Christian scholastic tradition and the later transcendental Thomist tradition. There is the possibility of sacramentality throughout all creation, since the world, the cosmos in its entirety, in its temporal, historical, and existential dimensions, is a possible locus for sacramentality, precisely because the world has been created by God. In Cousins's words cited above, the created world is "an organic, interrelated structure of the entire created universe, reflecting the divine archetype of this structure within the inner life of the Trinity." However, one might ask, *"Reflecting to whom?"* The following is an attempt to answer this question more carefully, because there appears to be some hermeneutical ease in the way in which Cousins speaks.

Because of this presence of God in an ongoing creation, there can be, and have been, sacramental events going on in all religions. There can be, and have been, sacramental events that take place whenever human individuals respond to this creative presence of God. Sacramentality cannot be restricted to a singular person, Jesus as primordial sacrament, or to a specific group of people, the church as a foundational sacrament, or to a numerically limited classification of ritual sacraments.

One could take it that "reflecting the divine archetype of this structure within the inner life of the Trinity" is a reflection back to the Trinity-God itself. This is not what Cousins implies. Rather, he implies that it is a reflection that is simply there in the cosmos for us to see. It is similar to the statement that Jesus is, in his humanity, a primordial sacrament. The humanness of Jesus is simply "there" as a primordial sacrament, whether or not one perceives his primordial sacramentality. Likewise, the church is simply "there" as a foundational sacrament, whether or not one perceives the church as a foundational sacrament. In a postmodern understanding, none of this makes sense. Indeed, the basic question of postmodern thought remains, How is understanding possible? How is the phrase that the cosmos is simply "there" reflecting the divine archetype even possible? Just as it is meaningless to speak of a revelatory God as a God who is continually saying, "I am revealing. I am revealing," such a God becomes a meaningless God if there is no one *to whom God is revealing.* So, too, it is meaningless to say that the world is reflecting, if there is no one who perceives this reflection. Jesus is not a primordial sacrament by his human nature if no one perceives that Jesus, in his humanity, is a primordial sacrament. The church is not a foundational sacrament by its very nature if no one perceives that it is a foundational sacrament. The *of what* someone or something is reflecting or is sacramentalizing cannot be understood unless there is a *to whom* someone or something is reflecting or sacramentalizing.

Much has been written about language and the so-called objective world in which we live. Chauvet reminds us that "to express oneself is not to give an exterior covering to a human reality already there interiorly, especially not in the sentimental and romantic sense of the 'need to express oneself' heard so frequently today."[19] Earlier, he had written, "Language creates—creates things."[20] He also writes, "The Word, Creator of the 'World.'"[21]

A word, like a sacrament, creates a world; it can create a world that reflects God. The word is not simply a naming of what was essentially and substantially already there, a something that already had a name. Lévinas makes the same point, "Language does not exteriorize a representation already existing within me—it offers to share a world that until then was only my own."[22]

It is precisely in the event of sacramentality that we find this kind of sharing a world that, until that time, was only one's own. It is, of course, God who reveals God's self in the world to us, but in our recognition of God's self-revelation and self-reflection we share in language, including sacramental and symbolic language, the world we find in this moment of *Haecceitas*. This is why language is not simply "out there" but includes an intention of expression (Merleau-Ponty). For Descartes, language and consciousness never meet each other. Were they to do so, Descartes would have made "I think, therefore I am," correlative to "I speak, therefore I am." This he never did. Unity of human beings in Descartes comes about by a rejection that consciousness is unique. This is not the approach in postmodern thought. It is in a world already spoken and speaking that we think.[23] This intentionality in linguistic expression, however, requires yet another step, the primacy of human perception.

THE PRIMACY OF HUMAN PERCEPTION OR THE NON-OBJECTIFIABILITY OF ANYTHING BEYOND HUMAN PERCEPTION

The other step in the identity-difference issue, belonging-together, is the framework within which all postmodern thought operates, to some degree, namely, the *primacy of human perception.*

It was Heidegger who provided a complex analysis of *Dasein* in the human framework as the *Ausgangspunkt* for his search for *Sein.* Since it is our own *Dasein* we know best,[24] we cannot begin by analyzing the world.[25] We do not and cannot know how a tree "trees." But we do have some perception of how a *Dasein* "daseins." It is with our own selves, the analysis of our own *Dasein,* that we begin to answer the question, How is understanding possible?

Merleau-Ponty moved the discourse on the primacy of perception even further. Naturally, all of these efforts—by Heidegger or by Merleau-Ponty, Husserl or Ricoeur, to name only a few—fall into the Cartesian-Kantian "return to the subject." All of these authors, however, move far beyond Descartes and Kant and their return to the subject. Merleau-Ponty, as we have seen above, centered on this aspect in a thorough and comprehensive way. In chapter 4 of *Phenomenology of Perception,* entitled "The Phenomenal Field," he draws together all the shortcomings of previous "objectifying" onto-epistemologies, including those of Husserl, and underscores the bypassing of the fundamental problem in all of these enterprises.[26] He writes:

> A philosophy becomes transcendental, or radical, not by taking its place in absolute consciousness, without mentioning the ways by which this is reached, but by considering itself as a problem; not by postulating a knowledge rendered totally explicit, but by recognizing as the fundamental philosophic problem this *presumption* on reason's part.[27]

Almost at the end of this volume, Merleau-Ponty, in his own way, confronts the position of Descartes and writes:

> What I discover and recognize through the *cogito* is not psychological immanence, the inherence of all phenomena in "private states of consciousness," the blind contact of sensation with itself. It is not even transcendental immanence, the belonging of all phenomena to a constituting consciousness, the possession of clear thought by itself. It is the deep-seated momentum of transcendence which is my very being, the simultaneous contact with my own being and with the world's being.[28]

All consciousness, he writes, is in some measure perceptual consciousness. "If it were possible to lay bare and unfold all the presuppositions in what I call my reason or my ideas at each moment, we should always find experiences which have not been made explicit, large-scale contributions from past and present, a whole 'sedimentary history' which is not only relevant to the genesis of my thought, but which determines its significance."[29]

The above citations indicate that our *only* perception is human perception, that we see things only through the horizons and intentionalities of our own selves. There is both a subjective element present in all perception and a sedimentary history that affects the genesis of our individual perception and, even more pointedly, our individual determination of significance. When we apply this way of thinking to the sacramental event, realizing that a sacramental event is a human response to a self-revealing God, we must say that in each sacramental event, *Ereignis,* God is indeed revealing God's own self, but each human person is responding. Each human response, however, is different. Merleau-Ponty said, as we noted in chapter 3, "I will never know how you see red, and you will never know how I see it." Likewise, one can say: The way I respond to God's action in a sacramental event and the way another responds to God's action in a sacramental event are different. The way you experience a given baptism and the way I experience a given baptism are different. There is no generic baptism. In a sacramental event, a multiple sacramental *Haecceitas* is present and active, because there are many individuals involved, each bringing his or her *sedimentary history,* his or her *genesis of consciousness and perception,* and his or her own *determination of significance.*

It is precisely *in the event of sacramental Haecceitas,* and *only in the event of sacramental Haecceitas,* that one begins to understand sacrament. A sacrament has both its reality and its meaning only in a concrete existential happening. This is why the world per se cannot be a sacrament, even though God is creatively present throughout the world. The world becomes a locus of sacramentality at a given existential moment when a human person perceives and responds to the self-revealing God, but the human person does this in and through the uniqueness of his or her own sedimentary history and his or her own determination of significance.

This onto-epistemological position—which not only Merleau-Ponty maintains, but which in some form or another can be found in almost all postmodern thinkers—radically changes the foundation of theological sacramentality. We do not understand sacramentality from some generalizing text about sacramentality, nor do we find sacramentality in generalizing canonical legislation on some aspects of sacramentality, nor do we find sacramentality in generalized de *fide definita* statements from the magisterium. All of these are important, but only in their abstract place and in their universal role. Sacramentality is primarily an event that is not abstract but concrete, not universal but individual.

Immediately, two protestations might arise. First, if each person perceives a sacrament in a subjective and individualized way, then is not the whole framework of sacramental worship challenged, since this fragments sacramentality into splinters of *Haecceitas?* Second, does not this way of thinking leave to one side any normative sacramental event, rendering statements such as "Jesus, the original sacrament," or "the church as the foundational sacrament" meaningless? Let us consider each of these seriatim.

Individual Subjectivity: *Haecceitas*

The return to the subject has indeed restructured the subjective as part and parcel of onto-epistemology. In some postmodern thinkers, subjectivity remains a common ground of their philosophical approach, but they presume that all subjectivities think and react in a basically similar way. It is with Merleau-Ponty that we explicitly see not merely a return to the subject, but a return to an individualized, temporalized, finite created subjectivity. Who and what is the "I" and who and what are the "Others"? This is a common issue among all Western philosophers from Descartes to Lacan and Derrida.

The reentry of subjectivity into a more commonly held "objective" onto-epistemology raises the issue of relativity. The issue of relativity has been deepened by the individualizing and, therefore, privatizing of subjectivity. Are we moving into a new form of nominalism? Even the selection of the term *Haecceitas* raises anew the shadow of this late medieval debate.

In the last hundred years, there has been considerable research on the works of Scotus.[30] Scotus was a medieval thinker with strong Aristotelian influence. Aristotle's predicamental categories provided a universal framework within which being and thought took place. Substance, quantity, quality, and relationship were the all-embracing categories of the cosmos, with primary substance clearly the dominant and controlling factor. Within a sort of philosophical cul-de-sac, dominated by the predicamental categories, scholastic thinkers constructed a marvelous objective and universal worldview and provided subsequent generations with a theological view as well. Scotus, at times, felt very confined by this cul-de-sac and attempted to move out of it and into a sort of unknown—unknown for that era because the predicamental categories did not provide a comprehensive structure for his thought.[31] His formal distinction, his understanding of contingency, and his understanding of *Haecceitas* provided him with a way out. These teachings do not fit well with the predicamental categories. Perhaps it is this outward move and openness to a different framework that has made Scotus's view of individuation of intense interest to contemporary Western thinkers.

Scotus and his own contemporaries did not ask psychological questions regarding individuation; namely, what are the intentional, cultural, and environmental factors that make one person distinct from another, "the necessary and sufficient conditions for something to be individual."[32] Nor is the question of individuation an issue about the source of individuality in general. Rather, Scotus focused on "the cause...of this designated singularity in particular, namely as it is determinately 'this.'"[33]

Scotus developed his thoughts on *Haecceitas* in a philosophical and theological dialogue with contemporary writers such as Peter Abelard, Richard Rufus of Cornwall, Thomas of York, Bonaventure, Robert Kilwardby, Henry of Ghent, and Godfrey of Fontaines. In these dialogues Scotus carefully honed his views on individuation. Because of the Aristotelian-scholastic framework, some of his ideas were perceived as *cantans extra chorum*. Today there seems to be a seminal interfacing of Scotistic *Haecceitas* and postmodern subjectivity.

An understanding of *Haecceitas* in Scotus requires an understanding of his view on contingency and freedom. The Scotistic view of contingency and freedom, as developed in *Lectura I, 39,* has been examined by A. Vos Jaczn, H. Veldhuis, A. H. Looman-Graaskamp, E. Dekker, and N. W. den Bokin in their book *Contingency and Freedom,* which includes the Latin original, an English translation, and a commentary on this section of Scotus's writings.[34] In *Lectura I, 39,* Scotus departs completely from the position of Aristotle as well as that of his contemporaries, and he formulates a doctrine on contingency and freedom that finds an echo in postmodern thought. Scotus's views of contingency have played no small role in my own discussion on subjectivity, individuality, temporality, and language.

My intention is not to bring a medievalist's view into postmodern discussion as if it might fit directly into this contemporary onto-epistemology. Rather, I am picking up an issue, *Haecceitas,* that, in the history of Western philosophy from the medieval period onward, has always been an outsider to the objectivistic approaches, both of the distant and recent past. The postmodern reaffirmation of subjectivity has only intensified this debate, but today the outsider has truly become the insider, and the objectivist who was the insider has become the outsider. Generic, mechanistic, or technological/scientific objectivity is yielding to the intrinsically subjective and has already lost much of its validity, which was based on generality, if not universality, on objectivity, if not on absoluteness. My incorporation of *Haecceitas* in this volume is to suggest that the role of outsider, which *Haecceitas* played in the medieval framework, runs parallel to the role of outsider-now-become-insider, which postmodern thought on subjectivity now has.

An enormous step in this return to subjectivity was made with the centralization of time into being. Temporality has stressed the limitedness, the finiteness, the individuality of being. Temporality has called into question, through a hermeneutic of suspicion, any and all claims for a "grand plan" and any and all claim for "universality"; to cite the words of Jean-François Lyotard an "incredulity toward metanarratives."[35] It is precisely this melding of being and time that seriously challenges the standard Christian approaches to sacramentality. In postmodern thinking, all sacramental events are intrinsically temporalized, historicized, individualized, so much so that one must develop a new phrase to encompass this. I have selected the phrase "sacramental *Haecceitas.*"

The event of a secondary personal response to a primary self-revealing God is a sacramental event. Therefore, both on the part of the primary self-revealing God and on the part of the secondary personally responding individual, neither the temporality nor the individuality of the event can be put to one side. A sacramental event can only be experienced and understood as an event of sacramental *Haecceitas.* But from the standpoint of one's secondary personal response, can the personal "I" be sure that it is really God revealing God to "me," at least in some inchoative way? Or is there some sort of self-delusion taking place?

When we are unsure about our own judgment, we turn to others, not just to others in general, but to other individual, temporal, living human beings. We share our experiences and judgments. In doing this, the "I" remains totally within the horizon and intentionality of human perception. There is no Archimedean place from which the "I" is able to adjudicate one's experiences. All perceptions are humanized, temporalized, relativized human perceptions. There is an inescapable primacy to human perception, an element of non-objectivity to human perception. I can indeed remain in my solipsistic world, but it is a world unto itself, an isolated world. To have some verification, some adjudication of my experiences, I turn to others. I understand myself in some way or another as a *Mit-Anderen-Dasein,* and I act accordingly.

With the introduction of the "Other," we might easily find ourselves back to the "objective" and "generalizing" framework of thought and being common to the Western approach. Indeed, Lévinas once noted that Western philosophy might be defined as the activity of assimilating all otherness into the Same.[36] Or as Rodolphe Gasché once said, "Western philosophy is in essence the attempt to domesticate Otherness, since what we understand by thought is nothing but such a project."[37]

This is precisely where the *onto*-epistemology begins to be more clearly seen. Many postmodern philosophers allude to the important section of Heidegger's *Being and Time* in which Heidegger introduces the words, *Vorhabe, Vorsicht, Vorgriff.*

> The ready-to-hand is always understood in terms of a totality of involvements. This totality need not be grasped explicitly by a thematic interpretation. Even if it has undergone such an interpretation, it recedes into an understanding which does not stand out from the background. And this is the very mode in which it is the essential foundation for everyday circumspective interpretation. In every case this interpretation is grounded in *something we have in advance—in a fore-having [Vorhabe].*[38]

Heidegger, in the same paragraph, speaks of something we see in advance, a fore-sight *(Vorsicht),* something we grasp in advance, a fore-conception *(Vorgriff).* There is a pre-thematized situation that one already has, sees, grasps, prior to all thematized understanding. In the section on the Other, as we noted above, Heidegger says, "By 'Others' we do not mean everyone else but me—those over against whom the 'I' stands out. They are rather those from whom, for the most part, one does *not* distinguish oneself—those among whom one is too."[39] This not distinguishing oneself, however, is different from the universality of consciousness that Merleau-Ponty found unacceptable in Descartes.

There is a "given" pre-thematized situation in which the I is I, and this given, non-thematized situation includes, in a special way, Others. This kind of pre-established *Vorhabe* and *Vorgriff* was alluded to in the distinction de Saussure made between *langue* and *parole*. Merleau-Ponty begins his major opus with a chapter on the phenomenal field, which is itself an unthematized *Vorgriff*. Gadamer speaks of tradition as an absolute given, a sort of *Vorgegeben*.[40] Habermas disputes Gadamer precisely on the claim for an absolute, *Universitalitätsanspruch der Hermeneutik*.[41] Lacan distinguishes the "I" in the Cartesian *cogito* from the "I" in the Cartesian *ergo sum*. None of these efforts moves out of the human field of perception; none really moves into an Archimedean standpoint (Gadamer, perhaps, excepted). A listing of other thinkers could be included, but there is a *Mit-sein* of some sort involved in these forms of onto-epistemology.

As regards an event of sacramental *Haecceitas,* one's response to the self-revealing God has its own *Vorhabe, Vorsicht, Vorgriff,* which includes the "other," who is also in one's world. This "other" includes the others of our own religious community, the others of our own religious tradition, and the others of different religious communities. This is why the history of the Christian sacramental tradition is important, why the history of our liturgical tradition is important, why the history of other religious sacramental traditions is important. Without them we would be speaking with a certain hermeneutical ease as we interpreted our idiosyncratic moments of sacramental *Haecceitas.* All of these givens not only affect our thematization in consciousness of a sacramental event, but they also affect the pre-thematization, the *Vorhabe, Vorgriff, Vorsicht,* of the "I" of *ergo sum,* prior to the "I" of *cogito.* There is truly no solipsistic sacramental event, but rather a relationship of *Dasein* and *die Anderen.* There is an active *Horizontsverschmelzung* long before this is known and designated by this term.

In the writings of postmodern thinkers, the issue of the I and the Other has not been presented in any final way. This comes as no surprise, because the discussion probably arose in Western philosophy with Parmenides's discussion on the principle of identity. What postmodern thinkers bring into this discourse is a radical pursuit of the subjective within all human knowledge and, in the writings of some authors, the radical pursuit of the temporalized individual. These writers do not allow the existential, finite, temporal individual to be swallowed up by some essentialist, objectifiable understanding of the human, much less by some sort of grand scheme of universal being. In Christian writings sacramental discourse has been focused on generalities, the physical and metaphysical nature of sacrament; on epiphenomenal, transcendental generalities, the humanness of Jesus as a primordial sacrament, or the church as a foundational sacrament. In all of these discussions, the "I" of the human person who experiences a revealing God is placed at the fringes of the discussion. Even such a statement as "Christ, the sacrament of the encounter with God" does not intrinsically centralize the "our" of the encounter or the "my" of the encounter with God. Somehow, *Haecceitas* is left to one side as *Generalitas* takes over. Postmodern thought raises fundamental questions about this entire way of thinking. This is why a complete reworking of sacramental theology and hermeneutics is needed, and why sacramental *Haecceitas* is such an important issue.

Normative Disclosure in the Events of Sacramental *Haecceitas*

The second issue has to do with a normative disclosure of the self-revealing God in any event of sacramental *Haecceitas*. In recent Roman Catholic theology, the claim has been made that Jesus, in his humanity, is the primordial sacrament and, in this theology, there is a claim of normative primordiality for the Jesus event. Jesus in his humanity is the normative and primordial sacrament through which and by which all other sacramentality is adjudicated. Likewise, the claim has been made that the church is a foundational sacrament, and this theology also involves a normative claim for a religious community through which and by which all other sacramental communities are to be judged. We have already mentioned the hermeneutical ease with which many theologians and church officials have used these phrases and the ideas behind them. They have made a normative claim with unreflected hermeneutical ease.

In the Anglican, Protestant, and Roman Catholic traditions, there has at times been a normative claim for two sacraments or for seven sacraments. In these approaches, only two or only seven sacraments are truly sacraments and these two/seven sacraments have a normative claim over all other usages of the term "sacrament." Once again, authors have made a normative claim and, in my view, made such claims with unreflected hermeneutical ease.

We have already discussed some of the basic philosophical issues involved in this manner of speaking, and I wish to present a more theological challenge to such claims. "Disclosure" is a term which postmodern thinkers have used in technical ways, and it is a term that aptly enters into the field of sacramental discourse. In a sacramental event, God is revealing and there is a human response. This event is thoroughly existential, temporal, historical, and finite. Existentiality, temporality, historicality, and finiteness all raise challenges to any claim of absolute normative status, since such a claim moves one from the existential to the essential, from the temporal to the atemporal, from the historical to the ahistorical, and from the finite to the unsurpassable. These challenges we have considered in the preceding chapters.

In Christian theology, and in other theologies as well, God is presented as the ineffable one. Thomas Aquinas states, "The believer's act [of faith] does not terminate in the propositions, but in the realities which they express."[42] Even though propositional language is a help to understanding God, there is something about God, in God's own self, that makes any disclosure about God problematic. The *Catechism of the Catholic Church* states:

> Our knowledge of God is limited, our language about him is also limited (no. 40).

> God transcends all creatures. We must therefore continually purify our language of everything in it that is limited, image-bound or imperfect, if we are not to confuse our image of God—"the inexpressible, the incomprehensible, the invisible, the ungraspable," with our human representations. Our human words always fall short of the mystery of God (no. 42, citing the Anaphora from the Liturgy of St. John Chrysostom).

> Admittedly, in speaking about God like this, our language is using human modes of expression; nevertheless it really does attain to God himself, though unable to express him in his infinite simplicity (no. 43).

The *Catechism* ends this section by citing Thomas Aquinas once again, "Concerning God, we cannot grasp what he is, but only what he is not, and how other beings stand in relation to him."[43]

God is so great, so inexpressible, so incomprehensible, so invisible, so ungraspable, that any disclosure of God is but a small window onto this inexpressibility, incomprehensibility, invisibility, and ungraspability of God. God is absolute freedom and, therefore, cannot be limited to any single event of sacramental *Haecceitas*. Jesus, in his humanity as an event of sacramental *Haecceitas,* discloses only a fraction of what the ineffable God truly is. The church, in whatever dimension of meaning one wishes to use this term, as an event of sacramental *Haecceitas,* discloses only a fraction of what the ineffable God truly is.

Not only does the existentiality, the temporality, the historicity, and the finiteness of the human response in the sacramental event preclude any unsurpassability, but the ineffability of the revealing God in the same sacramental event challenges any claim of a person or persons, or of a thing, to unsurpassability. God is simply greater than any particular sacramental event. Even more, whatever disclosure of God that occurs in any and every event of sacramental *Haecceitas* is minuscule compared to the ineffability of God. There is then a twofold challenge to the hermeneutical ease that one employs in saying that "Jesus in his humanity is the primordial sacrament," or "the church is a foundational sacrament," or that there are only two/seven sacraments.

The issues set forth in this section are not meant to challenge the uniqueness of Jesus or the claims of the Roman Catholic Church. *That* these two themes need to be reexamined from a hermeneutical—or better, onto-hermeneutical—basis is the point this discussion is making. *That* the reexamination needs to be made on the philosophical basis of the temporality, finiteness, historicity, and *Haecceitas* of Jesus' humanity and on the theological basis of the absolute ineffability and inexpressibility of God, is also part of this discussion.

Jesus is a unique human individual. Jesus, in his humanity, is an intrinsically temporal, historical, finite, created being. In the theological discussion of the Incarnation, the focus should not be one-sidedly on the splendor of the divine humility of God becoming human. One should also see in Jesus the splendor of human uniqueness. A human Jesus, in all his finiteness, temporality, historicity, and createdness—and therefore in all his limitedness and relativity—is seen in a theo-ontological dimension, a personal relationship of a self-revealing God and a human response to this self-revealing God.

Jesus is divine, not because the *esse substantiale* of Jesus is the *esse substantiale* of the Logos. This is simply one theological view among others and is, by no means, the official teaching of the church. When scholastic theologians discussed the way in which the Logos and the humanness of Jesus are united, they moved in these discussions far beyond any defined statements of the councils of Nicaea, of Ephesus, or of Chalcedon. This is why the theological value of their opinions on this matter of *how* the Logos and the human are united in Jesus were rightfully labeled *probabilior* (more probable), *communior inter theologos* (more common view of theologians), *sententia communis* (a common opinion). There is within Christian theology an enormous amount of latitude on the issue of *how* the Logos and the human Jesus are united.

When one asks today whether one could be truly human, perfectly human, consubstantial with all other human beings, born of a woman (all statements from the Council of Chalcedon), and yet not exist as a human being, the answer would either be no or that what has just been said is hermeneutically meaningless. If one were to say in response, "But if the human nature abstractly and therefore essentially were a truly abstract human nature, a perfect abstract human nature, a human nature abstractly consubstantial to our own human natures, able to be, abstractly speaking, born of a woman, would not this human nature be exactly as ours?" The answer again would be either no or that the statement is hermeneutically meaningless. For a human being truly to be a human being, a perfect human being, a human being similar to all other human beings, this human being needs to be intrinsically temporalized in his or her very being, needs to be individually historicized in his or her very being, needs to be manifestly like all other living human beings. To separate essence from existence and, on that basis talk about reality and objectivity, is hermeneutically meaningless. To speak of a real human being who does not have real human existence is to talk about a human nature in the abstract, and such a human nature has no hermeneutical objectivity.

Ricoeur aids us to understand this when he writes:

The gesture of hermeneutics is a humble one of acknowledging the historical conditions to which all human understanding is subsumed in the reign of finitude.[44]

. Hermeneutics places us in the humble historical process in which we know we all belong. Ricoeur continues:

> Would it not be appropriate to shift the initial locus of the hermeneutical question to reformulate the question in such a way that a certain dialectic between the experience of belonging and alienating distanciation becomes the mainspring, the key to the inner life, of hermeneutics?[45]

We have already mentioned the centrality of the experience of belonging, *Gehören/Zusammen,* as also distanciation and alienation *Identität und Differenz,* to every hermeneutical endeavor. In the sacramental event, God, in a self-revealing way, encounters us and we respond. It is this humble kind of an actual, existential, temporal, and historical encounter that is the mainspring of hermeneutics. "The most decisive break with Romantic hermeneutics is here: what is sought is no longer an intention hidden behind the text, but a world unfolded in front of it."[46] This unfolding is a disclosure:

> To understand is not to project oneself into the text but to expose oneself to it; it is to receive a self enlarged by the appropriation of the text which gives the reader his dimension of subjectivity; understanding is thus no longer a constitution of which the subject possesses the key.[47]

Ricouer

In every sacramental event there is a disclosure that the subjective does not fully control; self-projection on a text is a distortion of the self and the text; and yet in the encounter with the text there is a self *enlarged* by the appropriation of the text. Disclosure speaks to our very *Haecceitas* and enlarges the meaning of our *Haecceitas.*[48] In a sacramental event, God addresses God's own Word, Logos, to us, and it is a disclosure not only of God but of who we are as well.

✳

If Christian theologians want to say that the Logos truly became human, then the union of the Logos to a temporal, finite, historical, created, limited human being cannot be a union to a "human nature" but only to a human *Haecceitas.* The Word did not become human nature; the Word became a human person, Jesus. This indicates the splendor of human uniqueness. In this kind of union, we begin to see the mystery of the Incarnation. The doctrine of the Incarnation is a disclosure moment, not only of Logos becoming flesh, but of what

our flesh means. The doctrine of the Incarnation, as in all major doctrines of the church, discloses to us something about God, and at the
same time discloses to us something about ourselves. This is why a
theology that essentializes human nature when discussing the union
of God and human in Jesus can render the human nature meaningless
to us, since we only know temporal, historical, existential, finite, and
created human beings.

The human splendor of Jesus lies in his *Haecceitas,* his existential
individuality, to which we can relate and which discloses to us an
enlargement of our own self-understanding. This is an individuating
disclosure. The splendor of God, incarnate in Jesus, offers our understanding a glimpse of ultimacy, of primordiality, of foundationality.
God is the only basis on which a sacramental event can be called primordial, foundational, normative. The humanness of Jesus is, in itself,
not normative, not foundational, not primordial; the presence of God in
this humanness is primordially and foundationally normative. The
gathering of the *ecclesia,* the church, is not, in itself, foundationally
normative; the presence of God in this gathering of the *ecclesia* is foundationally normative.

On the other hand, we must once again state clearly that God is
the inexpressible, the incomprehensible, the invisible, the ungraspable,
and, therefore, no single human *Haecceitas,* even the human
Haecceitas of Jesus, and no single grouping of people, no *ecclesia,* can
claim an unsurpassability in sacramentalizing what God truly is.

RITUALS AS CELEBRATIONS
OF SACRAMENTAL *HAECCEITAS*

Up until now, little has been said about sacramental rituals such as
baptism and eucharist. After a long detour on the ecclesiality of scripture, Chauvet turns to the sacramentality of scripture and notes,
"Sacramentality is not an accident; it is a constitutive dimension of
Scripture."[49] On this basis Chauvet then moves to the sacraments as
precipitates of the scriptures:

> *Word-Scripture and Word-Sacrament.* The dynamic of the two
> tables [the table of the scriptures to the table of the sacrament]
> shows us that it is always the Word that deposits itself in the sacra-
> mental ritual as well as in the Bible. In more rigorous terms, it

would thus be better to speak, safeguarding the *sacramental essence* in each case, of a liturgy of *the Word under the mode of Scripture* and of a liturgy of *the Word, under the mode of bread and wine.*[50]

Chauvet offers us remarkable insight into the essential sacramentality of scripture, that is, of the Word proclaimed in the eucharist and the Word sacramentalized in the ritual meal. In both instances, the gathered community is celebrating the primacy of God's actions, the centrality of Christ, and the Spirit of Jesus.

The Primacy of God's Action

Liturgy centers on the spiritual blessings which God gives us (*Catechism of the Catholic Church,* no. 1083) and only on this prior basis does liturgy become a community's response of faith and love. Such an emphasis is basic to what ritual is all about. Christian liturgy is primarily a celebration of God's action and, only secondarily, a response of the church, an action of the people of God. On too many occasions emphasis has been placed on the individual's or the community's response, namely, on songs, readings, posture, and prayers, rather than on the celebration of God's action.

The Centrality of Christ

Liturgy primarily celebrates the paschal mystery by which Christ saved us (no. 1067). Liturgy is Christ's own prayer in which we share (no. 1073). Liturgy is Christ living and acting within his Church (no. 1076). Liturgy is Christ signifying and making present his paschal mystery (no. 1085). Liturgy is celebrating the presence of Christ—God—in all sacraments (no. 1088).

The Spirit of Jesus

The Holy Spirit is central to liturgy. The Holy Spirit prepares us for Christ (nos. 1093ff.; 1099ff.; 1104ff.). The Holy Spirit is sent to us in every liturgical action to bring us into communion with God. The Holy Spirit makes Jesus present in the eucharist.

When one takes these three issues into the heart of a baptismal ritual, into the heart of a eucharistic ritual, into the heart of a reconciliation ritual, into the heart of a matrimonial ritual, one finds in these rituals a disclosure of a self-revealing God to human persons who are responding to this grace of disclosure. However, when one speaks only in the abstract, as we ourselves have just been doing, then we are simply writing about or talking about sacramental *Generalitas.* Ritual sacraments all have their own *Haecceitas,* and only in an analysis or experience of an actual sacramental event will one truly understand, in an inchoative way at least, what existential, temporalized, historicized, personalized sacramental actions are all about. Abstract analysis by itself does not reflect what an actual sacramental event is all about.

Chauvet's analysis is extremely helpful, but in many ways it lacks the temporality and existentiality of a sacramental event. It too lacks sacramental *Haecceitas.* However, there is a dimension of Chauvet's work that most authors tend not to discuss or to discuss in only a transient way. This is the entire seventh chapter in *Symbol and Sacrament,* which he entitles "The Relation Between Sacrament and Ethic."[51]

Chauvet writes:

> Between "life" and "cult," between "prophecy" and "priesthood," between the "intention" and the "institution," there exists an authentic evangelical tension. Therefore, it is not self-evident that a religion which proclaims "worship in spirit and truth" (Jn. 4:23–24) should develop ritual forms of worship. For the "sacred" is not Christian by definition [*le "sacré" n'est pas chrétien à n'importe quelle condition*], even though faith cannot pretend to do without it.[52]

Chauvet says that his entire chapter focuses on a single question: How can one avoid the temptation to oppose ethical practice and ritual practice without yielding to the reverse temptation, namely, to reduce the tension by forgetting the tension between them?[53] In the contemporary world, he notes, such issues as social concern and prophetic engagement are highly praised, while such issues as religious institution, rituals, and priesthood are sometimes set to one side as though they have no value. Should one simply oppose ethics and sacramental ritual, or should one simply forget the evangelical tension between faith and ritual? Chauvet maintains that ritual is constitutively ethical. One without the other is inadequate.

Matthew Jayanth Koddekanal discusses the same theme at great length.[54] Koddekanal reviews the literature on liturgy, particularly eucharistic liturgy, written after Vatican II. He divides this material into four categories.

The first category focuses mainly on the scriptural basis of liturgy, the history of the liturgy, the historical evolution of the eucharistic prayer, and the structure of the eucharistic celebration. He includes the works of several well-known scholars in this category, such as Robert Cabie, Cheslyn Jones, Geoffrey Wainwright, Edward Yarnold, Paul Bradshaw, Gary Macy, and Enrico Mazza.[55]

In the second category, the concern is primarily with the systematic theology of eucharistic ritual. He includes in this category such authors as Regis Duffy, Edward Kilmartin, and David Power.[56]

The third category focuses on certain issues of injustice that are present in the eucharistic liturgy and on attempts to make the traditional teachings and dogmas on the eucharist meaningful for contemporary times. In this category he places such authors as James Empereur, Christopher Kiesling, Mark Searl, and William Willimon.[57]

In the fourth category, the concern is with the "testamentary tradition" of the eucharist (the term is from Léon-Dufour), and these authors argue for the necessity of social commitment to make eucharist sacramental liturgy meaningful. In this category, Koddekanal places Tissa Balasuriya, Avila Rafael, Monika Hellwig, David Power, and Juan Segundo.[58] Koddekanal is clearly moving in the same direction that Chauvet takes in this particular section of his own volume.

Chauvet first reflects on the status of cult in Old Testament Judaism. For these early Jewish people, God manifested God's own self in history more so than in the act of creation. Old Testament Jewish cult, then, memorializes moments of history, but this memorializing is not only a memory of the past but also a promise of and an ethical commitment to a future. The communal memory of the people, celebrated in various cultic actions, regenerates the community. But regeneration is meant to bring a new life, replete with serious ethical dimensions.

Chauvet employs the image of "tearing apart" when he considers the way the early followers of Jesus celebrated liturgical rituals. With the Easter event, something new has taken place: the heavens are torn apart;

old wineskins tear and burst; the high priest tears his clothing; the curtains of the temple are torn open. "In Jesus," Chauvet writes, "the religious fabric of Judaism has been torn."[59] Something new has taken place, and this newness must be enfleshed in one's existential and ethical life.

> The ritual story at each Eucharist, retelling why Jesus handed over his life, sends all Christians back to their own responsibility to take charge of history in his name.[60]

Only after the two sections on the historic-prophetic status of the Jewish cult in the Old Testament and then on the eschatological status of the early Christian cult does Chauvet address his third and final step, in which he wants to develop a more global theological reflection on the tension that characterizes the relation between sacrament and ethics. He attempts this, but briefly, in four pages.[61]

> The element *"Sacrament"* is thus *the symbolic place of the ongoing transition between Scripture and Ethics, from the letter to the body.* The liturgy is the powerful *pedagogy where we learn to consent to the presence* of *the absence of God who obliges us to give him a* body *in the world,* thereby giving the sacraments their plenitude in the "liturgy of the neighbor" and giving the ritual memory of Jesus Christ its plenitude in our existential memory.[62]

What Chauvet develops is powerful, but it is only a beginning. Four pages cannot do justice to the ethical dimension in today's globalized world. Husserl, Lévinas, Lyotard, and Baudrillard have all raised ethical issues with a sharp involvement in hermeneutics and ethics. To recall the memory of the Exodus or of the arrest and trial of Jesus is most often told and retold from the viewpoint of the victor. Issues that do not conform or are contradictory are marginalized or left out entirely. The voice of the voiceless is often not heard in liturgical and sacramental ritual. Because of this, liturgical texts can be read with hermeneutical ease, and the lack of an ethical dimension is one reason why a hermeneutics of suspicion finds a dwelling place even in liturgy.

Postmodern thought has raised for the Western world at large profound questions of contemporary ethics and justice. Docherty writes:

> Postmodern Pessimism derives from the realization that "the just" can never be formulated; the positive aspect of such Pessimism lies

in the realization that the just must be enacted, invented. History may not exist for the Subject; but the Subject must "just" exist.[63]

In sacramental *Haecceitas* there is a need not only to ritualize in celebration what God does for us, but the very response to this wondrous self-revelation of a compassionate God must be a response with life-activating and ethical dimensions.

7

Postmodern Onto-Epistemology
and Solemn Church Teachings

In the Roman Catholic Church, there are a number of solemn or official teachings, which are also called unchangeable or defined. In Latin they are called *de fide definita catholica* (of defined Catholic faith). For Roman Catholics, these teachings are of major importance.[1] In this chapter we reflect on the official teachings of the Roman Catholic Church regarding sacraments in general and on postmodern hermeneutical and onto-hermeneutical thought. To bring clarity to this section, we must first review a hermeneutical issue that major contemporary Roman Catholic theologians have presented on the interpretation of various Tridentine statements.[2]

One notices immediately that the number of official and solemn teachings of the Roman Catholic Church on the issue of general sacramentality is not large. Nonetheless, it is these kinds of conciliar statements that theologians of this century have analyzed thoroughly regarding their proper hermeneutic. This chapter is, therefore, divided into three main sections: first, we review what twentieth-century Roman Catholic theologians have developed on the interpretation of the Tridentine documents. Second, we consider the five issues Roman Catholic theologians have consistently taught as the solemn and defined teachings of the church on general sacramentality. Finally, we consider the insights postmodern onto-hermeneutics provides.

TWENTIETH-CENTURY THEOLOGICAL INVESTIGATION ON THE INTERPRETATION OF THE TRIDENTINE DOCUMENTS

At the Council of Trent a format had been adopted by the bishops in order to present agenda items such as the sacraments: (a) prepare a doctrinal statement, usually called a chapter; and (b) prepare a set of propositions, or canons, based on the doctrinal chapter. This indicates that the canons served as the major focus for the Tridentine bishops, regarding their discussion of a particular issue, and that the chapters provided a practical teaching/preaching background through which the canons can be interpreted.

In contemporary sacramental theology there has been considerable discussion on the theological value, technically called the *valor theologicus,* of the individual chapters and, above all, of the individual canons connected with the respective chapters. Each of the canons begins with the words, "If anyone shall say…" *(Si quis dixerit…)* and concludes with the words: "let that person be anathema" *(anathema sit).* Does this mean that if someone maintains the teaching expressed in the canon, he or she is ipso facto a heretic? Is the teaching there stated against God's own law, *de iure divino,* or merely against a church law, *de iure ecclesiastico?* One realizes, of course, that whatever is from God's law, *de iure divino,* brooks no rebuttal, while whatever is only from the church's law, *de iure ecclesiastico,* has, of itself, no such divine sanction.[3] With this distinction of divine and ecclesiastical law, one can ask whether in the Tridentine anathemas we have revealed truth, divine law, or merely a disciplinary regulation of the church, ecclesiastical law?

In 1929, J. B. Umberg, who was one of the editors of *Denzinger,* compared the censures of Pius VI against the propositions of the Synod of Pistoia with the canons found in the decrees of Trent.[4] Did the Synod of Pistoia, he asked, dissent from Trent, and, if so, were these instances of dissent heretical? Umberg found two instances in which the Synod of Pistoia clearly contradicted Trent, and which Pius VI had judged heretical. However, Umberg argued, what about the other one hundred and eighteen canons of Trent? Umberg pointed out that there were additional instances in which the Synod of Pistoia had clearly contradicted Tridentine canons, but which Pius VI had not judged heretical. Umberg concluded that the mere fact that something is contradictory to the canons of Trent cannot in itself be considered an adequate basis for heresy.

Following Umberg, H. Lennerz examined the canons of Trent and came to the conclusion that many of the canons must be interpreted as penalties, *latae sententiae*.[5] Lennerz states that if one is going to deny a tradition of the church, one must first know what that tradition is, and if one has such knowledge and still denies the tradition, then there is an anathema because of the contempt *(pro eius contemptu),* not specifically because of the denial of the tradition.

R. Favre continued this line of research on a number of the Tridentine canons.[6] He found that *anathema sit* had several meanings, even during the council. In turn, A. Lang reviewed the teaching of Melchior Cano, a major figure at the time of Trent, and concluded that *anathema sit* by itself cannot be taken to mean heresy.[7] Lang argues that other factors, from other sources, must be present and operative before a condemnation of heresy is warranted. H. Jedin, through his historical research on the Council of Trent, arrived at the same conclusion.[8] Piet Fransen also researched the material and came to a similar conclusion.[9] "Faith" and "heresy" have, in the documents of Trent, a meaning that is far more comprehensive than merely a divinely revealed truth (faith) or its denial (heresy). Under "faith," the documents of Trent refer not only to items found in scripture but also to items proposed for the universal church, including merely ecclesiastical laws. On this same topic Carl Peter states, "An anathema meant a major excommunication, as canonists have remembered better than theologians. Heresy, by the same token, involved disobedience to the religious leaders Christ left to guide us to salvation."[10]

On many occasions during the Council of Trent the issue under consideration focused more on the rejection of church authority by the Reformation theologians than on heresy. At times it was this contempt for authority that was anathematized rather than a specific dogmatic position. The mere recital of the canons, then, cannot be understood, by itself, as a statement of divinely revealed truth and its denial as a heretical position. In the analysis of each canon, an attempt is made in the following pages to state carefully the central issue or issues involved and to indicate which of these central issues are doctrinal and which are disciplinary.

If such a nuanced interpretation affects the Tridentine canons, an even wider berth must be accorded to the chapters. No effort was made by the Tridentine bishops during the development of these chapters to sort out in an academic way theological opinion and defined doctrine. Rather, the bishops simply presented a general overview of the sacraments as they were to be practiced and preached at that particular period of time.

THE SOLEMN AND OFFICIAL TEACHINGS OF THE ROMAN CATHOLIC CHURCH ON GENERAL SACRAMENTALITY

As far as sacramentality in general is concerned, five issues have customarily been considered by systematic theologians as solemn or defined truths.[11] An analysis of the works of these authors can be expressed in the following format.

The Sacraments Have Been Instituted by Christ

> If anyone says that all the sacraments of the new law were not all instituted by our Lord Jesus Christ...let that person be anathema (*Denz.*, 1601)

The central issue that the bishops at Trent wanted to define in this particular teaching was that *sacraments are primarily gifts of God*. Basically, sacraments are not of human origin; rather, sacraments are gifts from a loving God. What God has done for us and is doing for us is at the center of all sacramental life. This issue lies at the heart of the statement: sacraments have been instituted by Christ/God. Not what we do but rather what God first does on our behalf should be the major focus of sacramental life.

In this teaching the Roman Catholic Church has defined that Jesus as God instituted the sacraments. It is not part of Roman Catholic defined faith that Jesus as a human being instituted them. Many theologians have, on occasion, taught that Jesus instituted an individual sacrament at a given time in his life: baptism on the occasion of his own baptism, or the eucharist on the occasion of the last supper. One must realize that pinpointing an exact time in which the historical Jesus, acting in and through his humanity, is said to have instituted a given sacrament is only a theological opinion, not part of defined Catholic doctrine.

J. A. de Aldama, in one of the more important pre–Vatican II manuals of theology, presented his thesis as follows: Christ, insofar as he was human, immediately instituted all the sacraments of the New Law.[12] When he comes to the question of the dogmatic value of this position, *valor dogmaticus,* he says that the immediate institution of all the sacraments seems, *videtur,* to be *de fide divina et catholica definita*—but that "not all theologians speak this way." In actuality, the view that the sacraments were instituted by Christ, insofar as he is human, is a *sententia communior et probabilior.* The focus of the solemn teaching is on the action of God/Christ, not on the action of Christ as human.[13]

Sacraments Are Symbols of Something Sacred, and They Confer the Grace They Signify

> If anyone says that the sacraments of the new law do not contain the grace which they signify, or that they do not confer this grace to those who present no obstacle, let that person be anathema (*Denz.,* 1607).

The central issue of this defined teaching of the church focuses on the grace reality at the heart of every sacramental action. In the celebration of each sacrament the Christian community is celebrating the transcendent gift of God: first of all and primarily, the gift of God's own holy presence and life; second, the effects God's holy presence has on our Christian lives in making them holy. In this sense there is a real presence of God in every sacrament, not simply a real presence of God/Christ only in the eucharistic sacrament. The church is teaching us that the very holiness of God—the very presence of God—is active in every sacramental action.

As signs and symbols, sacraments confer grace. It is only in a generalized form that the statement that sacraments confer grace is a solemn teaching of the church. *That* sacraments confer grace has been defined. *How* the sacraments confer or cause grace has not been defined. Theologians, particularly Dominicans and Franciscans, have presented very different views on the way in which a sacrament confers grace. Dominican theologians, following Thomas Aquinas, explain the causality of grace through a theological view called "instrumental efficient causality." In this Thomistic view the words of a priest, as well as the matter and form, are considered "efficient instruments" used by God to produce grace. Franciscan theologians considered this efficient causality view to be a denial of God's freedom. God does not have to use any "instruments" to give grace, and if God does use created things

like priestly words, bread, wine, and oil, they cannot be seen as "causing grace." Grace is an absolutely free gift of God. Franciscan theologians explained the causality of sacramental grace in two ways. One
group, following Bonaventure, considered all the human elements
(words of a priest, bread and wine) to be "moral causes," similar to a
prayer that asks God to freely give grace.[14] The second group of
Franciscan theologians, following Scotus, taught that sacraments
"give" grace because of "occasional causality." When a community of
Christians celebrates eucharist in the way God has instructed, God
gives grace not because of anything Christians do, but basically
because *God promised* to give his grace on such occasions. It is the
promise of God, not the words of a priest or the use of correct materials,
that is the basis for sacramental grace. Other theologians, particularly
Jesuits, have refined or nuanced one or the other of these theological
views in explaining how sacraments confer the grace they signify. Only
the general notion that "sacraments truly do confer or cause grace" is
the defined teaching of the church. A more precise description of the
way in which this conferring or causing of grace takes place involves a
theological view or opinion. No explanation of sacramental causality is
the official teaching of the church.

The way in which de Aldama presents the issue of sacramentality
causality is helpful. His thesis is that the sacraments of the New Law
confer grace, *Sacramenta Novae Legis conferunt gratiam*. De Aldama
rightfully considers this statement as a teaching of the Roman Catholic
Church that is *de fide definita et catholica*.[15] When he touches on the
question of how the sacraments confer grace, he opts for the Thomistic
opinion and states that this view is *communis et certa*. He adds, correctly, that the bishops at the Council of Trent did not have this
Thomistic view in mind, *non enim est certa mens Tridentini*.[16]

Three different religious truths are intertwined in this official
teaching of the church: (1) it is God who acts through the sacrament to
give grace; (2) Christians can set up obstacles to grace, such as sin; and
(3) sacraments confer the grace they signify. The official teaching of
the church does not attempt to explain how these three ideas can be put
together. In their effort to unify these issues, theologians over the years
have offered a number of views. That these three truths are to be held as
official and solemn statements is a teaching of the Roman Catholic

Church. How these three truths are unified is not a teaching of the Roman Catholic Church.

There Are Seven Sacraments

> The Tridentine *Decree on the Sacraments* lists all seven sacraments by name. Each of these is defined as a true and proper sacrament of the Roman Catholic Church (*Denz.,* 1601).

Since the beginning of this century, many books have been written on the history of the sacraments, and, on the basis of this historical research, it is impossible today to state that the church has "always taught" that there are seven, and only seven, sacraments. For instance, prior to 1150 there was no official church teaching about "seven sacraments." This is most clear in the history of confirmation and marriage.

From about 1000 onward in the West, and only in the West, a ritual of confirmation, separate from baptism, began to be the norm. In the centuries prior to 1000 such a separate ritual in the West becomes less and less general. When one moves prior to 500/400 "confirmation" is an integral aspect of baptism.[17] Prior to 1000, then, it is difficult to maintain that there were seven sacraments, because confirmation as a sacrament separate from baptism developed slowly, a development that took place only in the West.

Second, only from about 1100 onward did the issue of marriage as a sacrament begin to be discussed by theologians and canonists. At first, most theologians and canonists refused categorically to consider marriage a sacrament. They argued that all sacraments give grace, but because marriage involves sex, which these same scholars considered at least venially sinful, it could not be a sacrament. How can anything sinful give grace? The theological and canonical documentation of this period makes it amply clear that this was the precise issue that blocked marriage from any consideration as a sacrament of the church. From 1150 onward, this gradually changed. Theologians and canonists arrived at a theological distinction that allowed marriage, understood as a contract or an interpersonal consent, to give grace, leaving the actual sexual aspect of marriage to one side. Consent, they argued, makes the marriage. Only then was marriage, separated from its sexual connection, considered a sacrament; only when this happened did Western theologians and canonists begin to speak about "seven sacraments."

Within a very short time this teaching of seven sacraments began to appear in official church documents. The bishops at the Council of Trent made this teaching solemnly official.

Likewise, a sacramental ritual of penance cannot be established, with any certainty, prior to 150, nor is there any sure data on a ritual of ordination prior to 200. Today, this kind of historical material is well known. Because of this history the question immediately arises, In what way can one teach that there is a dogma of the church regarding the seven sacraments?

Since vast amounts of material on the history of the sacraments are fairly new, theologians have not yet fully integrated the historical data with this dogma of the church. Some theologians have utilized the issue of development of doctrine, and undoubtedly something along this line will have to be involved as this matter becomes clearer. But, as yet, a satisfactory integration of the historical data and the "seven sacrament" teaching has not been developed.

Vatican II officially teaches that the church itself is a sacrament, indeed a basic sacrament. Moreover, respected Roman Catholic theologians, like Rahner and Schillebeeckx, teach that Jesus in his humanity is the most fundamental sacrament. This teaching on Jesus is, of course, a theological view; it has not been officially adopted by the magisterium. Both teachings—the church as a fundamental sacrament, and Jesus as the most basic sacrament—are new insights in sacramental theology. Contemporary theologians have attempted to relate the official teaching on seven sacraments with this new approach of two additional sacraments, but no satisfactory theological relationship of these positions with the solemn teaching at Trent has yet been firmly established. The position that there are seven, and only seven, sacraments seems to be one of those Tridentine statements that is more disciplinary than doctrinal.

In the acts of the Council of Trent it is clear that the bishops were very concerned about the denigration by various reform theologians who assailed bishops for "creating" sacraments other than baptism and eucharist. Calvin, for instance, castigated the bishops for the development of confirmation: "If they are without a command [that is, in scripture], they cannot excuse their sacrilegious boldness."[18] Or again:

> What can you say here but that they are plainly mad who are so fond
> of their own inventions that by comparison they carelessly despise

God's most holy institutions? O sacrilegious mouth, do you dare oppose to Christ's sacrament a grease [i.e. the oil of confirmation and extreme unction] befouled only with the stench of your own breath and under the spell of mumbled words and to compare it with the water sanctified by God's Word? Yet to your audacity this was but a trifle—and you even preferred it. These are the responses of the holy see, the oracles of the apostolic tripod [i.e., a reference to the oracle at Delphi, where the seat of the prophetess was supported by a high, upright, gilded tripod of wood].[19]

Many other citations could be mentioned, including citations from Luther. Clearly, there is sarcasm and scorn for the papacy and the bishops. The Tridentine bishops bristled at such language, since it was, in their minds, a challenge to episcopacy itself. The arguments against the sevenfold sacramental system were the lightning rods for an attack on episcopal and papal power, and it was the attack on episcopal position that underlies this particular statement from Trent on seven sacraments. The Tridentine bishops were saying that this is the Catholic Church as we know it, with seven sacraments. If you do not wish to abide by the regulations of this Catholic Church and accept the authority of bishops and popes, then leave, that is, *anathema sit.* The position is disciplinary.

Three Sacraments Confer a Character: Holy Baptism, Holy Confirmation, and Holy Orders

If anyone says that in three sacraments, namely, baptism, confirmation and orders, a character, that is a certain spiritual and indelible sign, is not imprinted on the soul, so that these sacraments cannot be repeated, let that person be anathema (*Denz.,* 1609).

The central focus of this official and solemn teaching of the church is that three sacraments confer a character. *What* this character is has never been defined by the church. Jean Galot states the position of his historical analysis clearly:

The Council of Trent defined the existence [of a character] as certain, but it refused to make a pronouncement on the nature of the character.[20]

At the time of Trent there were, and still are today, many theological views on what this character is. The major issue behind the

Tridentine teaching is that these three sacraments are not to be repeated. If one attempts to describe the nature of this sacramental character in any detail, one has entered the area of theological opinion. No description of the "what" can be presented as the "official" teaching of the Roman Catholic Church.[21]

As regards sacramental character, baptism and confirmation must be understood in a unified way, almost as a single sacrament. The historical reason confirmation is said to confer a character is due to its intrinsic connection to baptism. The major focus of this teaching on character centers, therefore, on the nonrepetition of two sacraments, baptism and orders. Confirmation is added, but only because of baptism.

God's Action in the Sacraments Does Not Depend on the Intention or the Holiness of the Minister

One cannot deny that a minister who intends to do what the church does is not a real minister of the sacrament; nor can one deny that a minister in the state of serious sin cannot truly minister the sacraments (*Denz.*, 1611, 1612).

Behind this solemn teaching of the church one finds centuries of dispute and controversy. Again and again individual or regional Christian communities would not accept sacraments celebrated by unworthy bishops or unworthy priests, or by those deemed to be in schism or heresy. Such communities simply called such "sacramental actions" null and void. In some instances, given communities of Christians would accept only holy bishops, holy priests, and holy deacons, and these holy ministers alone could celebrate "true" sacraments. At other times, it was an issue of "orthodox" or accepted faith. Even popes have not always been clear on this issue. Some popes demanded holiness and orthodox faith for true sacramental validity, and other popes did not.[22]

We still find today individual Christians and Christian communities who will only accept other individual Christians and other Christian communities who measure up to their own definition of "holy," or who profess their own understanding of "orthodox faith." In these situations, all other Christians who are not "holy," in *their* understanding of the term, or all who do not hold "orthodox faith," in *their* understanding of the term, have been called, at times, diabolical, evil, non-Christian, satanic, and anti-Christ. Roman Catholic communities have used such names for those

sacramental ministers whom they did not consider either holy or orthodox. Protestant communities have used the same names for Roman
Catholics, and, in some cases, for other Protestant groups.

When the bishops at the Council of Trent began their official discussions on the Christian sacraments, the schism with Protestant
groups had already taken place. In some of these separated Christian
Protestant groups there were bishops and priests who at that time did
not believe the same way that Roman Catholics did. For the bishops at
Trent the question arose whether these bishops, priests, and deacons
had "true" faith. If priests and bishops had married and were, in Roman
Catholic eyes, living in sin, could they celebrate the sacraments
validly?[23] These issues were very real for the bishops at Trent. After
much discussion the official and defined teaching of the Roman
Catholic Church was this: in a given sacrament, if one at least intends
to do what the church itself intends, the sacramental action is valid,
provided the minister is a validly authorized minister of the sacrament.
If a validly ordained priest or deacon celebrates a sacrament while in
the "state of sin," the sacrament is also valid. Unless one has some
understanding of the centuries-long fight over these issues, one might
not understand the exact focus of this teaching. By making the Roman
Catholic position regarding the intention and the holiness of the minister clear, the leadership of the church at Trent officially brought to an
end centuries of bitter struggle. This was, however, only an "official"
ending. In the practical order, the struggle over these very same issues
can be found, even in our own day and age, as theologians and
churches struggle over ecumenical issues that touch on the same
points.[24]

This has been a long section on the official teachings of the Roman
Catholic Church, and there are many historical factors, nuances, and cau-
tious interpretations to each of these five teachings. The length of this section and the complexity of the material indicate that an enumeration of the
solemn and official teachings of the Roman Catholic Church cannot be
done in any simplified way. It should also be apparent that the Tridentine
documents clearly indicate that sacraments are primarily and fundamentally God's activity. This emphasis in Trent finds re-expression in the
Catechism of the Catholic Church, which, as we have seen, emphasizes
the liturgy, especially sacramental liturgy, as the "work of the Holy
Trinity"; God as "the source and goal of all liturgy" (no. 1077); God

"blesses" us in the church's liturgy (no. 1083); "in the liturgy it is principally his own paschal mystery that Christ [as God] signifies and makes present" (no. 1084); it is the Holy Spirit who primarily teaches, fulfills, awakens faith, converts hearts, manifests Christ, recalls the meaning of salvation, gives spiritual understanding, and makes present the mystery of Christ (nos. 1091–1109). In its own words, the documents of Trent had already said this. God is the source of all sacraments, because God institutes all sacraments. God gives grace in all sacraments. God acts in all seven sacraments. God gives a character in three sacraments. God's action overrides any deficiencies in the intention and moral character of a minister. Each of the above five issues that the bishops at Trent taught focuses on God as source and goal of all sacramental liturgy. All sacramental liturgy is primarily the work of the triune God.

It is also clear that, in the above enumeration and explaining of these five teachings, I have used many words, phrases, and terms with hermeneutical ease. I made no effort to camouflage this facile use of standard theological terminology, a terminology most Roman Catholic theologians find meaningful and hermeneutically acceptable, because it is a terminology that in their specific circles has been and is still used with hermeneutical ease. In the next section, however, we will see that postmodern thinkers raise major challenges to this kind of hermeneutical ease and, therefore, major challenges to this form of terminology. However, the challenge goes beyond the area of technical terminology. The challenge strikes at the very *epistemé* in and through which official church statements are made.

POSTMODERN ONTO-HERMENEUTICS AND THE SOLEMN TEACHINGS OF THE ROMAN CATHOLIC CHURCH

Two different strands of postmodern thought need to be distinguished before we consider the ways in which postmodern onto-heremeneutics might help us understand the solemn teachings of the church on general sacramentality. The first strand is the issue of atheism, which one finds in *some* postmodern thinkers. The second of these strands deals primarily with the hermeneutical and the onto-hermeneutical level of discourse, which one finds in *all* postmodern thinking. It is necessary to keep these two aspects distinct, for not all postmodern thought is anti-theistic. Some Christian leaders summarily dismiss all postmodern thinking on the basis that it is anti-theistic, which is clearly not the case, and these same leaders argue that this (assumed) anti-theism of postmodern authors renders all discussion on hermeneutical aspects irrelevant, which it is not.

In this section we consider the material under three headings: the anti-theistic stance; postmodern hermeneutics and the statements of the magisterium; and onto-hermeneutics of postmodern thought and the magisterial statements.

The Anti-Theistic Stance of Some Postmodern Writers

There can be no doubt that some postmodern writers have been anti-theistic in an outspoken way. Jean Beaudrillard and Jean François Lyotard might be mentioned in this regard.[25] Jean-Paul Sartre is certainly another major anti-theistic voice. On the other hand, one must also concede that some postmodern writers are ambivalent regarding the existence or nonexistence of God. Heidegger and the later Merleau-Ponty are examples of this ambivalence. Some postmodern writers are avowedly God-fearing. Gabriel Marcel, Karl Jaspers, and Emmanuel Lévinas come to mind.[26] Ricoeur has written extensively on religion and faith.[27] Merleau-Ponty, in his later years, was more open to God and the transcendent than in his earlier years.[28] Gadamer and Habermas grappled with religious questions.

Some postmodern authors would indeed find any discourse on sacraments, on God, or on church authority absolutely inane, since such discourse is based on an ideological religious thought pattern. If there is a basic antireligious stance on their part, then little by way of interfacing sacramental thought and their specific postmodern insights can be done.

Nonetheless, the anti-theistic stance of some contemporary postmodern thinkers is directed against specific positions on God, and their opposition deserves serious consideration on the part of Christian leadership. William Luijpen states the case as follows:

> We must ask ourselves against whom and against whose ideas of God atheistic existentialists battle. Which God do they reject? Certainly they do not aim their criticisms at the gods of Eskimos, Maoris or Papuans. Nor do they solely deny the God of Hegel, though they reject him *also*. The God who is principally rejected by them is the God of Christianity.[29]

In the sacraments Christians celebrate the revelatory action of the Christian God, and it is precisely the theological presentation about *this God* that postmodern authors reject. Nor are these writers disposed to call back this kind of Christian God. To cite Luijpen once more:

> Modern man, then, will not, without more ado, call God back, when the time for it has arrived. Jupiter and Thor, after their fall, have never been restored to their altars, and rightly so. So also will the man of the future not call back a "God" who has to make up as a sort of physical energy, for the loss of energy in the macrocosm, who has to justify the injustices of the mighty of this world, who has to make the poor accept their wretched lot on earth, who must keep the oppressed in their social and political state of degradation.[30]

In sacramental theology and liturgy, one must be very sensitive to this refusal to call back the Christian God, if the Christian God in sacramental liturgy and theology is the kind of God just described. Nor should theologians and liturgists, bishops and popes, disparage this refusal, for the documents of Vatican II state very clearly that there is a Christian involvement in the appearance of modern atheism:

> Atheism springs from various causes, among which must be included a critical reaction against religions and, in some places, against the Christian religion in particular. Believers can thus have more than a little to do with the rise of atheism [*partem non parvam habere possunt credentes*] (*GS*, no. 19).

Since sacramental liturgy is so formative of one's faith in God, sacramental theologians and liturgists as well as magisterial documents on the sacraments need to reflect whether their presentations contain a basis for atheism, *partem non parvam habere possunt credentes*.

One of the major complaints of postmodern atheism is this: Christian theologians and church officials say too much about God. Luijpen remarks: "God will not be a God who lets theologians have a look at the maps of His Providence."[31] One cannot enter into a discourse on God with rolls of architectural plans and maps, outlining in detail what God is all about. In the area of sacramental theology, Christian leaders need to rethink the use of such a phrase as the "full revelation of God's economy." The *Catechism of the Catholic Church* states that God is incomprehensible and ineffable (nos. 202 203, 213), mysterious (nos. 206, 208), transcendent over world and history (no. 212). But later one reads that the Spirit has revealed, in its *fullness,* the mystery of the Trinity (no. 244); God has revealed *himself,* the mystery, his plan of loving goodness. God has *fully* revealed this plan by sending us his beloved Son (no. 50). On Pentecost, the Holy Trinity is *fully* revealed (no. 732); the church is the visible *plan* of God's love for humanity (no. 776). In all this fullness of revelation, is God still mysterious, still incomprehensible, ineffable? What signals are given and what signals are people hearing?

One could say that Christians have too often spoken about God with hermeneutical ease, and it is precisely in this area, although not only in this area, that postmodern thinkers have rejected the Christian presentation of God. The way in which Christian leaders present God in sacramental theology and liturgy is, then, not an issue that can be presupposed. Rather, postmodern atheists challenge the sacramental theology and liturgy of the third millennium precisely on the basis of the question of whether in sacramental theology and liturgy the church presents to contemporary men and women a credible God. This is clearly no small challenge. This challenge to theologians and to church officials arises precisely because *partem non parvam habere possunt credentes.*

Postmodern Hermeneutics and the Statements of the Magisterium

The issue of hermeneutics in postmodern thought has asked a fundamental question: How do we understand? In the words of Gadamer: "How is understanding possible? This is the question which precedes any action of understanding on the part of the subjectivity including the methodical activity of the 'understanding sciences' and their norms and rules."[32]

Prior to any norms and rules for interpreting the magisterial statements of the Roman Catholic Church, the question, or better the prequestion, is exactly this: How is understanding possible? Postmodern thinkers ask this same question of those involved in natural sciences, in literature, in history, and in theology. At this level the challenge of postmodern thought to magisterial statements is no different from the same challenge to scientific thought or historical thought. All of these disciplines may speak a language, but how is understanding of them possible? Here is where a presumed hermeneutical ease on the part of the speaker begins to become evident.

Foucault's *Les Mots et les choses* is an amazing analysis. Each of his chapters describes "two great discontinuities in the *episteme* of western culture: the first inaugurated the Classical age (roughly half-way through the seventeenth century), and the second, at the beginning of the nineteenth century, marks the beginning of the modern age."[33] The *episteme* of the Renaissance has ended. No one any longer understands things from such an *episteme*. Moreover, the *episteme* of the Enlightenment is no longer viable. Even more, a mechanistic, objectivistic, non-subjective *episteme* has been supplanted. How, then, is understanding itself possible? There is perhaps no single format, for as each new period develops its own *episteme*, the older format becomes irrelevant. Thus, statements from scientists, historians, and psychologists made in and through one *episteme* lose credibility when another *episteme* becomes dominant. The statements of Trent were made in the classical period, and the *episteme* used in that period is no longer meaningful. No person or group of people is capable of making unchangeable statements. To claim unchangeableness is to make a claim with a remarkable amount of hermeneutical ease, and any and all such claims are challenged at their roots by postmodern hermeneutics. Any and every form of speech *sub specie aeternitatis* has no validity for the third millennium.

At this hermeneutical stage, the challenge of postmodernism on the magisterial statements analyzed above is simply a question of how the understanding of these statements is possible today. An answer cannot be given without consideration of onto-hermeneutical factors, but the onto-hermeneutical factors cannot be understood if the basic question has not been heard in some degree of clarity. If one does not understand the question, one will never understand the answer. That is why this section, at least methodologically, is vitally important.

The Onto-Hermeneutics of Postmodern Thought and the Magisterial Statements

Even though many postmodern authors have shied away from the ontological approach of Heidegger, there is, in all of the writers, some form or another of ontic or ontological structure. There is no one postmodern onto-hermeneutic, but there are some factors that tend to appear in each writer, at least to some extent. Postmodern thought is not simply epistemological, although it clearly *is* epistemological, but

it is profoundly ontological as well.[34] We have already mentioned some
of these major factors, and they can serve as a pedagogical and methodological structure for the comments which follow. These factors are:

1. return to subjectivity;
2. individuality or *Haecceitas;*
3. temporality; and
4. language.

Return to Subjectivity

All human knowledge is inescapably subjective. This does not
mean that all human knowledge is only subjective in some sort of solipsistic way. Rather, it means that there is a primacy to human perception
that is inescapable and that human knowledge is not simplistically
objective. In the sixteenth century there were bishops, priests, and lay
people meeting at the Council of Trent, and their knowledge was, in
some fashion or another, subjective. The statements that they produced
came from their own subjective perception. They may have thought
that they were totally objective, that revelation could be recorded in
immutable sentences, but today such perceptions and apperceptions are
challenged as inconsistent. The epistemological subject is not merely
an epistemological being; the subject is also a limited, finite, historically situated, temporally pinpointed entity. Such a subject and such a
subject's intellection do not exist in some Archimedean vantage point
through which and in which one can see a full range of totality. Rather,
such a subject and such a subject's intellection, and the bishops of Trent
were in no other situation, are both finitely limited and temporally, as
well as historically, circumscribed. Such a subject knows only in part
and only through the primacy of his or her own perception.

But what is this limited, finite, temporal, and historical subject?
Ricoeur writes:

> We have introduced the "subject," but it is not in the sense of the
> "I" but in the sense of the *substratum. Subjectum* does not first
> mean "ego," but according to the Greek *hypokeimenon* and the
> Latin *substratum,* it is that which gathers everything to itself to
> become a basis. This *subjectum* is not yet man and not at all the
> "I." What happens with Descartes is that man becomes the first

and real *subjectum,* the first and real ground. There is a kind of complicity and identification between the two notions of the *subjectum* as ground and *subjectum* as "I."[35]

These words of Ricoeur remind us that, in postmodern thought, a major distinction is made between the "I think" of Descartes and his "I am." The "I" in "I think" and the "I" in "I am" are identical but different, with primordiality attributed to the "I" in the "I am." There is a someone prior to a someone who thinks. The foundational center of human existence is not found in consciousness. In one's subjective and personalized depth, one finds the locus in which all data is primordially gathered. Ricoeur immediately continues, "The subject as myself becomes the center to which the existent, *das Seiende,* is related. But this is possible only because the world has become a *Bild* (picture)."[36]

The critique of the Western emphasis on logos, to which Nietzsche provided great impetus, moved first in a fairly destructive manner. Habermas gives the following description:

> The embodied speaking and acting subject is not master of its own house; it draws from this the conclusion that the subject positing itself in knowledge is in fact dependent upon something prior, anonymous and transsubjective—be it the dispensation of Being, the accident of structure-formation, or the generative poser of some discourse formation.[37]

This destructive-of-logos movement has been very real and very effective in the Western world. Object-centered reason has lost its dominance. In Western thought logos-based knowledge had long served to maintain an interiority protected by power. Postmodern thought has shown it to be outwardly aggressive but inwardly hollow. Habermas asks, After such destruction, what follows? What then is the subject?

One answer came from the linguistic philosophers who moved in a methodological pattern, uncovering the weaknesses of the abstractions that a logos pattern of thought had built. These logos-driven abstractions were not bound by any language, were apparently universal in application, and were intrinsically disembodied. The logos simply encountered entities and classified them.[38] Linguistic philosophers affirmed that the linguistic function of representing states of affairs is the sole human monopoly. Only when linguistic communication is denotatively clear is there truth; language that is connotative is suspect.

Phenomenologists have not espoused linguistic analysis as the heir-apparent to the once prevailing Western logos dominance.

A second, multidimensional stage began to appear. If the logos-structure has been seen as interiorly hollow, what takes its place? Not language, as was just noted. For some authors, subject-centered reason "is the product of division and usurpation, indeed of a social process in the course of which a subordinated moment assumes the place of the whole, without having the power to assimilate the structure of the whole."[39] Marxism moved in this direction, with praxis taking over many of the centralizing roles that logos had once played. History plays a similar role, as a centering focus, or society is set up as an objective network of relations that provided either a normative order, which is somehow transcendent of the subject, or an instrumental order, through which the subject finds reciprocal objectification. For others, Habermas notes, it was body-centeredness that provided the centering dynamic (Merleau-Ponty). In this struggle to find a center to take the place of logos, Habermas concludes, "thought that is tied to the philosophy of the subject cannot bridge over these dichotomies but, as Foucault so acutely diagnosed, oscillates helplessly between one and the other pole."[40]

In many ways Habermas has outlined the landscape of Western thought that the deconstruction of logos hegemony has brought about. Nonetheless, there is no effort at all to move back to the logos hegemony with its "objective world." Not even Habermas moves in that direction. In some way or another there is clearly a return to the subject, and even Habermas's own communicative format is still subject-centered. Today, Western postmodern thinkers are oscillating between various poles on the matter of the subject, but the logos pole is not considered a reasonable option.

The implications this has for an interpretation of the Tridentine statements—or for that matter any conciliar or magisterial statement—are that all such statements are made with some sort of subjective bias; all such statements are finite, historical, temporal, and limited; and all such statements of the past not only have a message that the authors intended, but such statements have their own history, and so there is also something in front of the text and not simply behind the text. Moreover, because there will always be something "in front of the text," no particular generation can absolutize a text.

In the above description of the return to the subject I have used both Ricoeur and Habermas, but they are simply two voices among many. The struggle is not simply to avoid a solipsism of subject-centeredness or to avoid the abstractionism of logos-centeredness. These are indeed the negative sides of the discourse. The struggle is to find an area that as yet has no defined nomenclature. Some authors struggle to make a claim for the "universal," while others struggle to make a claim for the "normative." One cannot, however, maintain a universal in which the particular is disallowed, or a normative in which the existential, temporal/historical is disallowed. All of the above simply restates where postmodern thought is at the opening of the third millennium.

However, this current struggle to return to the subject needs a further step to make it meaningful.

Individuality or Haecceitas

The particularity, *Haecceitas,* of the subject cannot be overlooked. Some authors return to the subject and, in their view subjectivity is "common" to all individuals. Individuation is adjacent but not central to subjectivity. In Descartes' reduction, the "I think" and the "I am" are common to all human beings. Particularity is secondary. In the Kantian framework, both pure reason and practical reason are common to all human beings; particularity is not a core issue. In transcendental Thomism, the return to the subject is clearly part of the enterprise, but subjectivity is a common denominator, not individuality. This is evident, for instance, in Karl Rahner's *Spirit in the World* and *Hearers of the Word.*[41] Particularity, however, is clearly a constitutive part of the human condition.

In the 1986 Gifford Lectures, Ricoeur focused on the stated theme, "On Selfhood: The Question of Personal Identity." Subsequently, these lectures, in a revised form, were published as *Soi-même comme un autre.*[42] In this work Ricoeur notes that there is a confrontation between two major uses of the concept of personal identity.

On the one hand, there is personal identity as *sameness.*

Latin:	idem
German:	Gleichheit
French:	mêmeté

On the other hand, there is personal identity as *selfhood*.

Latin:	ipse
German:	Selbstheit
French:	ipséité[43]

Selfhood, Ricoeur states on many occasions, is not sameness. This is precisely what *Haecceitas* is meant to connote and denote. There is a subjectivity that one can designate as sameness, but there is also a subjectivity that one must designate as selfhood. Selfhood is not something adventitious to sameness. We have already moved in this direction with the section on identity and difference, and the distinction between identity and difference is clearly basic for much postmodern thought. The distinction between *mêmeté* and *ipséité* is equally important.

For Ricoeur, the issue of *permanence in time* is a first aspect exclusively connected to *idem*-identity. Sameness, *mêmeté*, is a sameness in numerical identity and the opposite is plurality. The notion of identification, actually understood as reidentification, is at the base of numerical identity. We do say, and with solid reason, that the same thing occurs twice or "n" times.

The second aspect of *mêmeté* is a qualitative identity or extreme resemblance. One can say that two people are wearing the same suit. There is here a mental operation without semantic loss.

A third aspect of sameness is an uninterrupted continuity between the first and last stages of some development. One can say that the same man or woman exists from birth to death; however, one need not say that the same person exists from birth to death.

This leads to the fourth aspect, permanence in time. One sees an invariable structure of a tool over a specific period of time, even though its molecular and subatomic parts have all changed. Given a long stretch of time, however, even the structure will change. In the human genetic code of a biologic individual, what remains is the organization of a combinatory system. The notion of a structure, rather than an event, places the idea of permanence in a different light. Structural permanence is different from the Aristotelian or scholastic notion of "substance," particularly "primary substance." It is to some degree similar to the Kantian notion of substance, since, for Kant, substance is placed within the category of relation, and this is what structural continuity and "permanence" seem to be.[44]

Having presented all of this, Ricoeur then asks the primal question:

> Does the selfhood of the self imply a form of permanence in time
> which is not reducible to the determination of a substratum, not
> even in the relational sense which Kant assigns to the category of
> substance; in short, is there a form of permanence in time which is
> not simply the schema of the category of substance?[45]

For human beings, this is the question of the "who"? Who am I?
Is the permanence of the "who" irreducible to any question of the
"what"? What is the overlapping of the *idem/ipse, mêmeté/ipséité,
Gleichheit/Selbstheit?* Ricoeur himself posits at this juncture a description of "character," a theme that has a recurring history in his writings.[46]
In *Soi-même comme un autre* Ricoeur places character at the limit point
where the problematic of *ipse* becomes indiscernible from that of *idem,*
and where one is inclined not to distinguish them from each other.

An individual person has certain traits, which one can call
"habits," and these habits tend to provide a person with individuality.
Likewise, an individual person has certain acquired identifications that,
when taken together, provide the person with personal singularity;
these traits are values, norms, ideals, models, and heroes. In these
areas, a person recognizes himself or herself, at least in personal
desire.[47] In this the *idem* and the *ipse* coincide to some degree, but there
remains a fundamental difference.[48]

This discussion leads from the contrast of sameness and selfhood
to a far deeper contrast, that of selfhood in its dialectic with otherness.[49]
After a lengthy discussion on Heidegger's existentiality of *Sorge*
[care], Ricoeur states the following:

> Only a being that is a self is *in* the world; correlatively, the world in
> which this being is, is not the sum of beings composing the universe
> of subsisting things or things ready-to-hand [*Vorhandenheit*]. The
> being of the self presupposes the totality of a world that is the horizon of its thinking, acting, feeling—in short of its *care.*[50]

This is another way to describe *Haecceitas.* It is also a way of
speaking about each and every single human person. This passage occurs
in an *ontological* chapter that Ricoeur deliberately entitles "What
Ontology in View?" There is a selfhood and bodiliness, so that consequently all unbodied selves are not selves but "sames."[51] There is as well

a selfhood in dialectical relationship to otherness, so that if there is no otherness there are no selves but only "one-and-the-same."[52] The interstice between self and other is, for Ricoeur, an interstice called *Gewissen,* conscience.[53] Ricoeur rejects Heidegger's approach to otherness as facticity of being-in-the-world. He rejects Lévinas's understanding that there is no other modality of otherness than one's externality. Rather, Ricoeur argues that the model for all otherness is the other person, a modality involved in the very structure of selfhood.[54]

Heidegger, Lévinas, Ricoeur, Merleau-Ponty, Habermas, and many more have spoken, in one way or another, about the difference between *mêmeté* and *ipséité.* However, one might ask, what has all this to do with solemn proclamations by a council of the Roman Catholic Church, especially when the theme of these proclamations focuses on sacramentality? Let me restate the challenging relationship that this aspect of postmodern thought brings to an understanding of these proclamations.

Every sacramental action, a sacramental *Ereignis,* is exquisitely unique. There are no replicated sacramental actions. In each sacramental action the unique God is revealing something of God's own self to unique selves, not to "sames." Each self is unique and irreducible. The sacramental event is a moment involving a unique God and a unique self, at a unique time, in a unique place, in conjunction with others who are uniquely part of the *Soi-même comme autre* event. Solemn proclamations about some sort of "objective," atemporal, ahistorical, nonexistential sacramentality become less and less hermeneutically meaningful as these proclamations move into an area of so-called atemporality, so-called ahistoricality, so-called nonexistentiality, so-called objectivity, all of which are only abstract generalizations about something that never exists, that never can exist. In every sacramental action God is revealing something of God's own unique being to a "me" as a self, not to me as a "same," to us as selves, not to us as "sames." Therefore the solemn statements are, at best, generalized pointers to help a "self" or "selves" experience God in a unique and unreplicable moment of sacramental *Haecceitas.*

The proclamations attempt to point to a unique God who acts, blesses, and transforms in a unique way on a self/selves, on a "me," or on an "us," who are selves not "sames." Recall the words of Ricoeur, "Only a being that is a self is *in* the world." This world is not the sum of beings composing a cosmos, but a world that is "the horizon of its thinking, acting, feeling—in short of its care." When, and only when, a proclamation speaks to this unique self is the proclamation both hermeneutically and onto-hermeneutically meaningful. When proclamations speak not to *Haecceitas* but to *Generalitas,* the proclamations are using a form of hermeneutical ease that bears little meaning to what sacraments, as events, are uniquely all about.

After one reads these solemn statements, generalized as they perhaps must be, the response of a postmodern person might be: Do these proclamations point me in the direction of a unique and credible God who reveals God's own self in a given sacramental event? In many ways these proclamations, by pointing in a general direction, also play a role by indicating that we should not seek a sacramental event in a contrary direction. These proclamations gather together a common wisdom of the Christian community, but it is a general wisdom and, therefore, has a large generalized scope, not the particularized scope of one's own individual "world." These proclamations may indeed speak to the "same" as permanence in duration, but they do not truly address the *ipséité,* the *Haecceitas.* Only the sacramental moment does this.

Temporality

We have already spent some time on temporality and postmodern thought, but a few additional ideas are in order at this moment. It is with deliberation that I have placed temporality after *Haecceitas.* Heidegger introduces care, *Sorge,* as the most basic existential of *Dasein,* not temporality. Indeed, it is because of care, *Sorge,* that temporality makes sense. William Richardson reminds us of the following:

> The question we are posing, then, is this: if the Being of There-Being is concern, what is the Being—sc. the ultimate ground of possibility—of concern? Heidegger answers: temporality *(Zeitlichkeit).*[55]

Heidegger is not speaking of chronological time but rather of ontological time. Chronological time consists of a series of "nows," with a preceding series of "pasts" and a drive into a yet-to-be series of "futures." Ontological time, on the other hand, is a fundamental part of *Dasein* and is much more a matter of the relationship of letting being come to presence in *Dasein,* of *Existenz,* of the ontic and the ontological differential, of the presence of past-present-and-future at every moment of time, *Zeitlichkeit.*

For Heidegger and for many other postmodern writers, ontological time belongs to *Dasein* ontologically, not adventitiously. Being is a continual coming to being, and Being is clearly older than any span of time that we use to measure. Being, however, is not older than time, for Being is time in its origin.[56]

Temporality is clearly and ontologically part of both Being and *Dasein.* Heidegger uses the term *Gründen,* which might be translated as the process of grounding, or the coming-to-pass of grounding. It is a process that constitutes the transcendence of *Dasein* and of *Sein.*

As a process, there are three stages or components:

1. *Stiften*—laying claim;
2. *Boden nehmen*—taking possession;
3. *Begründen*—founding.

It is with the final component that one begins to understand the transcendence of being. This level uncovers the Being and Being-structure of beings, and such an uncovering is precisely what is meant by ontological truth.[57] Transcendence is intrinsically connected to truth, *Aletheia,* and to time, *Zeitlichkeit,* and to ground, *Gründen.* Transcendence is therefore not something that *Dasein* possesses and is ontologically oriented to the infinite, to the timeless, to the absolute.[58] Richardson remarks, "Since transcendence [for Heidegger] is radically finite, so too must be ground (therefore truth). This is worth emphasis."[59]

One sees that temporality involves many other issues besides time—for example, care, ground, truth, transcendence—and, as a result, the temporalness of all human thought, language, and being is finite. The challenge that postmodern writers bring to the solemn statements of the church is twofold. Hermeneutically, on what basis can a statement be made about absolute non-finiteness (the epistemological or hermeneutical question)? And on what basis is a human being able to move beyond his or her own finiteness and finite transcendence (the onto-hermeneutical question)? The focus of this challenge is not on what is said in such church statements, but rather on the more basic question, what is understanding? If understanding and onto-understanding are radically finite and temporal, what meaning can be understood by a human person regarding something that is radically non-temporal, non-finite, non-grounded in *Dasein?*[60]

Language

Language has been a structural theme of this present volume, and the language of a church council or of the magisterium, in any form, is not beyond the restrictions and the latitudes of any and all language. Church language is not a language in and of itself. It is rather a human language and shares in human historicality, temporality, and finitude. Not only is language so constrained, but, as we have noted in the section on de Saussure, each language has its own structure and sphere of meaning, so that what is originally written in one language may not be understood equivalently when translated into a different language.

Languages have both their own uniqueness and their own limitations. Therefore, what is said or written in one particular language, at one particular time, within one particular *epistemé,* cannot assume any eternal hermeneutic or any Archimedean hermeneutic. What is understanding? This basic question involves not only the onto-hermeneutical structures of human understanding, but also the epistemological structures of linguistic communication. It is precisely in this area, not in subject matter per se, that postmodern thought raises serious questions about the understandability, both hermeneutically and onto-hermeneutically, of all so-called immutable statements of a religious body.

Postmodern philosophical issues on hermeneutics and onto-hermeneutics, with all their emphasis on subjectivity, individuality, temporality, and language, provide us with insights into the wonder of the human. It is a wonder that stresses the limitations of the human in all dimensions of life. Theologically, we believe that God does reveal God's own self to us and that, too, is a wonder, but God reveals God's own self to a very limited human being, not to a "same," but to a "self." Postmodern thought pushes us to speak of this revelatory action of God in humble terms, not grandiose and Archimedean terms. In these revelatory events, which we Christians call sacraments, we catch only a small glimpse of the transcendent God. Postmodern thinking strongly cautions us not to extrapolate our small glimpses of the divine into panoramic vistas. To speak as though we have some all-encompassing view may have been considered possible in a former logos-dominated, subject-object dichotomized *epistemé,* but such an *epistemé* is, for third millennium sacramentality, no longer viable. This volume has been constructed along the lines of many other theological endeavors, namely, toward a postmodern understanding of a sacramental event. When one begins to see the wonder of limited, temporal, and historical human existence, one can only marvel that, in an event of sacramental *Haecceitas,* it is God who discloses not only a small share of the mystery of God, but also discloses a powerful insight of the meaning of the *humanum* itself.

Conclusion

It should be clear from all that has been written above that post-modern writers have not spoken directly on the theme of sacramental theology. Nonetheless, serious challenges confront sacramental theology in the third millennium. By way of conclusion, let us consider two basic challenges: the first is a challenge from both a hermeneutical and theological standpoint. The second is a challenge from an onto-hermeneutical and theological standpoint.

THE HERMENEUTICAL AND THEOLOGICAL CHALLENGE

Early on, the phrase "hermeneutical ease" was employed to indicate that theologians and church officials use such terms as *sacrament, primordial, foundational,* and *the sacrament of the universe* in a very facile and, therefore, misunderstandable way. In the postmodern thinkers we have studied, one hermeneutical question dominates: What is human understanding? Translated into a theological framework the question becomes: How is an understanding of theological discourse possible?

The return to the subject, the question of temporality, the limits of language, and *Haecceitas,* or individuality, all raise serious objections to current sacramental discourse. It has been my aim to indicate that these four issues, in particular, do not dismantle sacramental theology but rather enhance it. When the postmodern hermeneutical challenge that involves these issues in a fundamental way is brought to the table of theological discourse, the challenge is no different from the challenge postmodern thought brings to the standard subject/object thinking of science, technology, and linguistics.

In Husserl's 1907 lectures on phenomenology he introduced his celebrated "phenomenal reduction," the purpose of which was to attain a decisive overcoming of what Lowit called "la situation phénoménal du clivage" or, in other words, the subject/object split that has presided over modern Western philosophy from Descartes to the twentieth century.[1] There was in this call for a phenomenological reduction a clear "deconstruction" of the central problematic of modern philosophy; namely, the epistemological problem of how an isolated subjectivity, closed in upon itself, can, nevertheless, manage to transcend itself in such a way as to achieve a knowledge of the external world.

The human mind in this view is not an open subjectivity, open to any and all objectivity that shares in being. In the phrase *cogito ergo sum,* the "I" of the *cogito* and the "I" of the *sum* are not identical. It is this understanding of subjectivity that is one of the main foci of postmodern thought, and the challenge of Husserl has been reiterated and expanded by scholar after scholar throughout the twentieth century. It is precisely the *epistemé,* in which sacramental theology has been generally presented by the various Christian churches, which is challenged.

To invoke the issues of "divine revelation" or of "divine authority" avoids the very challenge itself and misses the precise area of the challenge. Postmodern thinkers in large measure do not focus on the divine aspect, the God aspect. Rather, there is a clear focus on human receptivity, human intellection, and human communicativeness. Theological and magisterial sacramental statements, on every level, have been made within a certain *epistemé.* What is challenged today is the *epistemé* that was used and is still being used in the formulation of such theological and magisterial statements.

In contemporary theology and magisterial statements, as we have seen, a sacramental action or event is primarily a self-disclosure of God and secondarily a human response. When this understanding of sacramentality is taken as the basis of sacramental discourse—that God alone is the source and goal of all liturgy—then subjectivity, individuality, temporality, and language are involved. God is disclosing God's own self to a subjective human individual within the coordinates of a given time-space continuum and through a linguistic communication. This theological change from propositional revelation to personalist revelation is helped strongly by postmodern hermeneutical discussion. Retention of an outdated hermeneutic—the hermeneutic of scholasticism, neo-scholasticism, or transcendental Thomism—can only end in hermeneutical disaster.

The Onto-Hermeneutical and Theological Challenge

The basic onto-hermeneutical challenge includes subjectivity, individuality, temporality and language, and therefore challenges any claim for universality. In my view, the basis of sacramental theology itself—that sacraments are foundationally and primordially actions of God and only secondarily human responses—moves the universal claim to divine dimension. The human dimension, then, remains subjective, individual, temporal, and linguistic. In the human dimensions these same issues cannot be avoided; they must be faced honestly. In other words, universality in a primordial and foundational way belongs only to God, and in the dual action of sacramentality in which God reveals God's own self to a human person there can only be temporal, subjective, linguistically particularized *Haecceitas* or individuality.

Sacramentality cannot be seen, nor can sacraments be described in some form of human generality or universality. To speak about the essential elements of baptism, of eucharist, or of any other sacrament is insufficient. To speak about the factors that must be present for the validity of sacrament is equally insufficient. Sacraments exist only in unique situations. In most theological discourse on sacraments, the *Haecceitas,* the *ipséité,* is not even taken into account, or if it is, it is seen in some form of *opus operantis.* Baptism only has its being and meaning in a given sacramental event of baptism, which is uniquely temporalized by unique people in a unique place. To speak only of sacramental "sames," *mêmeté,* is to miss the reality that involves the "selves," *ipséité.*

Contemporary theology substantiates this approach. All liturgy, sacramental and nonsacramental, is the work of the Trinity and has the Father as source and goal of the liturgy. In a sacramental event Christians *primarily* celebrate God's action, that is, the paschal mystery. In a sacramental event the Holy Spirit acts, makes present, and gives life. There is a dual dimension in the liturgical event: God acting first and in a personal way, and only then is there an action of unique "selves," not "sames," responding.[2]

Chauvet, as we saw, states the issue clearly when he writes that the world is a *possible* place of sacramentality. By itself, the world is not sacramental, because sacramentality is an action or event that involves a unique self-revelation of God and a response by unique human beings. Sacramentality, in the dimension of its human response, is an event that is thoroughly existential, historical, temporal, singular, and unique. Universality, unsurpassability, and fullness are qualities only applicable to God.

A similar theological centering can be applied to authors who have described Jesus, in his humanness, as a primordial sacrament. These authors speak with hermeneutical ease, both regarding the terms "sacrament" and "primordial." But everything that is human is limited, finite, temporal, historical, existential, singular, and unique. This holds for the humanness of Jesus as well. To speak of a primordiality of something finite, limited, temporal, or historical is meaningless, because this way of thinking implies that there is an unsurpassability in something finite, limited, temporal, historical, and subjective. However, the limits, *fines,* of something finite can always be surpassed. In the issue of primordiality, it is God who is unsurpassable, and it is the presence of God in each and every sacramental action alone that can be designated as primordial. Jesus in his humanness cannot possibly be primordial and unsurpassable.

Some contemporary theologians speak of the church as a foundational sacrament and, in doing this, not only is "sacrament" used with hermeneutical ease, but also "foundational" and "church." We have seen the lack of clarity in church documents and theological writings surrounding the use of the word "church." Which church is meant? The lack of clarity in the meaning of this term is generally not acknowledged by theologians who use the phrase "the church is a foundational sacrament." This makes the phrase ambiguous and hermeneutically unclear. However, since the church, in whatever extension it may be given, is, in its human side, finite, limited, historical, and temporal, it too cannot be seen as a foundation that is unsurpassable. If there is any unsurpassable foundationality in the church, it arises only from the presence of God, who alone is foundationally unsurpassable. However,

God, the unsurpassable foundation, is not confined to the limitedness, the historicity, the singularity of ecclesial events.

Since there is a dual dimension to sacramentality—the unique revelatory event of God *and* the secondary response of human individuals—a sacramental event only takes place when this secondary response occurs. The human response is intrinsically temporal, intrinsically limited, intrinsically subjective, and intrinsically *ipséité*. The return to the subject is not simply a return to human nature, which is only a return to the "same." Rather, the return to subjectivity is a return to the "self." Between the "same" and the "self" there is identity and difference, but it is in the dialectical relation of the self to the other that *ipséité* finds meaning, *soi-même comme un autre*. A unique self has its own world and finds itself in shared intentionalities and in *Horizontsverschmelzung*. In all of this, a unique self is intrinsically temporal, and all that one experiences and knows is hermeneutically meaningful only within an intrinsically temporalized *in-der-Welt-mit-Anderen-Dasein*. Such an existence occurs in a major decentering of the subject through language, on the proviso that language is understood, not as an adventitious means of communication or as *parole,* but as *langue,* involving both synchrony and diachrony, both the scriptible and the lisible. For Western people, sacramental *Haecceitas* begins to be hermeneutically sound when it is experienced, communicated, and lived within a new *epistemé*.

If one were to ask whether a postmodern approach is the final answer for Christian sacramentality, the answer would be no. There is never anything final in postmodern thought, but even more than that one could think of writing a book similar to this present volume on the notion of sacramental thought and East Asian philosophy. Were I to write such a volume, I would use not only authors such as Confucius, Mencius, Lao Tsu, but also the writings of the I Ching, of the Wei-shih, of the summa of Hsüan-tsang, of Huai-nan Tsu. Wang Yang Ming and Fung Yu-lan would be of major importance as well. Such names may be, for a Western person, strange. Surely Heidegger, Ricoeur, and Merleau-Ponty are strange names to many people in Eastern Asia. It is not the names that I wish to highlight, although they add to the esoteric sense Westerners have in this regard. What is important is to realize that over half of the world today does not think in the "canonized" Western subject/object form of knowledge. Sacramentality, among the

Christian Asians, is a Western import, not only in regard to the name itself, but also the way in which it is considered. Were I to write a book from the Asian standpoint, it too would require a total deconstruction and reconstruction, so that the reality of God revealing God's own self to human beings of another culture and their response to this revelation, in other words, the entire dynamic of a sacramental event, would be understandable, but only within a different *epistemé.*

We, however, are Westerners moving into the third millennium, and a sacramental theology for the third millennium inherits all that the twentieth century has accomplished. As we saw in chapter 1, this material is, in its totality, revolutionary. It is my belief that postmodern hermeneutical and onto-hermeneutical thought will help, in a most extensive and intensive way, to make sacramental *Haecceitas* a meaningful reality for third-millennium Western individuals.

Notes

1. The Twentieth-Century Legacy of Sacramental Revolution

1. H. C. Lea, *A History of Auricular Confession and Indulgences in the Latin Church* (Philadelphia, Pa.: Lea Bros & Co., 1896).

2. A. Boudinhon, "Sur l'histoire de la pénitence: À propos d'un livre récent (celui du Lea)," *Revue d'histoire et de littérature religieuse* (1897), 2:306–44, 496–524.

3. F. X. Funk, "Zur altchristlichen Bußdisciplin," *Kirchengeschichtliche Abhandlungen und Untersuchungen* (Paderborn: F. Schoningh, 1896), 1:155–209.

4. Pierre Battifol, *Études d'histoire et de théologie positive* (Paris: V. Lecoffre, 1902).

5. E. F. Vacandard, *La pénitence publique dans l'Église primitive* (Paris: Bloud, 1903).

6. P. A. Kirsch, *Zur Geschichte der katholischen Beichte* (Wurzburg: Godel & Scherer, 1902).

7. F. Loofs, *Leitfaden zum Studium der Dogmengeschichte* (Tübingen: M. Niemeyer, 1959), newly edited by K. Aland; originally published in Halle in 1906.

8. J. Gartmeier, *Die Beichtpflicht, historische-dogmatisch dargestellt* (Regensburg: G. J. Manz, 1905).

9. P. Pignataro, *De disciplina poenitentiali priorum Ecclesiae saeculorum commentarius* (Rome: Juvenum Opificum A. S. Josepho, 1904).

10. A. Di Dario, *Il sacramento della penitenze dei primi secoli cristiani* (Naples, 1904).

11. Paul Galtier, *L'Église et la rémission des péchés aux premiers siècles* (Paris: Beauchesne, 1932); *De Paenitentia: Tractatus dogmatico-historicus* (Rome: Gregorian University, 1956). This is the last revised edition.

12. Bernhard Poschmann, *Buße und Letzte Ölung* (Freiburg I. B.: Herder, 1951). Eng. trans. by F. Courtney, *Penance and the Anointing of the Sick* (New York: Herder and Herder, 1964).

13. A. D'Alès, *L'Édit de Calliste: Étude sur les origines de la pénitence chrétienne* (Paris: Beauchesne, 1914).

14. K. Adam, *Die kirchliche Sündenvergebung nach dem heiligen Augustin* (Paderborn: F. Schoningh, 1917); *Die geheime Kirchenbuße nach dem heiligen Augustin* (Munich: J. Kosel & F. Pustet, 1921).

15. J. A. Jungmann, *Die lateinische Bußriten in ihrer geschichtliche Entwicklung: Forschungen zur Geschichte des innerkirchlichen Lebens* (Innsbruck: Rauch, 1932).

16. K. Rahner, "Vergessene Wahrheiten über das Bußsakrament," *Schriften zur Theologie* (Einsiedeln: Benziger, 1964), 2:143–83. Originally written in 1953.

17. On the history of holy baptism, see B. Neunheuser, *Taufe und Firmung* (Freiburg im B.: Herder, 1956); Eng. trans. *Baptism and Confirmation* (New York: Herder and Herder, 1964); Aidan Kavanagh, *The Shape of Baptism: The Rite of Christian Initiation*, (New York: Pueblo, 1978); Robert Hovda, ed. *Made Not Born: New Perspectives on Christian Initiation and the Catechumenate* (Notre Dame, Ind.: University of Notre Dame Press, 1976), esp. Reginald Fuller, "Christian Initiation in the New Testament," 7–31; Robert M. Grant, "Development of the Christian Catechumenate," 32–49; E. C. Whitaker, *The Baptismal Liturgy* (London: SPCK, 1981); Michel Dujarier, *A History of the Catechumenate: The First Six Centuries* (New York: William H. Sadlier, 1978); Adrien Nocent, *La Liturgia, i sacramenti* (Genoa: Marietti, 1986); Paul Bradshaw, *Essays in Early Initiation* (Bramcote, Eng.: Grove, 1988); Edward Yarnold, *The Awe-Inspiring Rites of Initiation* (Middlegreen, Eng.: St. Paul, 1971); Kilian McDonnell and George T. Montague, *Christian Initiation and Baptism in the Holy Spirit* (Collegeville, Minn.: The Liturgical Press, 1991).

18. On the history of holy eucharist, see Xavier Léon-Dufour, *Le Partage du Pain Eucharistique* (Paris: Les Éditions du Seuil, 1982), trans. Matthew J. O'Connell, *Sharing the Eucharistic Bread* (New York: Paulist, 1987); J. Jeremias, *Die Abendmahlsworte Jesu* (Göttingen: Vandenhoeck & Ruprecht, 1964); Eng. trans. by Norman Perrin, *The Eucharistic Words of Jesus* (London: SCM Press, 1966); Josef Jungmann, *The Early Liturgy,* trans. Francis Brunner (Notre Dame, Ind.: University of Notre Dame Press, 1959); idem, *Missarum sollemnia: eine genetische Erklärung der römischen Messe* (Vienna: Herder, 1962); Robert Daly, *The Origins of the Christian Doctrine of Sacrifice* (Philadelphia, Pa.: Fortress, 1978); Nathan Mitchell, *Cult and Controversy: The Worship of the Eucharist Outside the Mass* (New York: Pueblo, 1982); Gary Macy, *The Theologies of the Eucharist in the Early Scholastic Period* (Oxford: Clarendon Press, 1984); idem, *The Banquet's Wisdom: A Short History of the Theologies of the Lord's Supper* (New York: Paulist, 1992); D. Power, *The Eucharistic Mystery* (New York: Crossroad, 1989).

19. On the history of holy orders, see Bernard Cooke, *Ministry to Word and Sacraments* (Philadelphia, Pa.: Fortress, 1976); L. Ott, *Das Weihesakrament* (Freiburg: Herder, 1969); E. Schillebeeckx, *Ministry: Leadership in the Community of Jesus Christ*, trans. J. Bowden (New York: Crossroad, 1981); H. von Campenhausen, *Ecclesiastical Authority and Spiritual Power in the Church of the First Three Centuries,* trans. J. Baker (Stanford: Stanford University Press, 1969); C. Osiek, "The Ministry and Ordination of Women According to the Early Church Fathers," *Women and Priesthood* (Collegeville, Minn.: The Liturgical Press, 1978); Jean Galot, *Theology of the Priesthood*, trans. R. Balducelli (San Francisco: Ignatius Press, 1984); Patrick J. Dunn, *Priesthood* (New York: Alba House, 1990); James Puglisi, *The Process of Admission to Ordained Ministry* (Collegeville, Minn.: The Liturgical Press, 1996/1998), trans. vol. 1, Michael Driscoll and Mary Misrahi, vol. 2, Mary Misrahi; Ray Noll, *Christian Ministerial Priesthood* (San Francisco: Catholic Scholars Press, 1993); James Monroe Barnett, *The Diaconate: A Full and Equal Order* (Valley Forge, Pa.: Trinity Press International, 1995); K. Osborne, *Priesthood: A History of the Ordained Ministry in the Roman Catholic Church* (New York: Paulist, 1988); idem, *Ministry: Lay Ministry in the Roman Catholic Church* (New York: Paulist, 1993); T. O'Meara, *Theology of Ministry* (New York: Paulist,

1983); D. Power, *Gifts that Differ* (New York: Pueblo, 1980); E. Foley, *From Age to Age: How Christians Celebrated the Eucharist* (Chicago: Liturgy Training Publications, 1991).

20. On the history of holy confirmation, see G. Austin, *Anointing with the Spirit: The Rite of Confirmation* (New York: Pueblo, 1985); Gregory Dix, *The Theology of Confirmation in Relation to Baptism* (London: Dacre Press, 1946); James D. G. Dunn *Baptism in the Holy Spirit* (London: SCM Press, 1970); L. S. Thornton, *Confirmation: Its Place in the Baptismal Ministry* (London: Dacre Press, 1954); W. Bausch, *A New Look at the Sacraments* (Mystic, Conn.: Twenty-Third Publications, 1983); L. Ligier, *La Confirmacion: Sense conjoncture oecumenique hier* (Paris: Beauchesne, 1973); Sigisbert Regli, "Firmsakrament und christliche Entfaltung," *Mysterium Salutis* (Einsiedeln: Benziger, 1976), 5:297–348; Nathan Mitchell, "Dissolution of the Rite of Christian Initiation," *Made Not Born* (Notre Dame, Ind.: Notre Dame University Press, 1976), 50–82; Joseph Martos, *Doors to the Sacred: A Historical Introduction to Sacraments in the Catholic Church* (New York: Doubleday, 1982), 203–30.

21. On the history of holy marriage, see Theodore Mackin, *What Is Marriage* (New York: Paulist, 1982); idem, *Divorce and Remarriage* (New York: Paulist, 1984); idem. *The Marital Sacrament* (New York: Paulist, 1989); E. Schillebeeckx, *Marriage: Human Reality and Saving Mystery,* trans. N. D. Smith (New York: Sheed and Ward, 1965); George Joyce, *Christian Marriage: An Historical and Doctrinal Study* (London: Sheed and Ward, 1948); Henri Rondet, *Introduction à l'étude de la théologie du mariage* (Paris: Lethielleux, 1960).

22. On the history of holy anointing of the sick, see James Empereur, *Prophetic Anointing* (Wilmington, Del.: Michael Glazier, 1982); Al Janssens, *Het Heilig Oliesel* (Nijmegen: N. V. Dekker En Van De Vegt, 1939); Paul Palmer, *Sacraments and Forgiveness* (Westminster: Newman Press, 1959); Poschmann, *Buße und Letzte Ölung,* 233–57.

23. See Martos, *Doors to the Sacred*; Cooke, *Ministry to Word and Sacraments.*

24. One can also argue theologically that neither baptism nor eucharist were instituted during the lifetime of Jesus, since no sacrament existed prior to the resurrection and ascension of Jesus. All

Christian sacraments are post-resurrectional in their institution and their meaning.

25. See *Catechism of the Catholic Church*: for baptism, nos. 1226–28; for confirmation, nos. 1290–92; for eucharist, nos. 1345–47; for reconciliation, nos. 1434–39; for the anointing of the sick, nos. 1512–13; for orders, no clear historical section is presented, nor is there a clear historical section presented for marriage.

26. Hermes, *The Shepherd, Commandment*, 4. 3.

27. Hippolytus, *The Apostolic Tradition*, 1.2–4; 7–9.

28. Ibid., 5, 1.

29. See Mackin, *The Marital Sacrament*, 83–136, for pre-Nicaean indications, and 137–89 for post-Nicaean indications.

30. Peter Lombard, *Libri IV*, Distinctions 26–42. Peter Lombard was not the first to place marriage into the seven-sacrament schematic, but it is only in this period of time that theologians in the West began to consider marriage one of the church's sacraments. T. Mackin writes: "The Catholic authorities may have accepted marriage among the church's sacraments formally and definitively as early as the Second Lateran Council in 1139 during the pontificate of Innocent II" (*The Marital Sacrament*, 318).

31. See Nathan Mitchell, "Dissolution of the Rite of Christian Initiation"; and Sigisbert Regli, "Firmsakrament und christliche Entfaltung," for a historical development of a separate rite of confirmation.

32. Otto Semmelroth, *Die Kirche als Ursakrament* (Frankfurt am Main: Josef Knecht, 1953).

33. K. Rahner, *Kirche und Sakrament* (Freiburg: Herder, 1961).

34. E. Schillebeeckx, *Christus, Sacrament van de Godsontmoeting* (Bilthoven: H. Nelissen, 1960). Eng. trans. by C. Ernst, *Christ the Sacrament of the Encounter with God* (New York: Sheed and Ward, 1963).

35. Gérard Philips, *La Chiesa e il suo Mistero* (Milan: Editoriale Jaca Book, 1986), 72. See A. Grillmeier, "Dogmatic Constitution on the Church, Chapter I," *Commentary on the Documents of Vatican II*, ed. H. Vorgrimler (New York: Herder and Herder, 1967), 1:140: "It is thus the intention of the Council to take up once more this ancient usage and to ascribe to the Church the value of a sacramental symbolism and instrumentality in the whole of the divine economy of salvation for all

mankind and its history." See also Bonaventure Kloppenburg, *The Ecclesiology of Vatican II*, trans. by M. J. O'Connell (Chicago: Franciscan Herald Press, 1974), esp. "The Church as Sacrament of Christ," 22–24. All three of these theologians were *periti* at the council and wrote their commentaries shortly after the conclusion of the council, thus carefully reflecting the intentions and attitudes of the bishops at Vatican II.

36. In its section on ecclesiology, the *Catechism* mentions the church as a sacrament in nos. 738, 774, 775, 776, 780, 849, and 932. With these few statements it is clear that the sacramentality of the church as far as the *Catechism* is concerned is a marginal issue compared to such themes as church structure, governance, hierarchy, and teaching authority, which the *Catechism* treats at much greater length and in much greater detail.

37. Lambert Beauduin, *Le piété de l'église* (Louvain: Louvain Univ. Press, 1914). Eng. trans. by Virgil Michel, *Liturgy the Life of the Church* (Collegeville, Minn.: The Liturgical Press, 1929). Also see Keith Pecklers, *The Unread Vision: The Liturgical Movement in the United States 1926–1955* (Collegeville, Minn.: The Liturgical Press, 1998), 8–16.

38. Romano Guardini, *Vom Geist der Liturgie* (Herder, Freiburg im B, 1921). Eng. trans. by Ada Lane, *The Spirit of the Liturgy* (London: Sheed and Ward, 1935).

39. Odo Casel, *Das christliche Kultmysterium* (Regensburg: Pustet, 1932). Eng. trans. *The Mystery of Christian Worship* (Westminster, Md.: Newman Press, 1962); idem, *Art und Sinn der Ältesten Christlichen Österfeier* (Münster: Aschendorff, 1938).

40. P. Parsch, *Das Jahr des Heils* (Klosterneuburg: Volksliturgisches Apostolat, 1947).

41. See J. D. Crichton, *The Once and Future Liturgy* (New York: Paulist, 1977).

42. For a detailed consideration of Virgil Michel, see Pecklers, *The Unread Vision.*

43. For the details of this survey on the liturgical movement in the twentieth century I am indebted to Daniel P. Grigassy, "The Liturgical Movement," *The New Dictionary of Theology*, ed. J. Komonchak, M. Collins, and D. Lane (Wilmington, Del.: Michael Glazier, 1987), 586–91; and also to Ernest B. Koenker, *The Liturgical*

Renaissance in the Roman Catholic Church (Chicago: The University of Chicago Press, 1954).

44. See Pecklers, *The Unread Vision*, 18–149.

45. See Anscar J. Chupungco, *Liturgies of the Future* (New York: Paulist, 1989), esp. 207–11.

46. L. Charlier, *Essai sur le problème théologique* (Thuilles, 1938), 69.

47. See H. De Lubac, *Catholicism*, trans. E. Sheppard (London: Longmans, Green, 1950), 165.

48. T. Bokenkotter, *A Concise History of the Catholic Church* (New York: Doubleday, 1990), 376. For an understanding of *La nouvelle Théologie,* see also T. M. Schoof, *A Survey of Catholic Theology 1800–1970* (New York: Paulist, 1970), 201–9.

49. The *Catechism of the Catholic Church* (1992) and the *Ratio Fundamentalis Institutionis Diaconalis* (1997) are two official documents of the Vatican that continue to press for scholastic language and interpretation.

50. A litany of the major philosophers in the twentieth century is impressive; to name a few major figures: Edmund Husserl, Martin Heidegger, Jean-Paul Sartre, Albert Camus, Maurice Merleau-Ponty, Gabriel Marcel, Karl Jaspers, Emmanuel Lévinas, Ernst Mach, Pierre Duhem, Gaston Bachelard, Georg Lukács, Antonio Gramsci, Henri Lefebvre, Roger Garaudy, Theodor Adorno, Erich Fromm, Herbert Marcuse, Jürgen Habermas, Hans Georg Gadamer, Paul Ricoeur, Giovanni Gentile, Benedetto Croce, Ferdinand de Saussure, Claude Lévi-Strauss, Roland Barthes, Jacques Lacan, Simone de Beauvoir, Jacques Derrida, and Alfred North Whitehead. With these and many others one can only speak of a genuine philosophical renaissance.

51. See Babette E. Babich, "Philosophies of Science: Mach, Duhem, Bachelard," *Continental Philosophy in the Twentieth Century*, ed. Richard Kearney (London: Routledge, 1994), 175.

52. Thomas Docherty, "Postmodernist Theory: Lyotard, Baudrillard and Others," in Kearney, *Continental Philosophy in the Twentieth Century*, 8:480.

53. This negative approach is scattered widely throughout the Roman Catholic world. A comprehensive overview is presented by D. Menozzi, "Opposition to the Council (1966–1984)," *The Reception of*

Vatican II, ed. G. Alberigo, J.-P. Jossua and J. Komonchak (Washington D.C.: The Catholic University of America Press, 1987), 325–48.

54. More specifically, this period of time begins with the announcement of the Vatican Council by John XXIII on January 25, 1959, moves from the inauguration of the council on October 11, 1962, down to the official close of council by Paul VI on December. 8, 1965.

55. The conciliar text does not reject the celebration of Mass privately. However, private eucharistic celebration is not encouraged. The term "community" does not necessarily mean "parish congregation." For some sacramental rites, community could mean a smaller assembly.

56. The text is based on the encyclical *Summi pontificatus* of Pius XII, see *AAS* 31 (1939), 428ff.

57. Kloppenburg, op. cit., p. 264; Kloppenburg's list, *The Ecclesiology of Vatican II*, 263–64, is more extensive.

58. See e.g., G. Magnani, "Does the So-Called Theology of the Laity Possess a Theological Status?" *Vatican II: Assessment and Perspectives*, ed. R. Latourelle (New York: Paulist, 1988), 568–633.

59. See Jeffrey Gros, "Ecumenism," in Komonchak et al., *The New Dictionary of Theology*, 316–22, for an overview of contemporary Roman Catholic positions on ecumenism.

60. Grillmeier, "Dogmatic Constitution on the Church, Chapter I," 150.

61. Ibid., 150. Gérard Philips, *La Chiesa e il suo Mistero*, 108, says the same thing as Grillmeier on the understanding of the church as both mystery and yet existing here on earth "in forma concreta e tangibile." On the issue of the term "Roman," Philips agrees with Grillmeier, noting that Vatican II makes a statement which differs from the statement in the Council of Trent, 111 (see Denzinger-Schönmetzer, Enchiridion Symbolorum, Definitionum, Declarationum, 32nd ed. [Freiburg im B: Herder, 1963, 999 (1868)]). (Hereafter *Denz.*)

62. Grillmeier, "Dogmatic Constitution on the Church, Chapter I," 150.

63. Cited in Grillmeier, "Dogmatic Constitution on the Church, Chapter I," 150, no. 29. The proposed but unaccepted Latin text reads: "Haec igitur Ecclesia, vere omnium Mater et Magistra, in hoc mundo ut societas constituta et ordinata, est Ecclesia Catholica, a Romano Pontifice et Episcopis in eius communione directa."

64. Ibid. See Philips, *La Chiesa e il suo Mistero*, 111. For this entire issue, consult F. A. Sullivan, *Salvation outside the Church?* (New York: Paulist, 1992).

65. Chupungco, *Liturgies of the Future,* 122–23.

66. The lack of independence on the part of national conferences or regional conferences of bishops in many ways makes these conferences almost a gathering of "vicars" of the pope, a view of episcopacy that runs counter to the main theology on episcopacy as found in the documents of Vatican II.

67. See Juan Luis Segundo, *The Sacraments Today* (Maryknoll, N.Y.: Orbis Books, 1974), 3–41.

68. For historical details, see Alfred T. Hennelly, *Liberation Theology: A Documentary History* (Maryknoll, N.Y.: Orbis Books, 1990).

69. Perhaps the comment by Roger Haight, that "the Second Vatican Council, in particular its Pastoral Constitution on the Church in the Modern World, *Gaudium et Spes,* opened the way for what would become liberation theology," needs to be modified. Vatican II reflected liberation theology, but that it opened the way for what became liberation theology is too facile a statement. See R. Haight, "Liberation Theology," in Komonchak et al., *The New Dictionary of Theology,* 571.

70. In the United States the Civil Rights Movement took place in all its intensity during the 1960s. This movement helped not only the United States but the entire world come to grips, at least in some inchoative way, with the issues of racism and marginalization. Black Theology, as James H. Cone called it, is clearly another form of liberation theology, just as feminist theology is a form of liberation theology.

71. Jon Sobrino, *Jesucristo liberador: Lectura histórica-telóg-ica de Jesús de Nazaret* (Madrid: Editorial Trotta, 1991). Eng. trans. by Paul Barns and Francis McDonagh, *Jesus the Liberator* (Maryknoll, N.Y.: Orbis Books 1993), 79–82.

72. For a standard Roman Catholic view of *locus theologicus,* see Miguel Nicolau, "Introductio in Theologiam," *Sacrae Theologiae Summa* (Madrid: BAC, 1962), v. I: 21. One can find a similar explanation in almost all the manuals of theology in use prior to Vatican II. The name, *loci theologici,* is derived from the treatise by Agricola, *De inventione dialectica,* in which the author expounded on the various *loci dialectici.* The phrase was later used in theology as *loci theologici,*

which means that these are the fountains of theological thought. The classical work on these theological sources is that of Melchior Cano (1509–60), *De locis theologicis*. There is a long history to this technical phrase in Roman Catholic theology, and Sobrino's use of this phrase for the poor is indeed a radical step.

73. The citation of Benedict XV is taken from Erwin Iserloh, "History of the Ecumenical Movement," *History of the Church, the Church in the Modern Age*, trans. Anselm Biggs (New York: Crossroad, 1981), 10:466.

74. For a listing and discussion of these passages from the magisterium on the freedom, equality, and dignity of every human being and every Christian, see Osborne, *Ministry: Lay Ministry in the Roman Catholic Church*, 581–86.

75. Ferdinand Klostermann, "The Laity," in *Commentary on the Documents of Vatican II*, 1:239.

76. See Rosemary Radford Reuther, "Feminist Theology," in Komonchak et al., *The New Dictionary of Theology*, 391.

77. Almost concomitantly with twentieth-century Christian feminism, there was and is a feminist movement in politics and society with such well-known people as Betty Friedan. This social and political movement influenced the Christian feminist movement and vice versa.

78. Chupungco, *Liturgies of the Future*, 192–93; see also O. Nußbaum, *Sonntäglicher Gemeindegottesdienst ohne Priester. Liturgische und pastorale Überlegungen* (Würzburg, 1985); P.-A. Liége, "Accompagnement ecclésiologique pour les assemblées dominicales sans célébration eucharistique," *La Maison-Dieu* 130 (1977), 114–28. More recently from the Congregation for Divine Worship, *Directory for Sunday Celebrations in the Absence of a Priest* (Vatican City, 1988).

79. See also Paul VI, *Ad Pascendum* (Vatican City, 1972).

80. See USCC, *The Deacon, Minister of Word and Sacrament*, (Washington, D.C.: USCC, 1979); *Permanent Deacons in the United States* (Washington, D.C.: NCCB, 1984); T. Kraus, *The Order of Deacons: A Second Look* (Hayward, Calif.: Folger Graphics, 1997).

81. On the issue of the permanent deacons, see James M. Barnett, *The Diaconate: A Full and Equal Order; NCCB, Foundations for the Renewal of the Diaconate* (Washington, D.C.: USCC, 1993); K. Osborne, *The Diaconate in the Christian Church: Its History and*

Theology (Chicago: NADD, 1996). P. McCaslin and M. G. Lawler, *Sacrament of Service* (New York: Paulist, 1986). The Vatican has issued *Ratio Fundamentalis Institutionis Diaconalis* (1997).

82. Cardinal Hickey, for example, made the *Catechism* the standard for all theological and religious education and formation in the Archdiocese of Washington D.C.

83. John Paul II, "Letter to Cardinal Ratzinger," *L'Osservatore Romano*, April 18, 1988, 2.

84. Ibid.

85. Karl Rahner, *The Church and the Sacraments* (Freiburg: Herder, 1963); idem, "Zur Theologie des Symbols," *Schriften zur Theologie* (Einsiedeln: Benziger, 1964), 4:275–311.

86. See Schillebeeckx, *Christ the Sacrament of the Encounter with God;* and idem, *The Eucharist* (London: Sheed and Ward, 1968).

87. Louis-Marie Chauvet, *Symbole et Sacrement: Une relecture sacramentelle de l'existence chrétienne* (Paris: Les Éditions du Cerf, 1987). Eng. trans. by P. Madigan and M. Beaumont, *Symbol and Sacrament: A Sacramental Reinterpretation of Christian Existence* (Collegeville, Minn.: The Liturgical Press, 1995).

88. David Power, *Unsearchable Riches: The Symbolic Nature of Liturgy* (New York: Pueblo, 1984).

89. Regis Duffy, *Real Presence: Worship, Sacraments and Commitment* (San Francisco: Harper & Row, 1982); idem, *An American Emmaus: Faith and Sacrament in the American Culture* (New York: Crossroad, 1995).

90. Robert Sokolowski, *Eucharistic Presence: A Study in the Theology of Disclosure*, (Washington, D.C.: The Catholic University of America Press, 1994).

91. Bernard Lee, *The Becoming of the Church* (New York: Paulist, 1974); idem, *Religious Experience and Process Theology* (New York: Paulist, 1976).

92. Edward Kilmartin, "A Modern Approach to the Word of God and Sacraments of Christ: Perspectives and Principles," in *The Sacraments: God's Love and Mercy Actualized,* ed. F. A. Eigo (Villanova, Pa.: The Villanova University Press, 1979), 59–109; idem, "Theology of the Sacraments: Toward a New Understanding of the Chief Rites of the Church of Jesus Christ," *Alternative Futures for Worship*, ed. R. Duffy (Collegeville, Minn.: The Liturgical Press, 1987), 1:123–75.

93. P. Lakeland, *Postmodernity: Christian Identity in a Fragmented Age* (Minneapolis, Minn.: Fortress Press, 1997).

94. Aylward Shorter, *Toward a Theology of Inculturation* (Maryknoll, N.Y.: Orbis Books, 1994), 194.

95. Regis Duffy, "Sacraments," *Systematic Theology* (Minneapolis, Minn.: Fortress Press, 1991), 2:205ff.

2. Methodology and the Point of Departure

1. G. van der Leeuw, *Sakramentstheologie* (G. F. Callenback, 1949), 219.

2. See Ulrich Kuhn, *Sakramente* (Gütersloh: G. Mohn, 1985); Eberhardt Jüngel and Karl Rahner, *Was ist ein Sacrament? Verstöße zur Verständigung* (Freiburg: Herder, 1971).

3. See *Baptism, Eucharist, and Ministry* (Geneva: WCC, 1982).

4. The Greek in Matthew is generally translated as "whatever you bind on earth." For a condensed overview of the current New Testament scholarship on these three passages, see K. Osborne, *Reconciliation and Justification* (New York: Paulist, 1990), 17–24. R. Brown, B. Rigaux, and A. Nocent have compiled the judgments of the best contemporary Protestant and Roman Catholic biblical scholars on these passages.

5. See P. Adnés, *La Penitencia* (Madrid: BAC, 1981), 36–47.

6. For consideration of various biblical texts and their analyses regarding the relative sacramental reference, consult the best New Testament commentaries and study first what biblical scholars, not systematic scholars, say about the text and the context of each pericope.

7. Examples of this method can be found in Jospeh A. de Aldama, "Theoria generalis sacramentorum," *Sacrae Theologiae Summa*, 4:12 ff. In the first chapter Aldama presents the "existence of sacraments," and in the second chapter he presents the "essence of sacraments," which includes such well-known issues as matter/form, sacramental causality, sacramental character, the valid minister of a sacrament, the valid recipient of a sacrament, the institution of the sacraments by Christ. One finds a similar point of departure in E. Doronzo, *De sacramentis in genere* (Milwaukee: Bruce, 1946).

8. The term "onto-theological" is used extensively by Chauvet. It requires considerable space to explain its meaning in any full way, and this will be done in the various chapters that follow. For now, the

"onto" refers generally to the way in which being was understood philosophically by both Plato and Aristotle and to the way in which this same philosophical understanding of being came to be such a radical foundation of scholastic and neo-scholastic theology. There is also a connection to its use in Heidegger, but I would not want to suggest that postmodern thinkers agree with Heidegger on his interpretation of the ontological.

9. K. Rahner says the same thing: "The grace of God no longer comes (when it comes) steeply down from on high, from a God absolutely transcending the world, and in a manner that is without history, purely episodic; it is permanently in the world in tangible, historical form, established in the flesh of Christ as part of the world, of humanity and of its very history" (*The Church and the Sacraments,* 15–16).

10. *Catechism of the Catholic Church,* nos. 1076–1209.

11. Ibid., nos. 1210–1690.

12. See Segundo, *The Sacraments Today,* esp. 68 75.

13. For texts and analysis of this issue, see Osborne, *Priesthood,* 30–31, 89–111.

14. In the *Didache* the prophets are called the successors to the apostles. In Ignatius of Antioch the *presbyteroi* are presented as the successors to the apostles. In Irenaeus both the *episkopoi* and the *presbyteroi* are viewed as the successors to the apostles. *The Letter of Clement,* Polycarp's *Letter to the Philippians,* *Shepherd of Hermas,* *Letter of Barnabas,* and the writings of Justin are silent on the matter.

15. Luke connects the twelve and the apostles, but throughout the New Testament he is alone in this matter. On the issue of apostle and the twelve in the New Testament, see Hans Dieter Betz, "Apostle," *Anchor Bible Dictionary* (New York: Doubleday, 1992), 1.309–11, Raymond Collings, "The Twelve," *Anchor Bible Dictionary,* D. N. Freedman, ed (New York: Doubleday, 1992) 6:670-71; also Raymond Brown, "The Twelve and the Apostolate," in *The New Jerome Biblical Commentary,* ed. R. Brown, J. Fitzmyer, R. Murphy (Englewood Cliffs, N.J.: Prentice Hall, 1990), 1377–81.

16. As far as neo-scholastic Roman Catholic theologians prior to Vatican II are concerned, let Joachim Salaverri be the spokesman, since his essay appeared just prior to Vatican II. His thesis is stated as follows: "Apostolis in ordinario eorum munere iure divino succedunt Episcopi,

quorum singuli Ecclesiis particularibus singulis praesunt" ("De Ecclesia Christi," *Sacrae Theologiae Summa,* 1:601). [By divine right the bishops, each of whom presides over particular individual churches, succeed to the Apostles in their ordinary duties]. For the *valor dogmaticus* of this thesis Salaverri says that the thesis is *theologically certain* [*theologice certum*] when it states that the bishops exercise their power of ordination and jurisdiction by divine right [*iure divino*]. It is only *catholic doctrine* [*doctrina catholica*] when the thesis states that bishops succeed to the apostles. The first two parts of his thesis are clearly connected to the theological issue which from the Middle Ages down to Vatican II was strongly debated by theologians, namely: Is episcopacy part of the sacrament of order, or only an office and dignity delegated by the pope? When Salaverri was writing his essay the debate was still going on. Because of this debate both sections of the first part of his thesis are simply theologically certain and catholic doctrine. When he moves to the issue of bishops as successors of the apostles his basis is the following: an interpretation of Matthew 28:18; Mark 16:15; Acts 1:8; and John 21:19. Today, his interpretation would appear more as eisegesis than exegesis. Research by contemporary scripture scholars on the sections of 1 Timothy and Titus, which Salaverri also cites, would not substantiate his interpretation of these verses.

17. A similar *post factum* superimposition of a theological rationale is the "soldier of Christ" motif superimposed onto the sacrament of confirmation, a superimposition that took place in the tenth century and subsequently became popular.

18. See Paul McPartlan, *The Eucharist Makes the Church: Henri de Lubac and John Zizioulas in Dialogue* (Edinburgh: T&T Clark, 1993).

19. Chauvet, *Symbol and Sacrament,* 321–22.

20. Duffy, "Sacraments," *Systematic Theology,* 205–8.

21. Ibid., 205.

22. Ibid.

23. Ibid.

24. E. Kilmartin,"Theology of the Sacraments: Toward a New Understanding of the the Chief Rites of the Church of Jesus Christ," *Alternative Futures for Worship,* vol 1, *General Introduction,* 123–75, esp. 157–61.

25. Ibid., 158.

26. Ibid.

27. Ibid., 159. Kilmartin immediately goes on to mention that this in turn accounts for "the insensitivity of the fathers of the Council of Trent towards the objection of a minority group of theologians, who petitioned that the first canon of the *Decree on the Sacraments* not simply condemn the opinon that denies the sacraments of the new law are 'more or less than seven.' Obviously these theologians agreed that the sacraments are seven in number, but they wanted to include the notion that the concept of sacrament extends beyond the seven chief rites of the church." Kilmartin adds that these theologians saw the ritual sacraments as actions of the church, which could then itself be called a sacrament, but Kilmartin's conclusion perhaps oversteps a reading of the mind of the bishops at Trent, since there is little evidence that at that period of time the church itself was considered a sacrament.

28. Regis Duffy, *An American Emmaus: Faith and Sacrament in the American Culture*, 9–32.

29. See, for example, Zachary Hayes, *The Hidden Center: Spirituality and Speculative Christology in St. Bonaventure* (St. Bonaventure, N.Y.: The Franciscan Institute, 1992); see also Ambroise Nguyen Van Si, *La théologie du l'imitation du Christ d'après saint Bonaventure* (Rome: Edizioni Antonianum, 1991), Eng. trans by E. Hagman, *The Theology of the Imitation of Christ According to St. Bonaventure* (New York: Franciscan Institute, 1997).

30. Chauvet, *Symbol and Sacrament,* 551.

31. Ibid., 552.

32. See Rahner, *The Church and the Sacraments,* 76–117.

33. See Schillebeeckx, *Christ the Sacrament of the Encounter with God,* 91–152.

3. Sacramental Structures in the World at Large

1. Gary B. Madison, "Hermeneutics: Gadamer and Ricoeur," in Kearney, *Continental Philosophy in the Twentieth Century*, 8:297–98. Richard Kearney, in the introduction to this volume, seconds the radicalness of this clarion call by Husserl, naming it a "fundamental rethinking of the western intellectual tradition," 8:4. Ricoeur, Gadamer, Merleau-Ponty, Adorno, Derrida, and other postmodern thinkers can be added.

2. The term "desconstruction" in Derrida's writing is not easily understood. Derrida writes: "Within the closure, by an oblique and always perilous movement, constantly risking falling back within what is being deconstructed, it is necessary to surround the critical concepts with a careful and throrough discourse...to designate rigorously the intimate relationship to the machine whose deconstruction they permit; and, in the same process, to designate the crevice through which the unnameable glimmer beyond the closure of our epoch can be glimpsed" (Derrida, *De la grammatologie* [Paris: Éditions de Minuit, 1967]. Eng. trans. by G. C. Spivak, *Of Grammatology* [Baltimore: Johns Hopkins University Press, 1975], 14).

3. In this essay I am using "hermeneutical" most often from an epistemological base, and I am using "onto-hermeneutical" most often to indicate that the issues are not simply epistemological but are also concerned with reality. I am aware that the issue of "being" as used by Heidegger is questioned by many postmodern philosophers. Thus, my use of "onto" should also be understood in the widest possible ambit, and its focus should be seen as a move beyond the epistemological framework of the Enlightenment and the subsequent technological, scientific thought patterns of our contemporary world.

4. For the majority of the world population—59.4 percent in Asia and 12.7 percent in Africa—Western epistemology and ontology in no way reflect the various Asian and African forms of hermeneutics and onto-hermeneutics. This in itself indicates that Western ways of thinking and Western views of an "objective" world are demographically limited. When one adds to this large population of Asia and Africa the continued growth of what one might call postmodernist thought in Europe and in the Americas, then the challenge to the traditional Western mode of thinking becomes formidable. Consequently, when one begins to speak about sacraments within a global context, it is clear that the hermeneutical ease that church leaders and theologians in Europe and North America use on the issue of sacrament is indicative that these very leaders have clearly missed the signs of the times.

5. See Michel Foucault, *Le Mots et les choses* (Paris: Éditions Galimard, 1966). Eng. trans. *The Order of Things: An Archeology of the Human Sciences* (New York: Vintage, 1970). In chapter 2, "The Prose of the World," Foucault draws together the *episteme* of the sixteenth century in two sections, one on the four similitudes and one on

the signatures (17–30), and he then states: "Such, sketched in its most general aspects, is the sixteenth-century *epistemé*" (32) and "In an *epistemé* in which signs and similitudes were wrapped around one another in an endless sprial, it was essential that the relation of microcosm to macrocosm should be conceived as both the guarantee of that knowledge and the limit of its expansion" (32). Foucault shows how this *epistemé* comes to an end with the classical period's own *epistemé*, and how today we move into a different *epistemé*. Other pages that have entered into this paraphrase are xx–xxiv, 16, 29, 54–56, 64, 74, 120, 162, 244–48, and 337.

6. For the meaning of event, *Ereignis*, as used in this book, see David Tracy, "A Theological View of Philosophy: Revelation and Reason," *That Others May Know and Love: Essays in Honor of Zachary Hayes, O.F.M.* (St. Bonaventure, N.Y.: Franciscan Institute Publications, 1997), 198–204. Tracy is clearly indebted to Heidegger on this issue.

7. I use baptism and eucharist as examples, since within the Church Catholic these two ritualized sacraments have more extensive acceptability. However, from a Roman Catholic viewpoint, any of the seven ritualized sacraments might also be used as examples of sacramental *Haecceitas* (thisness).

8. P. Ricoeur, "Herméneutique et critique des idéologies," in *Démythisation et idéologie*, ed. Enrico Castelli, 25–64 (Paris: Aubier Montaigne, 1973). For an English translation of this essay, see P. Ricoeur, "Hermeneutics and the Critique of Ideology," *Hermeneutics and the Human Sciences*, ed. John B. Thompson (Cambridge: Cambridge University Press, 1981), esp. 75–76. In this essay Ricoeur is critiquing H. G. Gadamer.

9. Frederic R. McManus, "Book IV: The Office of Sanctifying in the Church," *The Code of Canon Law: A Text and Commentary*, ed. J. Corriden, T. Green, and D. Heintschel (New York: Paulist, 1985), 595.

10. Ibid., 595, also 594.

11. McManus alludes to a contemporary openness to adaptation and cultural integration. However, Aylward Shorter notes: "The ardent desire for liturgical inculturation—a new liturgical creation—has to compete with the view of liturgy as a field for the exercise of hierarchical power" (*Toward a Theology of Inculturation* [Maryknoll, NY, Orbis, 1988], 196). In contemporary official Roman Catholic documents on

liturgical inculturation of the sacraments the term "sacrament" is used with hermeneutical ease, and this distracts from the struggle that Shorter alludes to: liturgical changes have become in actuality not instances of intercultural adaptation, but rather instances of authority and power.

12. Kearney, in *Continental Philosophy in the Twentieth Century*, 8:4.

13. Jürgen Habermas, *Logik der Sozialwissenschaften* (Frankfurt: Suhrkamp, 1967), esp. "Zu Gadamer's *Wahrheit und Methode*," 251–90. Habermas develops this same theme in *Der philosophische Diskurs der Moderne* (Frankfurt a. M.: Suhrkamp, 1985). Eng. trans. by F. Lawrence, *The Philosophical Discourse of Modernity* (Cambridge, Mass.: The MIT University Press, 1987). For a brief bibliographical overview of this argument of Habermas and Gadamer, see Ricoeur, *Hermeneutics and the Human Sciences*, 299.

14. Ricoeur, "Hermeneutics and the Critique of Ideology," 64.

15. Ibid., 64–65. Ricoeur refers the reader to Heidegger's *Being and Time*, in which Heidegger accumulates many words that have the prefix *Vor* (*Vorhabe, Vorsicht, Vorgriff*, etc.), and proceeds to found the hermeneutical circle of the human sciences in a structure of anticipation that is part of the structure of *Dasein* (*Sein und Zeit* [Tübingen: Neomarius Verlag, 1953]. Eng. trans. by J. Macquarrie and E. Robinson, *Being and Time* [New York: Harper & Row, 1962], pp. 188–95).

16. Hans Georg Gadamer, *Wahrheit und Methode* (Tübingen: J.C.B. Mohr, 1965), 264ff. Eng. trans. by Garrett Barden and John Cummings, *Truth and Method* (New York: Seabury Press, 1975). On this same issue Ricoeur offers his critique of the solution that Habermas proposes and his reconstruction of the question in "Hermeneutics and the Critique of Ideology," 95–100.

17. The *Catechism of the Catholic Church* shies away from the theological position that the church is a sacrament in the sense of Rahner and Schillebeeckx when it states in no. 774: "It is in this analogical sense, that the church is called a 'sacrament.'" The authors of the *Catechism* did not want to see the church as sacrament in the same way that the ritual sacraments are sacrament. The church is only analogically sacrament, but the primary analogue throughout the *Catechism* remains the ritual sacrament. Rahner, Schillebeeckx, and others see the church as a primary analogue and the ritual sacraments as derivative from this "root" or basic sacrament. These theologians also

see Jesus' humanness as the primordial sacrament and therefore the *foundational analogue* for all sacramentality.

18. See A. von Harnack, *Das Wesen des Christentums* (Leipzig: J. C. Hinrichs, 1901). The subsequent debate on the absoluteness of Christianity progressed throughout the entire twentieth century.

19. Louis-Marie Chauvet, *Symbol and Sacrament,* 554; French original, 565: "Le 'profane' du monde et de l'histoire est ainsi reconnu comme le *lieu sacramentel possible* d'une histoire sainte."

20. The term "Father" is noninclusive and has been challenged by feminist theology. In this section I wish to present the argument of the *Catechism* as faithfully as I can, since it is the thought of the *Catechism* that substantiates the position on primordiality. The exclusivity of the language is not central to the argument, but a deviation or changing of the language might make my own argument less forceful.

21. In these passages from the *Catechism* I have added the emphases.

22. The presence of the Logos in sacramental celebration is reminiscent of the theology of the Eastern churches, but no mention of this relationship is made in the *Catechism* itself.

23. Heidegger, *Being and Time,* 277–78.

24. Friedrich Ast, *Grundlinien der Grammatik, Hermeneutik und Kritik* (Landshut, 1808), 165. Eng. trans. in *The Hermeneutic Tradition: From Ast to Ricoeur,* ed. Gayle Ormiston and Alan Schrift (New York: State University of New York Press, 1990), 39.

25. Karl Rahner remains thoroughly Thomist when he states that the human mind is open to all being and includes in this the possibility of revelation of Being itself, *esse ipsum.* The view on mind that Ast presents in this citation and the view on mind transcendental Thomists present have similarities. This is one of the reasons why, in my judgment, transcendental Thomism as a bridge to postmodern thought remains inadequate. The pan-opticon-image of J. Bentham appears in the writings of both Foucault and Habermas.

26. Heidegger, *Being and Time,* 65. It should be noted that Heidegger clearly eliminates from this understanding of Being and *Dasein* anything earlier metaphysics in the West had called God, *esse ipsum.*

27. Ibid., 67, note 1

28. The comparison of Husserl and Heidegger is based on the

analysis of Heidegger presented by Jacques Taminiaux, a director of the *Centre d'études phénomémologiques* at Louvain. See "Philosophy of Existence I: Heidegger," in Kearney, *Continental Philosophy in the Twentieth Century*, 8:38–73, esp. 39–47.

29. Heidegger, *Phänomenologische Interpretationen zu Aristoteles*, *Gesamtausgabe*, ed. W. Bröcker and K. Bröcker-Oltmanns (Frankfurt: Klostermann, 1985), 61:17: "The complete intentionality (the relatedness to, that towards which there is a relation, the accomplishment of the self-relating, the temporalism of it, the preservation of temporalisation) is nothing but the intentionality of the object which has the ontological character of factical life. Intentionality, merely taken as relatedness to, is the first phenomenal character, proximally noticeable of the fundamental mobility of life, that is of care." Cited in Taminiaux, "Philosophy of Existence I: Heidegger," 40–41.

30. See Taminiaux, "Philosophy of Existence I: Heidegger," 42.

31. In Schillebeeckx's volume *The Eucharist* (New York: Sheed and Ward, 1968), there is a section entitled "A New Approach Towards the Formulation of Faith," 89–150, in which Schillebeeckx presents this fundamental step from an Aristotelian framework (his first chapter on the Council of Trent) to the contemporary phenomenological understanding (see esp. 107–21).

32. Heidegger, *Being and Time*, 154.

33. This way of thinking has at least some ties with Asian ways of human self-understanding. See, for example, Fung Yu-lan, *A History of Chinese Philosophy,* 2 vols. (Princeton, N.J.: Princeton University Press, 1952–53); Wing-tsit Chan, *A Source Book in Chinese Philosophy* (Princeton, N.J.: Princeton University Press, 1973).

34. Maurice Merleau-Ponty, *Phénoménologie de la perception* (Paris: Gallimard, 1945). Eng. trans. by Colin Smith, *Phenomenology of Perception* (London: Routledge & Kegan Paul, 1962), 54. Merleau-Ponty immediately adds, however, the following: "The tacit assumption of perception is that at every instant experience can be co-ordinated with that of the previous instant and that of the following, and my perspective with that of other consciousnesses—that all contradictions can be removed, that monadic and intersubjective experience is one unbroken text—that what is now indeterminate for me could become determinate for a more complete knowledge, which is as it were realized in advance in the thing, or rather which is the thing itself."

35. Ibid., 60.

36. Ibid., vii.

37. Ibid., 61.

38. Ibid., 70.

39. Ibid., 150: "But I am not in front of my body, I am in it, or rather I am it."

40. Ibid., 196.

41. Merleau-Ponty, "Le Primat de la perception et ses conséquences philosophiques," *Bulletin de la Société Française de Philosophie* 41 (1947), 119–35. Eng. trans. by James Edie, "The Primacy of Perception and Its Philosophical Consequences," in *The Primacy of Perception and Other Essays* (Evanston, Ill.: Northwestern University Press, 1964), 17.

42. Allan B. Wolter, *Duns Scotus' Early Oxford Lecture on Individuation* (Santa Barbara, Calif.: Old Mission Santa Barbara, 1992), xxvii. Wolter immediately adds: "His remark is in answer to an objection that individuals do not pertain to the order of the universe, for order is based on priority and posteriority, and individuals are all on a par with one another. Not only do individuals pertain to the order of God's universe, Scotus replies, but in communicating his good as something befitting his beauty in each species, he delights in producing a multiplicity of individuals. And in those beings which are the highest and most important, it is the individual that is primarily intended by God. Viewed from this aspect, Scotus' doctrine of thisness applied to the human person would seem to invest each with a unique value as one singularly wanted and loved by God, quite apart from any trait that person shares with others or any contribution he or she might make to society." Cf. the involved historical dimension of this issue of individuation in Gordon Wilson, "The Presence of Henry of Ghent in Scotus's *Quaestiones super libros metaphysicorum*," in *John Duns Scotus: Metaphysics and Ethics*, ed. Ludger Honnefelder, Rega Wood, and Mechthild Dreyer, 114–16 (Leiden: E. J. Brill, 1996). In the same volume, see Jorge J. E. Gracia, "Individuality and the Individuating Entity in Scotus's *Ordinatio*: An Ontological Characterization," 229–49. Gracia cites Scotus: "The singular is not definable by a definition other than the definition of the species, although it is *per se* a being, adding an entity to the entity of the species. But the *per se* entity it adds is not a quidditative entity (Scotus, *Ord.* II, d. 3, p. 1, q. 6, n. 192, Vat. 7: 486)" (243).

43. Rega Wood, "Individual Forms: Richard Rufus and John Duns Scotus," in Honnefelder, Wood, and Dreyer, *John Duns Scotus: Metaphysics and Ethics*, 271.

44. Heidegger, *Being and Time*, 58.

45. Ibid., 56–57.

46. Ricoeur, "Consciousness and the Unconscious," *The Conflict of Interpretations*. Eng. trans. by Willis Domingo (Evanston, Ill.: Northwestern University Press, 1974), 120.

47. On this issue, see especially Ricoeur, "Psychoanalysis and the Movement of Contemporary Culture," *The Conflict of Interpretations*, 148.

48. Ricoeur, "Heidegger and the Question of the Subject," *The Conflict of Interpretations*, 237.

49. See ibid., 238: "The result of this is that consciousness itself becomes a symptom and thus only one system among others, namely, the perceptual system which regulates our access to reality. Certainly consciousness is not nothing;…It is at least the place of all the effects of meaning, the data to which the analysis is applied. But consciousness is not the principle, nor the judge, nor the measure of all things; and this is the challenge that counts for a philosophy of the *cogito*.

50. On the principle of sacramentality see Kenan B. Osborne, "Ministry as Sacrament," *Ecclesia, Leiturgia, Ministerium* (Helsinki: Loimann Kirjapaino, 1977), esp. 111–17.

4. Jesus and Primordiality

1. By "church," Roman Catholic authors most often mean the Roman Catholic Church, but the Christian Catholic Church is much larger than the Roman Catholic Church. The Roman Catholic Church clearly calls the Orthodox churches "church," and in the post–Vatican II period official church documents also call Anglican and Protestant churches "church" rather than "ecclesial communities," which was the preferred title in Vatican II documents.

2. Otto Semmelroth, *Die Kirche als Ursakrament*; Karl Rahner, *The Church and the Sacraments*; E. Schillebeeckx, *Christ the Sacrament of the Encounter with God*.

3. See *Im Dialog der Wahrheit, Documentation des römisch-katholisch-orthodoxen Theologischen Dialogs XLI, Pro Oriente*, ed.

Theodor Piffl-Percevic and Alfred Stirnemann (Innsbruck: Tyrolia Verlag, 1990), 12:29, 70, 95.

4. See E. Jüngel, "Die Kirche als Sakrament," *Zeitschrift für Theologie und Kirche* 80 (1982), 432–57.

5. Rahner, *The Church and the Sacraments*, 15–16.

6. Ibid., 18.

7. In this passage Rahner seems to contradict his main intention, for although he calls the church the fundamental sacrament and the wellspring of the sacraments, the sacraments that come from this foundation and this wellspring are then called "sacraments in the strict sense." If a foundational sacrament is the basis from which other sacraments are derived, then it is difficult to call the derived sacraments "sacraments in the strict sense." Rahner usually operates from the viewpoint that the church as foundational sacrament is the primary analogue for the ritual sacraments; Jesus as the primordial sacrament is the primary analogue for both the church and the ritualized sacraments.

8. Rahner, *The Church and the Sacraments*, 38.

9. Schillebeeckx, *Christ the Sacrament of the Encounter with God,* 13: "The dogmatic definition of Chalcedon, according to which Christ is 'one person in two natures,' implies that one and the same person, the Son of God, also took on a visible human form. Even in his humanity Christ is the Son of God. The second person of the most holy Trinity is personally man; and this man is personally God."

10. Ibid., 15.

11. Chauvet, *Symbol and Sacrament,* 453.

12. Ibid., 460.

13. Ibid., 466–67.

14. Ibid., 459.

15. Ibid., 465.

16. Ibid., 461.

17. Ibid., 491.

18. Raphael Schulte, "Die Enzelsakramente als Ausgliederung des Wurzelsakraments," *Mysterium Salutis* (Einsiedeln: Benziger, 1973), vol. IV/2, ed. J. Feiner and M. Löhrer, 46–155.

19. See the "Einleitung" by the editors in *Mysterium Salutis*, vol. IV/1, 18: "[Damit sollte] das Übergewicht in etwa korrigiert werden, das der herkömmliche Sakramententraktat im Gesamtaufbau der Dogmatik eingenommenen hat."

20. See Semmelroth, "Die Kirche als Sakrament des Heils," *Mysterium Salutis*, IV/1, 309–56. In this essay, Semmelroth studies the meaning and use of the phrase "the church as sacrament" and in particular "Kirche als Wurzelsakrament," 319–48.

21. Schulte, "Die Enzelsakramente als Ausgliederung des Wurzelsakraments," 47: "Wir haben hier gerade jene Ausführung im 4. Kapitel genau zu berücksichtigen, ja sie noch zu ergänzen, die von dem (nur) *analogen* Charakter des Begriffs 'Sakrament' sprechen, wenn dieser sinnvoll auf Christus, auf die Kirche und dann auch auf die speziell 'Sakramente' gennanten (und vielleicht auf noch andere) Vollzüge des Lebens der Kirche angewendet wird."

22. Ibid., 53. The German text reads: "Wenn Jesus Christus als Ur-Sakrament unseres Heils bezeichnet wird, so ist ja tatsäschlich an ihn persönlich gedacht, in seiner die göttliche und menschliche Natur vereinenden Person, im Sinne der andernorts erklärten hypostatischen Union, und sein Heilswerken für uns."

23. Semmelroth, op. cit. #20 above, 320.

24. Schulte, op. cit. #21 and #22 above, "Die Enzelsakramente als Ausgliederung des Wurzelsakraments," 53, "Von *einen* (Gott-) Menschen Jesus Christus als dem Ur-Sakrament des Heils her gesehen, ist die Kirche *Wurzelsakrament in Partizipation* am Sein ihres Hauptes und Herrn *derart*, daß sie eben nicht eine *andere* Person neben oder unter Christus darstellt, sondern eben das, was hier Leib Christi oder Volk Gottes meint: die (freilich als Mysterium zu begreifende) Gemeindschaft vieler Personen als Glieder dieser Kirche, die selbst *mit* Christus *zusammen* ihre Lebens-Aufgabe zu erfüllen hat, die Weiter-Verwikrlichung des vom Herrn (schon) Verwirklichten."

25. Ibid., 56: "Zu diesem Zweck kann man das Sakrament christlichen Verständnisses vorläufig, ohne daß dabei schon *alle* seine Wesensmomente auszusprechen wären, folgendermaßen umschreiben: Bei den Sakramenten handelt es sich um ein zwischenpersonales, unter zeichenhafter Verwendung von Dingen, Symbolen, Gesten und Worten vollzogenes personal-ekklesiales Geschehen, in welchem die innere Gesinnung der Beteiligten so manifest und bekundet wird, daß die verwendeten Media den in ihnen zum Ausdruck gebrachten Willens- (und Herzens-) Entschluß auch personallebens-bedeutsam sich auswirken lassen."

26. Ibid., 57.

27. In transcendental Thomism the mind is open to being in whatever aspect being might have. This is not what postmodern thinkers are talking about. Human intellection itself is limited to the analysis of *Dasein* (Heidegger); to the primacy of perception (Merleau-Ponty); to the reevaluation of human consciousness itself in virtue of the unconscious, i.e., the separation of the I in I think and the I in I am (Ricoeur, Lacan, Derrida).

28. Theodor W. Adorno and Max Horkheimer, *Dialektik der Aufklärung: Philosophische Fragmente* (Amsterdam, 1947). Eng. trans. by J. Cumming, *Dialectic of Enlightenment* (New York: Seabury, 1972), 83.

29. Gadamer, *Truth and Method*, xxv.

30. Gadamer, "The Problem of Historical Consciousness," *Interpretive Social Science: A Reader*, ed. P. Rainbow and W. M. Sullivan (Berkeley and Los Angeles: University of California Press, 1979), 106.

31. Ricoeur, "Existence and Hermeneutics," *The Conflict of Interpretations*, 19.

32. Gadamer, *Truth and Method*, 258.

33. Ibid., 264.

34. Ibid., 270: "Just as in a conversation, when we have discovered the standpoint and horizon of the other person, his ideas become intelligible, without our necessarily having to agree with him; the person who thinks historically comes to understand the meaning of what has been handed down, without necessarily agreeing with it, or seeing himself in it."

35. See, for example, P. Winch, *The Idea of a Social Science and Its Relation to Philosophy* (London: Routledge & Kegan Paul, 1958).

36. Ricoeur, *Hermeneutics and the Human Sciences*, 75.

37. In this and the following survey I am indebted to Gayle Ormiston and Alan Schrift, eds., *The Hermeneutic Tradition: From Ast to Ricoeur*, 11–35.

38. F. Schleiermacher, *Lecture on Hermeneutics* (1819).

39. Ormiston and Schrift, *The Hermeneutic Tradition*, 15. This refers to the move described above on the change from epistemology to onto-epistemology.

40. Gadamer, *Truth and Method*, 421.

41. Ricoeur, "Heidegger and the Question of the Subject," *The Conflict of Interpretation*, 266: "A hermeneutic philosophy must show how interpretation itself arrives at being-in-the-world. First there is being-in-the-world, then understanding, then interpreting, then saying. The circular character of this itinerary must not stop us. It is indeed true that it is from the heart of language that we say all this; but language is so made that it is able to designate the ground of existence from which it proceeds and to recognize itself as a mode of the being of which it speaks. The circularity between *I speak* and *I am* gives the initiative by turns to the symbolic function and to its instinctual and existential root. But this circle is not a vicious circle; it is the living circle of expression and being expressed."

42. Ricoeur, "The Problem of Double Meaning as Hermeneutic Problem and as Semantic Problem," *The Conflict of Interpretations*, 66.

43. See ibid., 67: "I will venture to summarize this in a few words: the sole philosophical interest in symbolism is that it reveals, by its structure of double meaning, the equivocalness of being.... Symbolism's *raison d'être* is to open the multiplicity of meaning to the equivocalness of being."

44. On the Council of Chalcedon I am indebted to the analysis by Ignacio Ortiz de Urbina, "Das Symbol von Chalkedon: Sein Text, sein Werden, seine dogmatische Bedeutung," *Das Konzil von Chalkedon*, ed. A. Grillmeier and H. Bacht (Würzburg: Echter Verlag, 1951), 1:389–418, esp. 404–10.

45. Rahner, "Christology within an Evolutionary View of the World," *Theological Investigations*, trans. Cornelius Ernst (Baltimore: Helicon Press, 1961), 5:157–92.

46. Ibid., 180: "The theologian...can first of all take note of the fact that the Hypostatic Union takes effect interiorly *for* the human nature of the Logos precisely in what, and really only in what, the same theology prescribes for *all* men as their goal and consummation, viz., the direct vision of God enjoyed by Christ's created human soul."

47. Ibid., 183: "The Hypostatic Union does not differ from our grace by what is pledged in it, for this is grace in both cases (even in the case of Jesus). But it differs from our grace by the fact that Jesus is our pledge, and we ourselves are not the pledge but the recipient of God's pledge to us. But the unity of the pledge, and the inseparability of this

pledge from the one who pledges (indeed, pledges *himself to us!*) must be conceived in accordance with the peculiar nature of the pledge."

48. Merleau-Ponty, "The Primacy of Perception and Its Philosophical Consequences," *The Primacy of Perception and Other Essays*, 16.

49. For the question of the knowledge of Jesus, see Rahner, "Dogmatic Considerations on Knowledge and Consciousness in Christ," *Dogmatic vs. Biblical Theology*, ed. H. Vorgrimler (Baltimore: Helicon, 1964), 241–67; R. Brown, *Jesus God and Man* (Milwaukee: Bruce, 1967); Anton Vögtle, "Exegetische Erwägungen über das Wissen und Selbstbewußtsein Jesu," *Gott in Welt*, H. Grillmeier, ed. (Freiburg: Herder, 1964) 1:608–67.

50. For a theological understanding of person as used in the early church, see A. Grillmeier, "Die theologische und sprachliche Vorbereitung der christologischen Formel von Chalkedon," *Das Konzil von Chalkedon*, 1:5–202; also Ignacio Ortiz de Urbina, "Das Glaubenssymbol von Chalkedon—sein Text, sein Werden, seine dogmatische Bedeutung," *Das Konzil von Chalkedon*, H. Grillmeier and H. Bacht, eds (Würzburg: Erhter-Verlag, 1951) 1:389–418.

51. See P. Schoonenberg, *The Christ* (New York: Herder and Herder, 1971).

52. Heidegger, *Being and Time*, 460. He adds on 463: "The 'there' is disclosed in a way which is grounded in Dasein's own temporality as ecstatically stretched along, and with this disclosure a 'time' is allotted to Dasein; only because of this can Dasein, as factically thrown, 'take' its time and lose it."

53. Heidegger, *Being and Time,* 363. Heidegger speaks this way since critics had accused him of a strange circularity. If one reproaches him on the hermeneutical circle, then that person has failed to see that in his view understanding is a basic part of *Dasein* and that care is constitutive of Being.

54. For the term "tensive," see N. Perrin, *Jesus and the Language of the Kingdom* (Philadelphia, Pa.: Fortress Press, 1976), 31–2.

5. The Church as Foundational Sacrament

1. It is true that the documents of Vatican II cite the passage from St. Cyprian, Epist. 69, 6, but beyond this single source for the use

of sacrament in reference to the church, no other documentation is given, nor is any truly available. This is clearly a twentieth-century description, even though there are a few equivalent passages in other writers of antiquity.

2. Originally, the title suggested for this section of the decree was "On Relations with the Separated Brethren." This was ultimately rejected by the bishops precisely because of the ecclesial character of the Orthodox churches (see Johannes Hoeck, "Decree on the Eastern Catholic Churches," in Vorgrimler, *Commentary on the Documents of Vatican II*, 1:328).

3. Throughout the documents of Vatican II care was taken to use the term "church" only in reference to the Catholic Church. Other Christian communities were deliberately referred to as "ecclesial communities." The non-uniate Eastern churches are nonetheless called "church." One should also note the use of "church" for Eastern churches in the decree on ecumenism, nos. 14, 15, 16, 17, 18.

4. See the statetment of the Secretariat for the Promotion of Christian Unity, *Réunis à Rome*, Feb. 22, 1975, in A. Flannery, ed., *Vatican Council II: More Post-Conciliar Documents* (Northport, N.Y.: Costello, 1982), 156: "the cooperation between churches and ecclesial communions"; "It is through the local church that the Catholic Church is present with many other Christian churches and communities in the same localities" (158). In the Sacred Congregation for the Doctrine of the Faith's statement of April 1981, "Reception of U.S. Episcopalians into the Catholic Church," we read: "In June, 1980, the Holy See, through the Congregation for the Doctrine of the Faith, agreed to the request presented by the Bishops of the United States of America on behalf of some clergy and laity formerly or actually belonging to the Episcopal (Anglican) Church for full communion with the Catholic Church" (186). In these official documents the term "church" is applied to Christian communities not in union with Rome.

5. *The Joint Declaration on Cooperation*, in A. Flannery, ed., *Vatican Council II: The Conciliar and Post-Conciliar Documents* (Collegeville, Minn.: Liturgical Press, 1975), 479.

6. Common Declaration by Pope John Paul II and the Archbishop of Canterbury, Robert Runcie, in A. Flannery, ed., *Vatican Council II: More Post-Conciliar Documents* (Northport, N.Y.: Costello, 1982), 156.

7. One finds a study of these factors in Kloppenburg, *The Ecclesiology of Vatican II*, 22–80. The value of Kloppenburg's presentation is his wide-ranging use of the documents of Vatican II. He clearly indicates that the bishops at Vatican II did not attempt to make any large-scaled explanation for these various uses of "church."

8. Semmelroth, "The Eschatological Nature of the Pilgrim Church and Her Union with the Heavenly Church," in Vorgrimler, *Commentary on the Documents of Vatican II*, 1:280–84.

9. Ibid., 1:281.

10. See the explicit statements in this regard in the Decree on Ecumenism, *Ad Gentes*, no 1.

11. Tracy, "A Theological View of Philosophy," 198.

12. Ibid., 199.

13. Ibid.: "Hermeneutically, this use of the category 'manifestation' is also…suggestive of the hermeneutical notion of truth as primordially an event of manifestation (or disclosure concealment). The subjective correlate to the objectivity of manifestation is 'recognition.' In an analogous manner, the theological counterpart to the event-gift-grace of revelation as divine self-manifestation is the gift, grace, happening (never 'work' or personal achievement) of faith as reorientation of trust in and loyalty to the God disclosing Godself in the Word, Jesus Christ."

14. Ibid., 202–3.

15. Ibid., 206.

16. Ibid., 202.

17. See *LG*, no 1: "Christ is the light of humanity…proclaiming his gospel to every creature.…[The Church] purposes for the benefit of the faithful and of the whole world, to set forth as clearly as possible…her own nature."

18. Chauvet, *Symbol and Sacrament*, 554 (emphasis added).

19. Mara Rainwater, "Glossary," in Kearney, *Twentieth-Century Continental Philosophy*, 8:508–9.

20. Ibid., 510.

21. Ibid. In using these descriptions of Rainwater, I intend only to present a frame of reference. Descriptions are not definitions, and Rainwater offers more of a historical consideration than a definitive position.

22. Hugh Silverman, "French Structuralism and After: De Saussure, Lévi-Strauss, Barthes, Lacan, Foucault," in Kearney, *Continental Philosophy in the Twentieth Century*, 8:391.

23. Ferdinand de Saussure, *Cours de linguistic générale*. Eng. trans. by R. Harris, *Course in General Linguistics* (La Salle, Ill.: Open Court, 1991), 77. This work of de Saussure was gathered together and published posthumously; see translator's introduction, xii–xiii.

24. Ibid., 81: "But in order to mark this contrast more effectively, and the intersection of two orders of phenomena relating to the same object of study, we shall speak for preference of *synchronic* linguistics and *diachronic* linguistics. Everything is synchronic which relates to the static aspect of our science, and diachronic everything which concerns evolution. Likewise *synchrony* and *diachrony* will designate respectively a linguistic state and a phase of evolution."

25. R. Harris, *Reading Saussure*, (La Salle, Ill.: Open Court, 1991), 220.

26. Ibid.: "The only necessary and sufficient condition for establishing the identity of any individual sign is that it be distinct from other signs. However, this can presumably only be so if the system as a whole is structured in such a way as to allocate to each sign its own unique semiological 'space.' Therefore Saussure accepts that adopting the principle that the linguistic sign is arbitrary forces us to conclude that it can only be the total network of interrelations which establishes individual connections between *significants* and *signifiés*."

27. R. Barthes, *The Pleasure of the Text,* trans. R. Miller (New York: Hill & Wang, 1977), 5.

28. Ibid. These are not the only codes possible, they are merely ones that Barthes mentions, leaving the door open for additional codes.

29. J. Lacan, *Television. A Challenge to the Psychoanalytic Establishment* (New York: Norton, 1992), 107: "At a crucial point of the Cartesian askesis...consciousness and the subject coincide. It is holding that privileged moment as exhaustive of the subject which is misleading....It is, on the contrary, at that moment of coincidence itself, in so far as it is grasped by reflection, that I intend to mark the site through which psychoanalytic experience makes its entrance. At simply being sustained within time, the subject of the 'I think' reveals what it is: the being of a fall. I am that which thinks: 'Therefore I am,' as I have commented on elsewhere, noting that the 'therefore,' the

causal stroke, divides inaugurally the 'I am' of existence from the 'I am' of meaning."

30. J. Lacan, ""The Subversion of the Subject and the Dialectic of Desire," *Ecrits: A Selection* (New York: Norton, 1977), 292.

31. Jürgen Braungardt, "The End of Metaphysics: An Analysis of the Transformation of Philosophical Discourse Through Adorno and Lacan," unpublished ms. (Berkeley, Calif.: GTU archives, 1997), 22–23.

32. Ibid.

33. Lacan, *The Four Concepts of Psychoanalysis* (New York: Norton, 1981), 139: "It is quite clear that the 'I am lying,' despite its paradox, is perfectly valid. Indeed, the I of the enunciation is not the same as the I of the statement, that is to say, the shifter which, in the statement designates him. So, from the point at which I state, it is quite possible for me to formulate in a valid way that the I—the I who, at that moment, formulates the statement—is lying, that he lied a little before, that he is lying afterwards, or even, that in saying I am lying he declares that he has the intention of deceiving."

34. Cf. Ricoeur, "Consciousness and the Unconscious: The Conflict of Interpretations." "We must be reduced to a similar admission: the question of consciousness is just as obscure as that of the unconscious" (99); "I cannot understand the unconscious from what I know about consciousness or even preconsciousness" (100); "I no longer even understand what consciousness is" (100).

35. Cf. Heidegger, *Being and Time*, 163–68, but especially the summation, 166: "In these characters of Being which we have exhibited—everyday Being-among-one-another, distantiality, averageness, levelling down, publicness, the disburdening of one's Being, and accomodation—lies that 'constancy' of Dasein which is closest to us. This 'constancy' pertains not to the enduring Being-present-at-hand of something, but rather to Dasein's kind of Being as Being-with."

36. Gadamer, "Practical Philosophy as a Model of the Human Sciences," *Research in Phenomenology* (1980):83: "The best definition for hermeneutics is: to let what is alienated by the character of the written word or by the character of being distantiated by cultural or historical distances speak again. This is hermeneutics: to let what seems to be far and alienated speak again."

37. G. Madison, "Hermeneutics: Gadamer and Ricoeur," 8: 316. Cf. Gadamer, *Truth and Method*, 335, 345, 489.

38. Madison, Ibid., 8: 316.

39. Gadamer, *Truth and Method*, 237.

40. Gadamer, "The Problem of Historical Consciousness," *Interpretive Social Science: A Reader*, ed. P. Rabinow and W. M. Sullivan (Berkeley and Los Angeles: University of California Press, 1979), 107. See also Gadamer, "Zur Problematik des Selbstverständnis," *Kleine Schriften I: Philosophie—Hermeneutik* (Tübingen: J.C.B. Mohr, 1976), 70–81.

41. Gadamer, *Truth and Method*, 278.

42. See Gadamer, "The Problem of Historical Consciousness," 108.

43. Habermas, "Zu Gadamer's *Wahrheit und Methode*." Eng. trans. in Ormiston and Schrift, *The Hermeneutic Tradition*, 213–44.

44. Habermas, "Der Universalitätsanspruch der Hermeneutik," *Hermeneutik und Ideologiekritik* (Frankfurt: Suhrkamp, 1967), 120–58. Eng. trans. in Ormiston and Schrift, *The Hermeneutic Tradition*, 245–72.

45. Ibid., 253.

46. Ibid., 254.

47. Ibid., 268. In fairness, one should consult Gadamer's "Replik," also in *Hermeneutik und Ideologiekritik*, 283–317.

48. Ricoeur, *Hermeneutics and the Human Sciences*, 141.

49. Ibid., 202.

50. Ibid., 277.

51. Ricoeur, "The Hermeneutics of Symbols and Philosophical Reflection: II," *The Conflict of Interpretations,* 332: "All symbols invite thought, but the symbols of evil demonstrate in an exemplary manner that there is always something more in myths and symbols than in all of our philosophy and that, hence, a philosophical interpretation of symbols will never become absolute knowledge. The symbols of evil, in which we can read the limits of our own existence, announce at the very same time the limits of all systems of thought which would try to incorporate these symbols in an *absolute knowledge*. This is one of the reasons, perhaps the most striking, why no absolute knowledge but only the *symbols of the sacred* lie beyond the figures of Spirit."

52. Ibid., 333.

53. Aemilius Guano, "Oratio Quoad Prooemium et cap, I Schematis de Ecclesia," *Acta Synodalia Vaticani II* (Vatican Typis Polyglottis, 1971) 2/1:455–56.

6. Postmodern Sacramentality

1. Gadamer, "Foreword to the Second Edition," *Wahrheit und Methode*, Eng. translation in Ormiston and Schrift, *The Hermeneutic Tradition,* 203.
2. See *Cathechism of the Catholic Church*, nos. 1077–1112.
3. Thomas Aquinas, *Summa Theologica*, I, q. 45, a. 2, ad 2. See also I, q. 45, a. 1 (c): creation is "the emanation of all being from a universal cause."
4. See Paul Tillich, "Kairos—Theonomie—Das Dämonische," *Begegnungen, Gesammelte Werke* (Stuttgart: Evangelisches Verlagswerk, 1971), 12:310–15, originally written in 1959. See K. Osborne, *New Being* (The Hague: Martinus Nijhoff, 1969), pp. 26–30, 94–108.
5. Paul Tillich, *Systematic Theology* (Chicago: The University of Chicago Press, 1965), 9th ed., 1:14.
6. Paul Tillich, "Das Religiöse als kritisches Prinzip: Die protestantische Verkündigung und der Mensch der Gegenwart," *Religiöse Verwiklichung, Gesammelte Werke,* 7:31. "Die menschliche Grenzsituation is da erreicht, wo die menschliche Möglichkeit schlechthin zu Ende, die menschliche Existenz unter eine unbedingte Bedröhung gestellt ist." One cannot miss the Heideggerian overtone in these passages, namely, his *Sein zum Tode.* One also notes, however, that Tillich correlates *Esse Ipsum* and *Sein*, a position which Heidegger would never accept.
7. Bonaventure, *Collationes in Hexaemeron,* I, 17. Bonaventure's use of the term "metaphysics" is indicative of his Aristotelian scholastic philosophical base, in which philosophy and theology were intertwined.
8. Ewert Cousins, *Bonaventure and the Coincidence of Opposites* (Chicago: Franciscan Herald Press, 1978).
9. Ewert Cousin, "Bonaventure's Christology: A Resource for the Third Millennium," *That Others May Know and Love,* ed. M.

Cusato and F. E. Coughlin (St. Bonaventure, N.Y.: The Franciscan Institute, 1997), 214–15.

10. See Joan Stambaugh, "Introduction," in Martin Heidegger, *Identity and Difference,* trans. J. Stambaugh (New York: Harper & Row, 1969), 7. German text and English trans. by J. Stambaugh.

11. Heiddeger, *Identity and Difference,* 23; the German text reads: "Der Satz der Indentität lautet nach einer geläufigen Formel: A = A. Der Satz gilt als das oberste Denkgesetz" (85).

12. Ibid., 36. The German text reads: "Im Ge-Stell waltet ein seltsame Vereignen und Zueignen. Es gilt, dieses Eignen, worin Mensch und Sein einander ge-eignet sind, schlicht zu erfahren, d.h. einzukehren in das, was wir das *Ereignis* nennen" (100).

13. Ibid., 36. The German text reads: "Das Wort Ereignis meint hier nicht mehr das, was wir sonst irgendein Geschehnis, ein Vorkommnis nennen. Das Wort ist jetzt al Singulare tantum gebraucht. Was es nennt, ereignet sich nur in der Einzahl, nein, nicht einmal mehr in einer Zahl, sondern einzig" (101).

14. Ibid., 38: "The appropriation appropriates man and Being to their essential togetherness. In the frame, we glimpse a first, oppressing flash of the appropriation. The frame constitutes the active nature of the modern world of technology. In the frame we witness a belonging together of man and Being in which the letting belong first determines the manner of the 'together' and its unity. We let Parmenides' fragment: 'For the Same are thinking as well as Being' introduce us to the question of a belonging together in which belonging has precedence over 'together.' The question of the meaning of this Same is the question of the active nature of identity." The German text reads: "Das Ereignis vereignet Mensch und Sein in ihr wesenhaftes Zusammen. Ein erstes, bedrängendes Aufblitzen des Ereignisses erblicken wir im Ge-Stell. Dieses macht das Wesen der modernen technischen Welt aus. Im Gestell erblicken wir ein Zusammen*gehören* von Mensch und Sein, worin das Gehörenlassen erst die Art des Zusammen und dessen Einheit bestimmt. Das Geleit in die Frage nach einem Zusammengehören, darin, das Gehören den Vorrang vor dem Zusammen hat, ließen wir uns durch den Satz des Parmenides geben: 'Das Selbe nämlich ist Denken sowohl als auch Sein.' Die Frage nach dem Sinn dieses Selben ist die Frage nach dem Wesen der Identität" (103).

15. Ibid., 103. It should be noted that in some places throughout this volume the German text and the English text are not precisely congruent.

16. Ibid., 39. The German text reads: "Das Wesen der Identität ist ein Eigentum des Er-eignisses" (103).

17. Ibid., 39. The German text reads: "Satz der Identität sagt jetzt: Ein Spring, den das Wesen der Identität verlangt, weil es ihn braucht, wenn anders das Zusammen*gehören* von Mensch und Sein in das Wesenslicht des Ereignisses gelangen soll" (104).

18. Ibid., 24–25. The German text reads: "Die gemäßere Formel für den Satz der Identität A ist A sagt demnach nicht nur: Jedes A ist selber dasselbe, sie sagt vielmehr: Mit ihm selbst ist jedes A selber dasselbe. In der Selbigkeit liegt die Beziung des 'mit,' also eine Vermittelung, eine Verbindung, eine Synthesis: die Einigung in cinc Einheit" (87).

19. Chauvet, *Symbol und Sacrament*, 90; French text, 95.

20. Ibid., 89; French text, 94.

21. Ibid., 88; French text, 93.

22. Emmanuel Lévinas, "Totalité et infini," *Autrement qu'être* (The Hague: Martinus Nijhoff, 1974), 149.

23. Merleau-Ponty, *Phenomenology of Perception*, 184.

24. Heidegger, *Being and Time*, 34.

25. Ibid., 91–168; see especially his differentiation for the term "World," 98, and his detailed analysis of Descartes' position 122–35.

26. Merleau-Ponty, *Phenomenology of Perception*, 52–63. In these few pages Merleau-Ponty summarizes his key issues.

27. Ibid., 63.

28. Ibid., 377.

29. Ibid., 395.

30. See, for instance, Gustav Bergmann, *Logic and Reality* (Madison, Wis.: Univ. of Madison Press, 1964); idem, *Meaning and Existence* (Madison, Wis.: University of Madison Press, 1968); W. Park, "Scotus, Frege and Bergmann," *The Modern Schoolman* 67 (1972), 259–73; David Armstrong, *Nominalism and Realism* (Cambridge: Cambridge Univ. Press, 1980); idem, *A Theory of Universals* (Cambridge: Cambridge Univ. Press, 1980); R. M. Chisholm, "Possibility Without Haecceity," *Midwest Studies in Philosophy,* vol. 11, *Studies in Essentialism,* ed. P. French et al. (Minneapolis, Minn.: Univ. of

Minnesota Press 1986); G. S. Rosenkrantz, *Haecceity: An Ontological Essay* (Boston: Kluwer Publishers, 1993); O. Boulnois, "Genèse de la théorie scotiste de l'individuation," *Le problème de l'individuation*, ed. A. Bitpohl-Hespériès (Paris, 1991); G. Sondag, *Le principe d'individuation* (Paris, 1992); T. Barth, "Individualität und Allgemeinheit bei J. Duns Skotus," *Wissenschaft und Weisheit* 18 (1955), 192–216.

31. See, e.g., Scotus's argument that definitions must of necessity be universal not individual, and therefore "since individual forms are not predicable of many, Scotus is entitled to conclude that individual forms cannot be part of a definition, and consequently individuals are not definable" (Wood, "Individual Forms: Richard Rufus and John Duns Scotus," 266; see Scotus, *In Met.* VII, q. 13, nos. 89–91).

32. Jorge J. E. Gracia, "Individuality and the Individuating Entity in Scotus's Ordinatio," 230.

33. Scotus, *Ord.* II. d. 3, p. 1, q. 4, n. 76 (Vat. ed. 7:427): "Causa…'huius' singularitatis in speciali, signatae, scilicet ut est 'haec' determinate" (The cause…of this designated singularity in particular, namely, as it is determinately 'this'"). A phrase common among scholastic writers from 1150 on was "the principle of individuation." Scotus deliberately avoids using it. Principle of individuation refers to the *source* of individuality, whereas Scotus's focus is on the *thisness* of the individual.

34. A. Vos Jaczn, H. Veldhuis, A. H. Looman-Graaskamp, E. Dekker, N. W. den Bok, *Contingency and Freedom* (Dordrecht: Kluwer Academic Publishers, 1994).

35. See Jean-François Lyotard, *La Condition postmoderne* (Paris: Minuit, 1979). Eng. trans. by G. Bennington and B. Massumi, *The Post Modern Condition: A Report on Knowledge* (Manchester: Manchester Univ. Press, 1984), xxiv.

36. See Emmanuel Lévinas, "Transcendence et hauteur," *Bulletin de la Société Française de la Philosophie* 56 (1962), 92, in S. Critchley, "Derridean Deconstruction," in Kearney, *Continental Philosophy in the Twentieth Century*, 8:447.

37. R. Gasché, *The Tain of the Mirror: Derrida and the Philosophy of Reflection* (Cambridge, Mass.: Harvard Univ. Press, 1982), 101.

38. Heidegger, *Being and Time*, 191. In the same paragraph he says: "Die Auslegung gründet jeweils in einer Vorsicht, die das in

Vorhabe Genommene auf eine bestimmte Auslegbarkeit hin 'anschnei-det'"(191, German text in footnote 3).

39. Ibid., 154. This is not an isolated sentence. The entire paragraph 26 belabors this point.

40. See Walter Schulz, "Anmerkungen zur Hermeneutik Gadamers," *Hermeneutik und Dialektik*, ed. Rüdiger Bubner, Konrad Cramer, and Reiner Wiehl (Tübingen: J.C.B. Mohr, 1970), 1:308–9: "Grundsätzlich gesagt: Alle inhaltlichen Einheiten—so etwa die Idee des Fortschrittes—sind relativierbar, nur die *formale* Einheit des Gespräches mit der Vergangenheit ist nicht relativierbar....Dies aber eben bedeutet, daß nicht ich, *sondern das Gespräch der eigentliche Akteur ist.* Das Gespräch ist ja das geschichtliche Geschehen selbst, in dem ich schon immer stehe und durch das ich immer schon vermittelt bin. Dies Gespräch geschieht als die Geschichte selbst."

41. Habermas, "Der Universalitätsanspruch der Hermeneutik," 265 70.

42. Thomas Aquinas, *Summa Theologiae* II-II, 1, 2, ad 2. This particular statement is cited at the very beginning of the *Catechism of the Catholic Church*, no. 170.

43. Thomas Aquinas, *Summa Contra Gentiles* I, 30.

44. Ricoeur, "Hermeneutics and the Critique of Ideology," 87. Ricoeur contrasts hermeneutics with ideology: "[The gesture] of the critique of ideology is a proud gesture of defiance directed against the distortions of human communication."

45. Ibid., 90.

46. Ibid., 93.

47. Ibid., 94.

48. We see that the "I" is not a solipsistic "I," since the text enlarges us and makes our own self better understood. *Gehören und Zusammen* are once more part of the picture.

49. Chauvet, *Symbol and Sacrament*, 213.

50. Ibid., 221.

51. Ibid., 228–316; French text, 233–71.

52. Ibid., 228; French text, 233.

53. Ibid.

54. Matthew Jayanth Koddekanal, *Eucharist and Social Ethics*, Ph.D. diss. (Berkeley, Calif.: Graduate Theological Union, 1997).

55. Ibid., 241.

56. Ibid.

57. Ibid.

58. Ibid., 242. Koddekanal devotes a lengthy analysis to their position on liturgy and ethics, 243–53.

59. Chauvet, *Symbol and Sacrament,* 249.

60. Ibid., 261.

61. Ibid., 262–65.

62. Ibid., 265. The French text reads: "L'élément 'Sacrement' est ainsi le lieu symbolique du passage toujours à faire de l'Écriture à l'Éthique, de la lettre au corps. La liturgie est le grand pédagogie où nous apprenons à acquiescer à cette présence du manque de Dieu qui nous requiert de lui donner corps en ce monde, accomplissant ainsi le sacrement en 'liturgie du prochain' et la mémoire rituelle de Jésus-Christ en mémoire existentielle" (270–71).

63. Docherty, "Postmodernist Theory," 8:501.

7. Postmodern Onto-Epistemology and Solemn Church Teachings

1. In the *Catechism of the Catholic Church* these teachings are described as follows: "The Church's Magisterium exercises the authority it holds from Christ to the fullest extent when it defines dogmas, that is, when it proposes truths contained in divine Revelation or having a necessary connection with them, in a form obliging the Christian people to an irrevocable adherence of faith" (no. 88).

2. Denzinger-Schönmetzer, *Enchiridion Symbolorum, Definitionum, Declarationum,* nos. 1602, 1604, 1606, 1609, 1611, 1612, 1639; to a lesser degree the *Decree for the Armenians* (1439) and the *Decree for the Jacobites* (1442), see nos. 1310–28; 1352–53. In the *Index systematicus rerum* (pp. 850–52) references that are considered *locus sollemnior (ad materias praestantiores)* are indicated by the use of bold print.

3. See Canon 11. In *The Code of Canon Law: A Text and Commentary,* ed. James Corriden, Thomas Green, and Donald Heintschel, 31: "'Merely ecclesiastical laws' (can. 11) are human laws enacted by an ecclesiastical legislator. They must be distinguished from ecclesiastical laws which are also articulations of divine laws. Thus many norms for the celebration of the Eucharist are mere ecclesiastical laws; that the Church should celebrate the Eucharist is a divine law."

4. J. B. Umberg, "Die Bewertung der Trienter Lehren durch Pius VI," *Scholastik* 4 (1929), 402–9. See H.-P. Arendt, *Bußsakrament und Einzelbeichte* (Freiburg: Herder, 1981) for a detailed examination of the theological valency of the Tridentine canons.

5. H. Lennerz, "Das Konzil von Trient und theologische Schulmeinungen," *Scholastik* 4 (1929), 38–53; idem, "Notulae Tridentinae, Primum Anathema in Concilio Tridentino," *Gregorianum* 27 (1946), 136–42.

6. R. Favre, "Les condemnations avec anathème," *Bulletin de Litterature Écclésiastique* 17 (1946), 226–41; 18 (1947), 31–48.

7. A. Lang, "Die Bedeutungswandel der Begriffe 'fides' und 'haeresis' und die dogmatische Wertung der Konzilsentscheidungen von Vienne und Trent," *Münchener Theologische Zeitschrift* 4 (1953), 133–56.

8. H. Jedin, *A History of the Council of Trent*, trans. E. Graf (St. Louis, Mo.: B. Herder Book Co, 1961), 2:381.

9. P. Fransen, "Réflexions sur l'anathème au Concile de Trente," *Ephemerides théologiques lovanienses*, 29 (1953), 657–72.

10. Carl J. Peter, "Auricular Confession and the Council of Trent," *The Jurist* 28 (1968), 287. Peter cites other theologians who are in agreement with this position, 287; cf. A. Duval, *Les Sacrements au concile de Trente* (Paris: Les Éditions du Cerf, 1985), 170–71. J. Leclercq, H. Holstein, P. Adnès have also addressed this theme. C. Lefebvre, *Trent* (Paris: Éditions de l'Orante, 1981), 550–51, repeats the same conclusion: "On voit dès lors avec quelle prudence il faut traiter les canons avec anathème dans les décrets dogmatiques du concile de Trente. La contradictoire de chacun des canons n'est pas nécessairement de 'foi divine' au sens précis des terms. Chaque cas est à étudier pour lui-même. Les propositions de 'foi divine,' irrévocables, parce que l'Église y a engagé toute son autorité, sont à distinguer des conclusions théologiques, des propositions dites de 'foi ecclésiastique,' de décisions touchant la discipline générale, que l'Église pourrait un jour soumettre à révision."

11. See, e.g., Ludwig Ott, *Fundamentals of Catholic Dogma*, trans. P. Lynch (St. Louis, Mo.: Herder, 1954); A. Pesch, *Praelectiones Dogmaticae: De Sacramentis*, vol. 1 (Freiburg im B.: Herder, 1950); A. Tanquerey, *A Manual of Dogmatic Theology* (New York: Desclée, 1959). Eng. trans. by J. Byrnes, vol. 1; L. Lercher, *Institutiones theologiae dogmaticae* (Innsbruck: Rausch, 1948), IV/2.

12. J. A. de Aldama, "Theoria generalis sacramentorum," *Sacrae Theologiae Summa*, 4:96: "Christus, secundum quod homo, omnia sacramenta Novae Legis immediate instituit."

13. It should be noted that this is not merely a contemporary view. In the Middle Ages Scotus argued that Christ in his human nature could not have instituted any of the sacraments, since it is beyond the power of the human will to unite efficacious grace infallibly to any sensible sign. Many Scotistic theologians followed in this line of thought (see Scotus *Questiones in IV Libros Sententiarum* 4, d. 1, q. 3 [Paris: Vives, 1894] 126–30). At the Council of Trent not quite half of the bishops' theologians were Scotistic and would not have been mute if the Scotistic position were meant to be invalidated.

14. Moral causality is similar to views that Eastern Catholic theologians hold when they discuss the holiness of the sacred mysteries.

15. De Aldama, "Theoria generalis sacrmentorum," 33 and 35.

16. Ibid., 57 and 59.

17. In the Eastern churches the sacred mysery of baptism never became divided into two rituals.

18. John Calvin, *Institutes of the Christian Religion*, ed. John T. McNeill, trans. Ford Lewis Battles (Philadelphia, Pa.: Westminster Press, 1960), 2:1453.

19. Ibid., 2:1458.

20. Jean Galot, *La Nature du caractère sacramentel* (Paris: Desclée de Brouwer, 1958), 231: "La concile (de Trente) définira l'existence (du caractère) comme certaine, mais refusera de se prononcer sur la nature du caractère." Galot's study is a seminal historico-theological analysis on sacramental character. Galot writes, "Mais le concile a voulu expressément éviter toute détermination concernant la nature du caractère, et ne condamner aucune des opinions d'école, meme pas celle de la pure relation de raison proposée par Durand" (224). Again, "Le Concile s'est donc limité, dans la théologie du caractère sacramentel, à déclarer l'existence d'un signe spirituel et indélébile imprimé dans les sacrements de baptême, de confirmation et d'ordre, en relation avec la non-réitération de ces sacrements" (224).

21. In the *Catechism of the Catholic Church*, the authors are not clear on the issue of sacramental character. In no. 698 one reads: "The image of the seal *(sphragis)* has been used in some theological traditions to express the indelible 'character' imprinted by these three unrepeatable

sacraments." Sacramental character is seen in this sentence as theological not doctrinal. In no. 1121 the text goes beyond the mere existence of sacramental character and presents a description of its nature: "It [the character] remains forever in the Christian as a positive disposition for grace, a promise and guarantee of divine protection, and as a vocation to divine worship and to the service of the Church." As a theological understanding of sacramental character such a view cannot be considered defined teaching of Trent. In no. 1272 on the baptismal character the text merely notes the existence of baptismal character, offering no description of its nature. In no. 1304 the text mentions the sacramental character of confirmation with a theological description of the nature of this character: "[It] is the sign that Jesus Christ has marked a Christian with the seal of his Spirit by clothing him with power from on high so that he may be his witness." This theological position cannot be considered defined doctrine. The title for nos. 1581–84 reads: "The indelible character." Sacramental character is presented as one of the effects of the sacrament of holy orders. The existence of sacramental character in holy orders is defined, but what this character is has not been defined. In no. 1581 the text offers a theological description: the configuration of the one ordained so "that he may serve as Christ's instrument for his Church. By ordination one is enabled to act as a representative of Christ, Head of the Church, in his triple office of priest, prophet and king." Such a description is not a defined teaching of the church. In no. 1582 the emphasis of the text is basically on the non-reiteration of holy orders, but there is mention of a sharing in Christ's office, which again is descriptive of the nature, the "what" of a character, which is not defined doctrine. In no. 1583 the text links sacramental character to the vocation and mission of an ordained person. In no. 1584 the focus is on the holiness or lack of holiness of the one ordained. In all of this the *Catechism* should have made clear the distinction between the solemn teaching of the church on the issue of sacramental character, and the area of theological opinion. As the text stands, there is an implication that all that the *Catechism* says on this issue is the teaching of the church, which it is not.

22. See the situation with Pope Stephen I (256) and Bishop Cyprian of Carthage; also Augustine, *Contra Cresconium*, iv, 21, 26. The Pelagian situation with Pope Zozimus is another case in question.

23. At the time of Trent the office of bishop was not considered to be part of the sacrament of holy orders. Nonetheless, at this time all

bishops, even Protestant and Anglican bishops, had been ordained priests, and it was in virtue of their priesthood, not their episcopacy, that sacramental celebrations were judged valid or not valid.

24. This is part of the ecumenical discussion today. The mainline churches agree for the most part on the theological meaning of baptism, eucharist, and holy orders, but the issue of a valid ordination to diaconal, priestly, and episcopal orders as required in the Roman Catholic Church prevents the Roman Catholic Church from accepting the validity of eucharist and orders in Anglican and Protestant churches.

25. See J. Baudrillard, *La Gauche divine* (Paris: Grasset, 1985); J. F. Lyotard, *La Condition postmoderne* (Paris: Minuit, 1979). See Lakeland, *Postmodernity*, 44.

26. See William Desmond, "Philosophies of Religion: Marcel, Jaspers, Lévinas," in Kearney, *Continental Philosophy in the Twentieth Century*, 8:131–74.

27. Ricoeur, "Religion and Faith," *The Conflict of Interpretations*, 381–497. Ricoeur once mentioned to me that he and his wife visited Taize annually.

28. Merleau-Ponty, *Le Visible et l'Invisible* (Parish: Gallimard, 1964). Eng. trans. *The Visible and the Invisible*, ed. Claude Lefort, trans A. Lingis (Evanston, Ill.: Northwestern University Press, 1968). Remy Kwant, *From Phenomenology to Metaphysics* (Pittsburgh, Pa.: Duquesne University Press, 1966), 241–43, shows how Merleau-Ponty changed in his later years. In an earlier volume Kwant had stressed the atheistic stance of Merleau-Ponty and indicated the reasons for this atheism (see Kwant, *The Phenomenological Philosophy of Merleau-Ponty* [Pittsburgh, Pa.: Duquesne University Press, 1964], 128–49).

29. Luijpen, *Phenomenology and Atheism* (Pittsburgh, Pa.: Duquesne University Press, 1964), 227.

30. Ibid., 336.

31. Ibid., 337.

32. Gadamer, "Foreword to the Second Edition," 203.

33. Foucault, *The Order of Things*, xxii.

34. Neo-Kantianism of the early twentieth century was dominantly epistemological, but Kantian philosophy is much more than epistemology. It is ontological as well. So, too, postmodern thought focuses strongly on the question: What is understanding? But there is

an ontological foundation for the epistemological or hermeneutical discussion.

35. Ricoeur, "Heidegger and the Subject," *The Conflict of Interpretations*, 228.

36. Ibid. To this consideration Ricoeur adds a passage from Heidegger himself: "Where the world becomes a view [Bild], the existent as a whole is posited as that with respect to which a man orients himself, which, therefore he wishes to bring and have before himself, and thus, in a decisive sense, re-presents to himself" (Heidegger, *Holzwege* [Frankfurt am Main: Klostermann, 1972], 82). Heidegger's representational character of the existent is the correlate of the emergence of man as subject.

37. Habermas, "An Alternative Way out of the Philosophy of the Subject: Communicative versus Subject-Centered Reason," *The Philosophical Discourse of Modernity*, trans. F. Lawrence (Cambridge: MIT Press, 1987); reprinted in *From Modernism to Postmodernism: An Anthology*, ed. Lawrence E. Cahoone (Oxford: Blackwell, 1996), 602–3.

38. Cahoone, *From Modernism to Postmodernism*, 603: "The relationship of the human being to the world is cognitivistically reduced: ontologically, the world is reduced to the world of entities as a whole (as the totality of objects that can be represented and of existing states of affairs); epistemologically, our relationship to that world is reduced to the capacity to know existing states of affairs or to bring them about in a purposive-rational fashion; semantically it is reduced to fact-finding discourse in which assertoric sentences are used."

39. Ibid., 606.

40. Ibid., 608.

41. See, e.g., Rahner, *Hearers of the Word* (New York: Herder and Herder, 1969), 10: "In light of factual Christian revelation the concrete ability to hear the divine word of revelation is constituted by two moments: by the spiritual transcendence of man (his 'subjectivity') and by its 'elevation' through grace, or its 'illumination.'...Since this 'supernatural existential' does not imply a new, added ability, but an inner illumination of spiritual subjectivity or transcendence itself without admitting the possibility of being created as such from it, the ability to hear the word of revelation can be considered in the light of the basic constitution of the human spirit." This basic constitution of the human

spirit with its subjectivity is common to all human beings in Rahner's approach, and this same kind of thinking applies to all the major authors in transcendental Thomism. In the phraseology of Ricoeur, Rahner and others lead subjectivity back only to the "same," but not to the "self."

42. Ricoeur, *Soi-même comme un autre* (Paris: Editions du Seuil, 1990). Eng. trans. by Kathleen Blamey, *Oneself as Another* (Chicago: University of Chicago Press, 1992).

43. Ricoeur, *Oneself as Another,* 116.

44. Ibid., 116–18.

45. Ibid., 118.

46. See Ricoeur, *Freedom and Nature: The Voluntary and the Involuntary*, trans Erazim Kohak (Evanston, Ill.: Northwestern University Press, 1966); and idem, *Fallible Man,* trans. W. Lowe (New York: Fordham University Press, 1986).

47. Ricoeur, *Oneself as Another*, 121.

48. Hume renounced the idea of sameness, considering it impossible, and he maintained only the selfhood, which leads to solipsism.

49. Ricoeur, *Oneself as Another*, 297.

50. Ibid., 310.

51. On Ricoeur's approach to this issue, see ibid., 319–29.

52. Ibid., 329–41.

53. Ibid., 341–55.

54. Ibid., 354: "To the reduction of being-in-debt to the strange(r)ness tied to the facticity of being-in-the-world, characteristic of the philosophy of Martin Heidegger, Emmanuel Lévinas opposes a symmetrical reduction of the otherness of conscience to the externality of the other manifested in his face. In this sense, there is no other modality of otherness for Lévinas than this externality. The model of all otherness is the other person.To these alternatives—either Heidegger's strange(r)ness or Lévinas's externality—I shall stubbornly oppose the original and originary character of what appears to me to constitute the third modality of otherness, namely being enjoined as the structure of selfhood."

55. W. Richardson, *Heidegger: Through Phenomenology to Thought* (The Hague: Martinus Nijhoff, 1963), 85, see also 173.

56. Heidegger, *Erläutering zu Hölderins Dichtung* (Frankfurt: Klostermann, 1951): "'Nature' is the oldest time—not at all that which is 'beyond time' in the metaphysical sense and certainly not the 'eternal' as Christians understand it" (in Richardson, *Heidegger,* 425). The

German text reads "'Die Natur' ist die älteste Zeit und keineswegs das metaphysisich gemeinte 'Überzeitliche' und vollends nicht das christlich gedachte 'Ewige'" (57).

57. Heidegger, *Vom Wesen des Grundes* (Frankfurt: Klostermann, 1949), 45: "In ihn ist die Transzendenz als solche begründend. Weil darin Sein und Seinsverfassung enthüllt werden, heißt das transzendentale Begründen die *ontologische Wahrheit*."

58. Karl Rahner's understanding of the supernatural existential does not fit with this understanding of ontological human transcendence and is therefore subject to the same challenge of postmodern thought as any religious claim for human transcendence toward the ultimate.

59. Richardson, *Heidegger*, 172.

60. Ibid., 181. "The ontological structure of the self is the ecstatic nature of existence; it is essentially not a substance enclosed within itself but a process which comes-to-pass as finite transcendence." Heidegger remarks in *Das Wesen des Grundes:* "Die Selbstheit des aller Spontaneität schon zugrunde liegenden Selbst liegt aber in der Transzendenz" (41). In the same work Heidegger had said: "Diesen Grund der ontologischen Differenz nennen wir vorgreifend die *Transzendenz* des Daseins" (15).

Conclusion

1. This section is a restatement of the explanation by Gary Madison, found above, p. 55.

2. These ideas are found in the *Catechism*, nos. 1077–1109.

Index of Authors